ADVANCE PRAISE FOR *HOPE OVER FATE*

"With all his humility and kindness and belief in the potential of others, Fazle Hasan Abed was also the most visionary, the most entrepreneurial, and the most transformational leader I have met. This beautiful book tells his story—and shows how he changed the world and what we can learn from him." —**Wendy Kopp**, CEO and cofounder, Teach For America

"*Hope Over Fate* fluidly traces the formative influences in the incredibly inspiring story of Abed *Bhai* as he eschewed paternalism toward the poor in favor of learned self-sufficiency. This book evocatively describes his simple demeanor, one that belied his enormous impact on the reduction of poverty. It rings true to the role model I had the privilege of knowing in the last two decades of his eventful and fully lived life." —**Tarun Khanna**, Jorge Paulo Lemann Professor, Harvard Business School

"Are you a wonk, keen to know how the world's largest nonprofit came to be (while maintaining a fairly low profile) and how it uses evidence and business savvy to deliver effective, scaled programs around the world? Or are you keen to understand the human stories behind the scenes of one of the best but untold stories of fighting poverty one household at a time? Either way, this book will grab you as it follows the story of the unsung hero Fazle Hasan Abed and the path to scale for fighting poverty." —**Dean Karlan**, professor of economics and finance at Northwestern University and founder of Innovations for Poverty Action

"Abed was an extraordinary man who built one of the largest and most effective anti-poverty organizations in the world. He did this with humility, attention to rigor and evidence, and relentless pursuit of the innovation and scale needed to be truly transformative. This book tells his remarkable story and provides important lessons to all those who care about development." —**Minouche Shafik**, director of London School of Economics and author of *What We Owe Each Other: A New Social Contract*

"If you aspire to be a great changemaker or even social entrepreneur, this book is for you. Scott MacMillan brings us a living Fazle Abed, one of the first and absolutely most creative, pattern-changing entrepreneurs for the good of the last hundred years." —**Bill Drayton**, founder and CEO, Ashoka

"A beautiful tribute to a man who inspired awe but was profoundly relatable—always reminding us that we, too, could choose to live consequentially. A giant of history, Fazle Abed believed deeply in the power of hope and personal agency and in the fundamental dignity of all people. He proved that given a dose of inspiration, a door to opportunity, and a community of support, individuals and communities facing poverty could and would change their own lives. Like his life, his story is a treasure trove—a gift to the world!" —**Reeta Roy**, president and CEO of the Mastercard Foundation

"In the soul of every Bengali is a poet and an entrepreneur, yearning for a voice and an opportunity. *Hope Over Fate* is a lyrical biography chronicling the origin story of Sir Fazle Hasan Abed and the noble enterprise that was both his life's work and his greatest poem. Sir Fazle found his opportunity in the aftermath of the Bangladesh Liberation War. He gave up life as a rising corporate executive and committed himself to a life of service in liberating the voices and entrepreneurial potential of his fellow Bengalis. Speaking softly and ever in search of new ideas, he combined entrepreneurial genius with servant leadership to build BRAC, the most elaborate, sustainable, and successful nonprofit network of poverty alleviation programs in the world. He achieved at scale what governments and other global nonprofits only dream of." —**Raymond Offenheiser**, director, Pulte Institute for Global Development, Keough School of Global Affairs, University of Notre Dame

"This book tells the story of a true genius, Fazle Hasan Abed, who above all was a teacher: he made BRAC into an organization where programs were built on a constant updating of knowledge and experience, creating an institution that was never afraid to change course when necessary. Despite all the awards and praise that Abed received, it was always about BRAC, never himself—so much so that he was even uncomfortable sharing his remarkable story with the world." —**Richard Cash**, senior lecturer on global health, Harvard T. H. Chan School of Public Health

"The inspiring story of a brilliant, self-effacing man, the incredible organization he created, and the largest, most successful poverty eradication effort in history." —**Ian Smillie**, author of *Freedom from Want*

HOPE OVER FATE

Fazle Hasan Abed and the Science of Ending Global Poverty

SCOTT MACMILLAN

ROWMAN & LITTLEFIELD
Lanham • Boulder • New York • London

Published by Rowman & Littlefield
An imprint of The Rowman & Littlefield Publishing Group, Inc.
4501 Forbes Boulevard, Suite 200, Lanham, Maryland 20706
www.rowman.com

86-90 Paul Street, London EC2A 4NE, United Kingdom

Distributed by NATIONAL BOOK NETWORK

British Library Cataloguing in Publication Information Available

Library of Congress Cataloging-in-Publication Data

Names: MacMillan, Scott, 1974– author.
Title: Hope over fate : Fazle Hasan Abed and the science of ending global poverty / Scott MacMillan.
Description: Lanham : Rowman & Littlefield, [2022] | Includes bibliographical references and index. | Summary: "This book tells the story of Fazle Hasan Abed (1936–2019), a former finance executive with almost no experience in relief aid who founded BRAC in 1972. Abed's methods have changed the way global policymakers think about poverty"— Provided by publisher.
Identifiers: LCCN 2021052272 (print) | LCCN 2021052273 (ebook) | ISBN 9781538164921 (cloth) | ISBN 9781538164938 (epub)
Subjects: LCSH: Abed, F. H. | Bangladesh Rural Advancement Committee. | Social service, Rural—Bangladesh. | Poverty. | Economic development.
Classification: LCC HC79.P63 M33 2022 (print) | LCC HC79.P63 (ebook) | DDC 362.5—dc23/eng/20211122
LC record available at https://lccn.loc.gov/2021052272
LC ebook record available at https://lccn.loc.gov/2021052273

∞™ The paper used in this publication meets the minimum requirements of American National Standard for Information Sciences—Permanence of Paper for Printed Library Materials, ANSI/NISO Z39.48-1992.

To Alexandra and Isabella

হেথা যে গান গাইতে আসা আমার হয় নি সে গান গাওয়া

The song that I came to sing remains unsung to this day.

—Rabindranath Tagore

CONTENTS

INTRODUCTION

This book was originally supposed to be a memoir: the story of Fazle Hasan Abed, the mild-mannered accountant who would rid the world of poverty, as told by the man himself. For the last several years of his life, I was privileged to be the speechwriter for Abed, a man whose work changed the lives of millions. We would sit together for hours at a time in his office in Dhaka, or in hotels in Miami, Des Moines, and elsewhere, working through his speeches line by line. During these sessions, he would share stories from the previous eight decades of his life, of long train rides to Calcutta during his childhood in British India, and of his uncles, the last generation of Muslim Indians to learn Persian, the court language of the Mughals. He spoke of his friendship with the elderly E. M. Forster, his flight from war over the Khyber Pass to Kabul, his love life in London in the 1960s, his three marriages, and how, in 1972, with a few thousand pounds from the sale of his flat in Camden, he launched a small nonprofit organization to aid refugees, originally called the Bangladesh Rehabilitation Assistance Committee. Queens, presidents, and Nobel laureates would later call BRAC the world's most effective anti-poverty organization. He led it until he died in 2019.

That seemed like a story worth telling in full, and after some coaxing, he gave me permission to begin ghostwriting his autobiography. Abed was an exceptionally private man, however. He cringed at anything with a whiff of pomposity or self-promotion. "You have me pontificating!" he scolded me after an early draft of his speech to accept the World Food Prize in Iowa. He much preferred to let BRAC's work speak for itself—which may explain why so few people outside his native Bangladesh knew who he was or the magnitude of what he had accomplished.

I was about halfway done with his memoir when he told me to stop. The story, as I had written it, did not feel right coming from him.

His standards for the written word were high. He was an accountant, but he loved poetry and put great stock in the creative capacity of the human species, that which makes us, in Hamlet's words, "the paragon of animals"—our ability to create, reflect, and build—and it pained him that others might love literature the same way but could not, only because they had the bad fortune of growing up illiterate.

In the last year of his life, Abed came around to the idea that his story needed to be told by someone, even if it would not ultimately be him. He asked that I use the material I had gathered to write this book myself, in my own words. I did so knowing many of these words would fall short of the task.

★ ★ ★

Abed told stories, but he was not a great storyteller in the typical sense. He did not sprinkle his speeches with anecdotes of the "ordinary" people he had met, as politicians often do. He devised systems to accurately gather the input of the people he served, but he was more comfortable at his desk, looking at spreadsheets, than visiting program participants in person.

I once pointed out that he seemed more comfortable with numbers than with stories. "But the numbers tell the stories," he replied.

Here is the story he would tell of his native Bangladesh—no names or faces, no cast of characters, just a chorus of statistics. At the moment of its independence in 1971, Bangladesh was the world's second-poorest country after the Republic of Upper Volta (now Burkina Faso), with a per capita GDP of less than $100, a nation of sixty-six million living on a patch of flood-prone land the size of Iowa. One in four children died before their fifth birthday, one of the highest rates of childhood death in the world. Population growth was out of control, with the average woman bearing more than six children, usually on the dirt floor of her home, with no medical personnel present. Many died in childbirth. As late as 1990, the country still had one of the highest maternal mortality rates, at 574 per 100,000.

But in the 1990s, almost miraculously, things began to change, and quality of life improved at a historically unprecedented rate. By 2013, under-five mortality had plummeted from 250 per 1,000 live births, the rate at the time of independence, to just 40; maternal mortality had dropped similarly. The fertility rate had gone from seven to just over two per woman, or roughly replacement level. These changes constituted "some of the biggest gains in the basic condition of people's lives ever seen anywhere," rivaling the pace of Japan's breakneck modernization after the Meiji Restoration of 1868, according to *The Economist*.[1] A British medical journal, *The Lancet*, wrote that Bangladesh's transformation, which took place despite widespread poverty and low per capita spending on health, was "one of the great mysteries of global health."[2]

What happened? Abed's work had a lot to do with it. He was an unlikely revolutionary, having studied naval architecture and accounting in Britain before taking a job as the finance director at Shell Pakistan. With BRAC, using novel methods drawing from his business background, he began working in a remote corner of the country to uncover the "felt needs" of exploited landless people, especially women. He trained and mobilized them, giving them a sense of self-worth that many had never felt before. They began standing up for themselves against landlords, corrupt government officials, and imams opposed to women's rights. Often, he found what people really needed was hope—a sense that, with a modicum of outside help, their fate could be in their own hands.

He scaled up the programs to reach millions, and he did so more cost-effectively than any government would have. Incentive-based training gave health information to mothers so they could save their own children's lives. Women took small loans from BRAC to buy cows and handlooms, the first time they had owned anything of substance. Since they had nowhere to sell the milk and fabric they produced, he built up the dairy and textile industries by launching enterprises that bought the women's goods. These enterprises, owned by BRAC, turned out to be profitable, so he plowed the money back into the poverty programs. The women's children grew up without education, so Abed launched fifty thousand schools, plus a commercial bank and a university. He adapted these solutions to other countries. BRAC now likely reaches more than one hundred million people in about a dozen countries in Africa and Asia.

Abed's own life was a tapestry of love and sorrow. At least one of these statistics, maternal mortality, had both a name and a face. His first wife, Bahar, his soulmate and partner in BRAC, died in his arms from complications of childbirth. He rarely shared the details, and never publicly—how he ran down the street to find a doctor who might help, how the clinic's oxygen canister was empty, and how, after she lost consciousness, he tried to resuscitate her himself.

There was a part of him, I learned, that would have preferred to be completely alone, working in isolation, never having to tell his story. He often said that satisfaction comes when one's occupation becomes one's preoccupation. But Abed was no ascetic, self-abnegating Gandhi; he left the office at a reasonable hour and enjoyed coming home to the comforts of domestic life, to the sound of family and the warm smell of spices from the kitchen. When he spoke of his loneliness between his marriages, he told me he could never bear to return to an empty house or sleep in an empty bed for long. He loved the messy world of humans, with both its problems and its pleasures.

★ ★ ★

I suspect there was one more reason Abed questioned whether his own story was worth telling. In his mind, BRAC had done relatively little to help Bangladesh rise from the ranks of one of the poorest nations on earth. All it did was create the enabling conditions; it was the poor themselves who worked tirelessly, once the conditions were in place, to change the condition of their lives and those of their children. His own story, therefore, did not deserve as much attention as the women who had long labored on the fringes of society, who would one day, in his words, "be their own actors in history, and write their own stories of triumph over adversity."

In that spirit, this book starts not with an anecdote about Abed but with the story of Shahida and her goats.

1

THE FOX THAT KILLED MY GOAT

When the fox killed Shahida Begum's goat, she was so inconsolable it was as though her own child had been murdered. Shahida lives in the panhandle of Bangladesh's far north, where the Brahmaputra pours in from India. In some respects, this is the start of Bangladesh itself, a country created by mighty rivers making their last few hundred miles to the sea, where the land, fertile but often flooded, and its people, constituting more than 2 percent of humanity subsisting on a small patch of the earth's surface, exist in a fragile equilibrium. Here in the north, the Brahmaputra is seven miles wide, its murky gray waters flowing around islands called *chars* made of Himalayan silt, their shapes changing from season to season. A thousand tributaries and distributaries merge and split and merge again like chaotic lace.

Shahida owns three acres of land in a fishing village on one of these sub-streams. Even when the paths turn to muck, she walks a mile every afternoon, surefooted in her flip-flops, to sell her cow's milk. "Since you're from a different country, you don't know about my land," she tells me. Her face is broad and leathery with a stain-toothed smile, her gray hair covered by a yellow sari—a single piece of cloth draped over her head and wrapped around her body. It is 2016, and we're sitting outside her home, a one-room mud hut with a thatched overhang to give cover during the rain. The neighbors' walls are made of rusted corrugated iron and woven reed, lined by tattered plastic tarps. Nothing stays dry for long during the summer monsoon here, although, when the sun is out, the midday heat is stifling.

"When I first came to this village, its condition wasn't as good as what you see here," she continues. She speaks loudly, with the confidence of someone who has overcome great odds. "It was in shambles! People barely had roofs over their heads or walls to keep them safe, and if it rained, you couldn't keep anything dry. Some people didn't even have clothes to cover themselves decently, so they just wore scraps. Our house would often get flooded, but we couldn't afford to repair it."

Shahida was one of the first participants in a "graduation program," a term, now common in development jargon, for a program that aims to boost people out of a poverty trap with a sequence of interventions that usually include training, livestock, cash, and—this is crucial—in-person coaching. Long after Shahida went through the pilot in 2002, the graduation approach gained worldwide recognition as one of the most effective ways to fight extreme poverty.

Shahida thinks she's about fifty years old. In her generation, people born into poverty rarely know their age. There were no birth certificates and no reason to keep track of the years, since so little changed. However, for anyone old enough to remember 1971, one milestone stands out: the Bangladesh Liberation War, in which the Pakistan Army ran a campaign of genocidal rape and slaughter that ended with Bangladesh's independence. "I am older than Bangladesh itself," Shahida said. "I don't remember much of the war, but I remember hiding a lot."

Shahida's father plowed others' land as a day laborer. On most days, he earned enough to provide one meal a day for four children. Since the family couldn't afford wood for the cooking fire, young Shahida spent her girlhood collecting leaves to burn, often cutting her fingers on dried fronds. "And we didn't have a latrine," she added. "We defecated in the open."

She married at eleven, which was not uncommon. Even today, child marriage remains endemic in Bangladesh. Families in poverty tend to be eager to arrange their daughters' marriages as soon as possible, since girls rarely contribute to a household's income. A traditional marriage almost always means the girl is sent to live among strangers in a distant village. Shahida's husband was decent and hardworking. She was luckier than many in that respect. He bought bamboo and dry reeds from other villagers and used them to weave conical hats called *jhapis*, which farmers wore to protect themselves from the sun's heat. "My husband was very poor, but he was a good man," she said. "Our days were hard, but filled with love." The sale of *jhapis* provided their only income. They remained childless.

That was Shahida's life well into her thirties. On one extremely hot day in 2000, her husband came back from the market where he had been selling *jhapis* all morning and collapsed, gasping on the ground in front of their hut. "He said he felt suffocated and was having trouble breathing. My neighbors and I rushed him to the hospital around 1:30 p.m., but by three o'clock my husband was dead." It may have been heatstroke, a heart attack, or any number of underlying conditions that proper medical care, were it available and affordable, likely would have treated.

Shahida had always managed their household, gathering fuel, carrying water from the river, repairing the thatch, and cooking the daily meals. But she had never worked for money. "I didn't know what to do," she said. "I'd wake up and worry about how I would survive. I had no husband, no food, not even a handful of rice. I went hungry for days." She became a burden on the other villagers, who asked her how long she planned to scavenge from others' scraps.

At the time, urbanization was giving rise to brick factories around the Bangladeshi countryside. Giant kilns filled the air with soot. The neighbors suggested she join other women digging and hauling clay at a brickyard several miles away. "I remember not having had anything to eat for three days when I decided to go," she said. "I walked an hour to the brickyard south of here on an empty stomach. All day, I dug mud and carried it half a mile back to the factory in a bowl balanced on my head." Payment depended on how much clay she hauled. On some days, she received twelve Bangladeshi taka, or about 24 US cents at the time. The most she ever earned in a day of work was 25 taka. "We hardly got time to take a break to eat. My workday started at 10 a.m. and ended at 6 p.m. We were allowed to take a lunch break, but taking long breaks meant I'd get paid less. So there was no time to rest." Life was a static misery, and she had no notion that anything could ever be different.

In 2002, a group of strangers came to the village. They said they were from BRAC, a Bangladeshi organization known mainly for making microloans to poor women, although they provided other services as well. Their intentions seemed vague and cryptic, and Shahida wanted nothing to do with them. "I didn't know who they were," she said. "I didn't want to take their money. How would I return a loan? I didn't believe a word they said, and I was scared of them."

The BRAC people conducted "a long and tedious survey," she said, and then selected eight destitute women, including Shahida—and promptly left the same day without much explanation. "They didn't tell us anything." A little more than a week later, they returned and informed the eight women that they could choose to receive cows, goats, or chickens. "We refused. We said, 'We don't have the money to pay for any of that.' I didn't want anything to do with BRAC."

"We don't want your money!" the lead BRAC officer told the women. "You don't have to pay us anything. We will give you cows, goats, or chickens, whichever you choose." This was not microfinance, he explained, but a program designed for people too poor for microfinance. If she chose to join, Shahida would stay with the program and receive training and support for two years, after which she would be on her own. The program was in its pilot stage, and it had a cumbersome name in English: Challenging the Frontiers of Poverty Reduction—Targeting the Ultra-Poor (CFPR-TUP).

Founded by a former accountant in 1972, BRAC was now by far the largest development organization in the country and, by some measures, the largest nongovernmental, nonprofit organization in the world. In 2002, it had about sixty thousand employees, ran almost thirty-four thousand schools, and worked in sixty-one thousand villages across Bangladesh, its services reaching an estimated seventy million people, or more than half the country's population at the time. But it had yet to build trust in Shahida's community. Several neighbors said BRAC planned to send them to a foreign country—"a very frightening thought," said Shahida. "My life was already miserable. I didn't want any added trouble." Though it was an organization founded in Bangladesh, a Muslim country, the neighbors warned the women that BRAC would convert them to Christianity. "We all thought it was a foreign agency preying on our situation." Some of the eight women approached the *matabor*, the "village leader," who encouraged them to participate. A BRAC *apa*, the Bengali term for "older sister," came and talked to them several times. Another BRAC *bhai*, or "older brother," held multiple courtyard sessions.

After a month of this, Shahida and the seven other women made a group decision to join. She recalled what the BRAC *apa* told her: "You are still young and physically fit. You are able to offer manual labor. But you don't have a husband or any children—no one to look after you when you're older. If you take this opportunity to improve your life, you can save up enough to take care of yourself. You will be independent."

Shahida chose to receive a native breed of goats, "because it sells for a good price, is easy to manage and take care of, and its meat is tastier than other breeds." In August 2002, BRAC gave her five female goats and a three-day training on how to feed them, care for them, and keep them healthy. The CFPR-TUP program also allotted her a stipend of 70 taka ($1.40) per day, far more than she ever earned at the brickyard, to give her breathing room while she learned to raise the goats. "Three days after I got the goats, I took them to a neighbor who had rams. In no time, all five goats were pregnant. I was so happy!"

By this point in telling the story, the sun has risen farther in the sky. Shahida invites me into her mud-brick hut, to avoid both the heat and the small crowd of villagers who have gathered to hear the conversation. Her home is about the size of a pickup truck, the only light coming from a crude, round window opening. The interior is decorated with pictures cut out from newspapers. She said she can't read the papers and doesn't know what they mean, but she likes having these images, even black-and-white faces of strangers, decorating her walls.

She sits down on the bed to continue. "Back then, I didn't even have this bed," she said. "I slept on the ground in my old straw hut, out where the courtyard is." There is still no electricity. "My village received electricity only five or six months ago, but I haven't gotten the connection yet. Those electric wires frighten me."

The BRAC *bhai* would visit at least once a week to check on her progress. The combination of a gift of goats, the stipend, and in-person coaching had a remarkable effect on Shahida. She could now imagine a better future and began working toward it. In December 2002, four months after she received the five goats, they gave birth to thirteen kids. This was the first time she had felt something akin to motherhood. She named each of the goats, and they came when called. "By now it was winter, so I couldn't leave the baby goats outside. They would die if they got cold. I kept them inside my hut with me. The babies slept on my bed. I covered them with my blanket and kept them warm. When I got up to use the washroom, the goats would get up too. They would run outside and do their business and drink milk from their mother. When I got back to my bed, they would jump in and take their spots again. They never urinated or defecated in my bed. They were so well mannered."

About a week after the birth of the thirteenth goat, a BRAC *bhai* came to visit. It was early morning, and Shahida hadn't yet risen. The *bhai* couldn't find any goats in the courtyard. The neighbors looked and couldn't find them either. The *bhai* knocked on her door. "I heard your goats delivered, so I came to see the babies," he said. "But I can't find them anywhere, neither the babies nor the mothers. Your neighbors are also looking for your goats. Where are they?"

"You know, he was worried," Shahida said, suppressing a giggle. "I told him to come inside. He came in with a few neighbors. They looked around. Then I pulled back my blanket and uncovered my baby goats! Everyone was ecstatic! My neighbors couldn't believe how much I loved my baby goats."

She could not keep tragedy at bay for long, however. One afternoon, Shahida was visiting a neighbor when she heard the goats screaming in her courtyard. They ran out to see a fox dragging one of the baby goats away.

She and the neighbor gave chase. "We beat the fox! How dare he! But I couldn't save her. My baby goat died. I buried her. My heart was broken. I didn't know where all the tears came from."

The next day at a group training at the BRAC office, Shahida broke down in tears. The staff tried to tell her it was "only a goat." One of the senior BRAC officers pulled her aside and admonished her: "Stop crying now! You'll have more goats. It will be okay."

"It wasn't just a goat," she sobbed. "It was my baby goat!"

I cautiously point out to Shahida that she herself chose this breed because she likes the taste of goat meat. "Yes, it's true what I said earlier," she admits. "But I would never harm my own goats. If I have to eat goat meat, I'll go to the market and buy it. If I sell one and the person who buys it eats it, that's their business. But I will never eat my goats."

⋆ ⋆ ⋆

I visit Shahida again in 2019. Her hair seems a bit grayer and her voice even louder than I remember. Due to recent violence against foreigners, I arrive with a police escort—unnecessary, in my view. "Everyone gets along here!" she shouts at the officers. "You never come here, because we never have any problems!" It is hard to imagine the woman she described earlier, half-starved and working at the brickyard, talking to the police like that.

The tattered plastic tarps on her neighbors' walls are gone, replaced by brick. Shahida now has electricity, though she admits she was terrified of the switches for the first several weeks. She is planning to build a new house out of brick. Shahida's three acres produce everything she and her household require: rice for herself and, from the husks and straw left over from the threshing, fodder for a cow, a calf, and three goats. She also has fifteen chickens. From the sale of milk, dung (used for fuel and fertilizer), eggs, and the young animals she fattens, Shahida continues to build a better life. She has bought a new milk cart since I last saw her, which she rents out for additional cash.

I suggest to Shahida that if the world around her were to disappear and she were the last person on earth, she would still be able to live as she does, off the fruit of her land. She replies thoughtfully, almost philosophically. "Everyone wants to build a good life, to live honestly and eat well, but all that requires good health," she says. "Even if all that were to happen, I could go on and continue building my life, as long as I have good health. But not if God gave me some illness."

It occurs to me that Shahida's surefootedness is deceptive. Rising from poverty must be like walking on a knife's edge, the threat of an illness or a bad harvest always looming. For those accustomed to living in constant stress and hunger, even a single dead goat can be devastating. Surely Shahida's confidence today is partly a result of the vast material improvements in her life. Yet a growing body of evidence suggests the causality might also run in the opposite direction—that rising from poverty may have been a result of her newfound confidence, not just its cause. Research from Abhijit Banerjee and Esther Duflo, MIT economists who won the 2019 Nobel Prize, suggests that activating people's confidence and giving them hope can lead to material improvements that cannot otherwise be accounted for by goats, cows, cash, and the like.

To be sure, this theory is potentially misleading, perhaps even dangerous, since it risks creating the impression that poverty is somehow self-inflicted and that all that Shahida really needed was a good pep talk. This is plainly not the case. In the case of Shahida and countless others, despair is well founded, for no matter how hard they work, nothing ever seems to make a difference. Poverty results from factors outside their control, including routine mistreatment by others; oppression and exploitation, especially for women, are a huge part of the equation. Even so, when material conditions do change via a sudden positive shock—through the gift of a goat, as with Shahida, or through livelihood training or a one-time cash transfer—it is likely that psychological factors, including a sense of despair rooted in generations of lived experience, will remain an obstacle.

Others who participated in the CFPR-TUP pilot also faced problems with their livestock and found themselves similarly overwhelmed. There were tales of stolen chickens and even a poisoned cow, the full story of which is told in chapter 21. Shahida was ultimately able to work through her grief with the support of a coach, who visited weekly to check in on her progress. As of 2022, the CFPR-TUP program (now under the manageable name Ultra-Poor Graduation) had scaled up to reach more than two million households, with one hundred thousand continuing to "graduate" from the program every year. Like many BRAC programs, this one started with a small pilot that was ultimately successful because it treated not just the material aspects of poverty but many of the underlying psychological and social causes as well, including, in the case of Shahida and many others, a deep-seated sense of hopelessness.

* * *

The road here was a long one. It is largely the story of the accountant himself, a lover of Shakespeare, T. S. Eliot, and Tagore, who had little patience for lofty ideas and speeches. Fazle Hasan Abed, the founder of BRAC, understood that poetry would never awaken the consciousness of the world when so many people could not even read. Only a well-managed intervention, driven by the structures of a large organization, could ignite the spark of self-worth in people like Shahida, giving them the power to change their own lives and the world around them. That power would come, in large part, from their recognition that a better world was possible. This is a book about overcoming the despair of centuries and replacing it with hope.

It began with a storm.

2

A MOMENT OF AWAKENING

The patrons of the Chittagong Club knew a cyclone had been gathering force over the Bay of Bengal and was due to make landfall that night. The wind picked up around 7 p.m., whooshing through the colonnades on the deep veranda. It was November 12, 1970, and Fazle Abed, who ran the finance department at Shell Pakistan, ordered a scotch and soda from the bar and stared out the tall windows at the trees whipping in the gale on the manicured grounds. The club was four miles inland, perched on a hill overlooking Chittagong, the main port city in what was then East Pakistan. None of the patrons felt they were in any danger there.

The Chittagong Club was a colonial relic, a gated remnant of the Raj, the era of British rule. On its veranda, the wives of English tea planters once sipped their gin and tonics and complained about the natives, in scenes reminiscent of E. M. Forster's *A Passage to India*. Twenty-three years had passed since the dismantling of British rule on the subcontinent and the subsequent partition of British India into Hindu-majority India and Muslim-majority Pakistan. The only thing that had changed at the Chittagong Club was the members' skin color. Waiters in white gloves, turbans, and tight-fitting trousers called *churidars* continued to serve roast beef, curries, and mulligatawny soup. The postcolonial elites of East Pakistan, Abed among them, had adopted the habits of the former rulers, including a set of arcane club rituals. Membership required a recommendation from a current member and an appearance at an initiation ceremony in black tie and cummerbund. One could be blackballed for failing to meet the club's standards. Abed, a pipe-smoking Anglophile in a pinstriped suit, who had spent fourteen years in Britain and could recite Shakespearean soliloquies, easily made the cut. A bachelor with no family to go home to, he dined at the club three nights a week.

Abed moved away from the windows and mingled with the other patrons, the ice clinking in his glass. He wondered how many people would die that night. Nobody knew how big the cyclone would be but, on the unprotected islands offshore, people's lives were already precarious. They were directly in the storm's path.

His driver took him home—a rented house with several empty guest-rooms. In the morning, he was woken by loud knocking and leaped out of bed to discover the front door banging open and shut, the wind having nearly blown it off its hinges. On the way to work, he saw several downed trees, but, apart from that, everything seemed normal.

How many would die? The answer, when it came, surpassed anyone's worst expectations. In the early 1970s, communication lines were poor, so it was forty-eight hours before the general public learned that the Bhola cyclone, as it was called, had been a cataclysm of historic proportions. The death toll was between three and five hundred thousand, making it one of the worst natural disasters in recorded history. On coastal islands, where people lived in thatched huts five feet above sea level, the cyclone had struck at high tide, causing a thirty-five-foot storm surge that swept away settlements, farms, and fishing villages. Those who survived were on the brink of starvation.

Abed was in a better position than many to organize rescue and relief. He had a well-paid job and perks that included corporate housing. Shell had given him the entire four-bedroom floor of a house in one of the city's upscale neighborhoods, plus a cook, a gardener, and a domestic servant. His position at the oil company allowed him to requisition Shell's transport, including motor launches and speedboats. He was also well connected, with friends in public health who were itching to help. "I always had a hankering for doing something good for my country," he said, years later. "That was there in the back of my mind. But I didn't know how to go about doing it." Now the opportunity had arrived.

Abed's friends from Dhaka, the capital, soon descended on his house in Chittagong. These included Viquar Choudhury, a barrister whom he had met while living in London, where they had become best friends; Viquar's wife, Runi Khan, who was also an old family friend of Abed's; Jon Rohde, an American doctor at Dhaka's Cholera Research Lab, who had come to Dhaka to avoid being sent to Vietnam; and Candy Rohde, Jon's wife. None had any experience in disaster relief, but few others seemed to be doing anything to help.

Abed stayed behind on the mainland to play an administrative role while his friends gathered whatever food and relief supplies they could find and boarded an old coastal steamer, landing the next day on Hatiya, a large, low island, halfway to Bhola, where the cyclone had made landfall. They knew there must be more survivors farther to the west, so Jon and Viquar attached an outboard motor to one of Shell's twelve-foot aluminum dinghies and, without any navigational equipment and only a single tank of gas, headed straight into the horizon toward the deltaic islands at the mouth of the Ganges. Fifty miles west of Chittagong, they found an island called Manpura, where groups of famished survivors kept themselves alive with banana roots, the occasional coconut, and whatever else they could claw from the mud. It was eleven days after the cyclone, and still nobody had come to help them. Jon and Viquar, who had no radios, stayed on Manpura until Candy spotted them from a crop duster flown by a pilot working for a Swiss aerial spraying company, who had dropped what he was doing to assist.

Back in Chittagong, people packed into Abed's home, creating an assembly line to stuff hard-boiled eggs and puffed rice into burlap sacks for airdrops. Abed worked the phones, calling on colleagues and their wives to volunteer or to help with accommodations or donations. Candy made runs in the crop duster, pushing the bags from the open door before circling back to the mainland. She and Jon developed a system of signal flags to communicate what was needed on the ground: clothing, utensils, matches, medicine, or kerosene. Abed would put in a day's work at Shell and return to the smell of the beef curry his cook had made to feed the volunteers packed into his home.

Weeks after the storm, Abed still hadn't seen Manpura himself, so he hitched a ride on one of the helicopters that was now making runs to the island on a regular basis. Manpura is a shifting expanse of silt and palm trees about two miles wide and nine miles long, formed by the deposits of the Ganges and Brahmaputra river systems. From the helicopter, Abed saw an image that would haunt him for the rest of his life: in the shallow waters of the bay surrounding the island lay countless bodies of adults, children, and livestock; he also saw bright streaks of color in the palm trees and soon realized they were women's saris hanging from bloated bodies tangled in the fronds.

Manpura had been densely populated before the cyclone, with about thirty-two thousand people. Only thirteen thousand survived. Very few were women, as only the men had been strong enough to cling to the trunks of palm trees for hours, buffeted by the waves and howling wind. The saris tangled in the palm trees belonged to young mothers who had died trying to save their children from the surging sea.

As the blades whirred above, Abed's conscience felt a jolt from which it never fully recovered. He understood now, on a visceral level, the reason for the massive death toll. The dead had lived in thatched huts, doing what little they could for their families. Most were illiterate; many suffered frequent illness and daily hunger. They never had the means to build solid roofs to protect themselves or their families. There were no doors to be blown from their hinges. Their circumstances had killed them, not the cyclone itself. They were born poor and died poor, and they died because they were poor.

Abed considered the cozy life he had been leading. He thought of his job at a multinational corporation, the thrice-weekly visits to the Chittagong Club, and the house with its cook, gardener, and servant. He looked back on everything that had led him here, including his privileged upbringing and his carefree years as a London expatriate. He was thirty-five years old. It had taken him years to decide what he wanted to do with his life. Now, in a single instant, it all seemed meaningless.

3

A SHY BOY

Understanding how Abed reached that moment requires a dive into the past, starting with his childhood in British India. His earliest memories were a series of standalone images, like frames from a lost film: the façade of his grandfather's house in rural Bengal, a house aglow with lights in Calcutta, and his favorite uncle, Sayeedul, sliding the yolks of his breakfast eggs onto his plate.

That first image, his grandfather's home, can still be viewed today in the Hasan family's walled compound in the village of Baniachong, now in northern Bangladesh. Abed was perhaps three, looking up at a one-story concrete dwelling as the servants brought the midday meal to the family table, just inside the main doors. Behind him, concrete steps led down to a pond rimmed by areca palms, which towered over the estate like giant broomsticks. To the left was a smaller house built by his father, its façade perpendicular to the main house. Set amid hedged walkways and mango trees, the two houses were close enough that people on each veranda could have a conversation without raising their voices. For the boy, this was the entire universe.

Baniachong sits at the southern edge of the *haor*, a vast watery lowland that stretches north to the hills of Assam, India. Just outside the compound's main gate, an expanse of grass stretches out in front of the local mosque. This served as the compound's outer courtyard, where Abed's grandfather, Rafiqul Hasan—a man small in physical stature but huge in charisma—would hold court and mediate disputes. The grass also served as the pitch where Abed, as he grew older, would play soccer with other local children, whose parents were the field hands and servants living in the surrounding village, in thatched huts set amid bamboo thickets. Outside the walls of the compound, in the village proper, Baniachong's dirt roads ran along embankments surrounding artificial ponds, the only source of drinking water until the family installed a well in the 1940s, the land having been built up by hand over centuries to protect the homes from the summer floods. Beyond the village, the rice paddies sprawled outward into the *haor*, turning bright green once a year just before harvest.

★ ★ ★

Abed was born in the waning days of the old feudal system of the Raj. His family, the Hasans, were the local Muslim zamindars, the landowning aristocracy, their compound the Bengali equivalent of a European manor and the center of power for the surrounding community. The voice of his grandmother, the matriarch, would rise above the hubbub of the compound. "There are only thirteen people in this family," she would often say. "But the kitchen cooks meals for fifty-six people!" Her extended headcount included the servants, the workers who tilled the fields, their wives, the imam of the mosque, the muezzin who led the call to prayer, and all of their children.

Indoors, on hot nights, woven bamboo fan blades affixed to the ceiling would sway back and forth, attached to a mechanism of ropes and pulleys. A servant outside pulled the ropes or operated a crank while the family rested under the fan. Abed's father and three uncles were the last link to a forgotten world, part of the last generation to learn Persian, the court language and lingua franca of the Mughal Empire. His father told stories of great-uncles who would pass the time composing Persian poetry, collaborating on verses even while in distant villages. One would write a few lines, send a servant on horseback to carry it to his brother, and await the reply.

Rafiqul Hasan, Abed's paternal grandfather, dominated the extended clan. His job as government sub-registrar, or magistrate for land registration, understates his importance, for he was one of the most prominent men in the region of Sylhet, where Baniachong sits. The British viceroy of India had granted Rafiqul the title Khan Bahadur, an honorific bestowed on Muslim nobility for acts of public service. Rafiqul Hasan was a small man who walked fast and commanded the room. During the days-long journey from Calcutta to Baniachong, he would circulate through the train, asking fellow passengers about upcoming marriages and events. When he returned, he would immediately send letters inquiring about their well-being.

Interviewed at his home in Los Angeles in 2019, shortly before his death at eighty-eight, Abed's cousin Nayeemul Hasan, along with Abed, was one of the last living relatives to remember Rafiqul Hasan. "I can't compare anyone with my grandfather," he said. "He freely mixed with everyone, from the highest to the lowest person. He was the type of person who, even if he was sleeping when somebody called to discuss a problem, would immediately go out and talk to that person. My grandmother used to say, 'What is this? You are going to run when any ordinary person comes?' And he would say, 'But he really wants to talk to me. He is my subject!'"

The Khan Bahadur had married well. His wife, Abed's paternal grandmother, Rabeya, was the only sister of Syed Shamsul Huda, an eminent Muslim scholar and political leader in Calcutta, who had a British knighthood and the title of nawab, an honorific the British had retained from the Mughals. Syed Shamsul Huda would feature prominently in the early life of all of Rafiqul's sons, for Rafiqul had sent them to Calcutta to be educated, and they were effectively raised in the nawab's palace, since the nawab and his wife had no natural children of their own. These men, Abed's father and three uncles, would in turn feature prominently in Abed's life.

Such stories of privilege—the nawab's palace in Calcutta, the servants, the titles, and the landholdings—likely give an exaggerated sense of the Hasan family's wealth. In fact, the buildings in the Baniachong compound are tin-roofed, concrete bungalows, not mansions, and the family holdings were never large enough that the sons of Rafiqul Hasan did not have to find work. Abed's father, Siddique Hasan, was the oldest and thus was expected to return to Baniachong after completing his studies to take up residence in the ancestral seat. When he did so, he took a job similar to his father's, working as a civil servant in the land-registry department of the nearest town, Habiganj. The other uncles stayed in Calcutta to pursue their careers: Abed's oldest uncle, Rashidul (Nayeemul's father), had the demeanor of a judge and ultimately became one; the second-oldest, Obaidul, who was more free-wheeling, became a dentist; and the youngest, Sayeedul, who was by far Abed's favorite, became a businessman and patron of the arts.

Though five hundred miles away, Calcutta, the capital of Bengal, was never far from the family's mind. When Abed was four, his oldest sister was married there. Though he could not recall the overnight train journey, he remembered the house his father rented for the event, completely aglow. The boy had never seen so many electric lights. The family would visit Calcutta for extended stays every year or two, as the ties were strong on both parents' sides: Abed's mother, Syeda Sufya Khatun, was the daughter of a minister in the provincial government.

Abed's youngest uncle, Sayeedul (pronounced "Saidul") Hasan, would often visit from Calcutta, and it was in Baniachong that Sayeedul would offer him the yolks of his eggs, cooked sunny-side up. It is hard to overstate Sayeedul Hasan's influence on Abed. "Throughout my life, I have heard many people say they never met a person as fundamentally kind as Sayeedul Hasan," Abed said. The other uncles were strict disciplinarians, but Sayeedul was warm, approachable, and cultured. Baniachong was a backwater compared to Calcutta, and when Sayeedul visited, young Abed felt a breeze of worldliness and sophistication. Sayeedul loved poetry and often spoke the name of Rabindranath Tagore, the great poet, still alive at the time of Abed's birth, who is to Bengali what Shakespeare is to English. Sayeedul also revered Kazi Nazrul Islam, a revolutionary poet who was then at the height of his influence. He gave his nieces and nephews long passages of verse by Tagore and Nazrul and asked that they recite them. In part due to Sayeedul's influence, Abed became a voracious reader and reciter of poetry.

⋆ ⋆ ⋆

Born at home, Fazle Hasan Abed entered this sprawling household on March 19, 1935, though the official record gives a different day and year, for it was the norm for parents to make up a birthday more convenient for schooling. Abed's name can also be confusing to a Westerner, since Bengalis did not adhere to Western norms of given name and surname. Parents would often give children a nickname at birth, and "Abed" became both name and surname. It stuck for life. Nobody close to him ever called him Fazle.

His father, Siddique Hasan, already had three children from a previous marriage and two from Abed's mother; two more would come later. This large family split its time between Baniachong and a rented house in the town, where the children attended primary school. Young Abed did not inherit his grandfather's extroversion, for he was a shy boy who clung to his mother, and, once he learned to read, he found himself more comfortable around books than people. Of his siblings, he grew closest to his sister Nurani, less than two years older, who looked after her kid brother at Habiganj Primary School. As his awareness expanded, his sister, his mother, and the Baniachong compound remained the nucleus of Abed's early world.

Syeda, Abed's mother, was a woman of quiet intensity, and it is likely that she passed on much of her personality to her bookish son. Deeply religious, she prayed five times a day without fail, and though Abed never shared her piety, he recalled being captivated by her retelling of religious parables and stories from *The Thousand and One Nights*. Syeda is described by those who knew her as a woman of compassion meted out equally to all, and Abed often called her his greatest teacher. She took great interest in the welfare of the servants, fetching the doctor when they fell ill, advising them on whom to marry, and caring for their children as if they were her own. Nayeemul, Abed's cousin, said his *borochachi*, or "oldest aunt," was the type of person who made you feel like you were the most important person in the world just by talking to you. "My aunt was so loving, so accommodating, so affectionate, that I used to feel shy just looking at her," he said. "Whenever I would see her, I felt she was looking right at me."

Abed's father was more distant, constrained by rules of propriety and class. When the time came to enroll his children in school, he would send one of the assistants from his office rather than going himself, as Abed noticed other fathers doing. Siddique Hassan did not believe a man of his upper-class background should be taking a child to school. Abed described how his first day at school led to the recording of his official birthday: "My father's assistant took me to school, and the headmaster said, 'How old is he?' And the assistant said, 'Three,' even though I was actually four. He didn't know. And the headmaster probably thought, 'Oh my God, this is Siddique Hasan's son,' and let me in. That was April 27, 1939." Abed never had a birth certificate. The date April 27, 1936, was copied from one record to another and recognized as his date of birth throughout his life.

His first inkling that he lived in a bubble of privilege came at the age of seven or eight, depending on how you count the years. Far beyond the village, India was changing. In 1943, in the midst of World War II, Bengal was struck by a terrible famine. News arrived from relatives in Calcutta, where Abed's maternal grandfather had become minister of agriculture, that rural people were coming to the city in droves, carrying their emaciated children and driven mad with starvation. The corpses began piling up on the streets. Abed's grandfather fasted as though it were Ramadan, refusing food and drink during daylight hours.

More than three million people died in the great Bengali famine of 1943. Historians still debate its causes. Some blame the Japanese invasion of Burma, which cut off supplies of rice. Others point to Winston Churchill's diversion of food from the rest of India to feed British soldiers. Churchill did not think highly of South Asians in general and expressed more concern for Nazi-occupied Greece, also suffering from famine, than the British Empire's own Indian subjects, arguing in a 1943 British Cabinet meeting that "starvation of anyhow underfed Bengalis is less serious than that of sturdy Greeks."[1] He also once asked the viceroy, if conditions in India were truly so bad, why Gandhi, whom he despised, hadn't died yet.[2]

Abed was aware of something terrible happening outside his familial cocoon. Baniachong was never severely affected by the famine, but it was bad enough to the south and west that skeletal migrants arrived in the village to beg for food, having walked hundreds of miles. Abed said the famine made him aware, for the first time, of two starkly divided classes of people: "One class serves us, and the other *is* us." The children with whom he played football on the pitch in front of the mosque were in one category; he was in another. There were those who sat indoors beneath the fans on hot nights, and there were those who sat outside and operated the fans. This was not something he questioned—and to an extent he never did, for he employed servants throughout his life, as do most middle- and upper-class South Asians. Gradually, though, he began to understand that, despite the stirring poetry of Tagore, for the vast majority of Bengalis, life was no pastoral idyll.

* * *

When Rafiqul Hasan died in 1943, Abed's father became the patriarch, but by most accounts he lacked the charisma and magnetism of his predecessor. It probably would have been difficult under any circumstances for Siddique Hasan to fill his father's shoes, but, in any case, personal and geopolitical changes conspired to cut off the possibility.

When Abed was twelve, the world around him began to change rapidly. In the distant Bengali capital, Sayeedul Hasan had long remained one of Calcuttan high society's most eligible bachelors. While studying, he had lived with his older brother Rashidul, a high-court judge who had been Syed Shamsul Huda's favorite. The nawab had chosen Rashidul to marry his niece, Razia, whom the nawab had raised as his adopted daughter, since he had no children of his own, and when Razia died in 1933, Rashidul married another of the nawab's nieces. The judge had a wide circle of influence in Calcutta with both Hindus and Muslims. After graduating, Sayeedul Hasan, the youngest of the Hasan sons, remained single, living for a time with his best friend, Mohammed Ismail, and his wife, Roshanara, a woman of great poise—and, discordantly, fierce leftist convictions—whom the nieces and nephews called auntie, or "Ismail *chachi*." Sayeedul and Ismail started several businesses together, mainly in industrial detergents. Eventually, through the judge's circles, Sayeedul found a suitable bride.

Her name was Farida, but she was known to everyone as Baiju, after the French *bijou*, meaning "jewel." She came from the well-to-do Rahman family, which owned tea estates in the far north of Bengal, close to Darjeeling. She was a fashionable girl, described as beautiful and popular. Baiju was sixteen and Sayeedul was thirty-five when they became engaged.

In 1947, Siddique Hasan, Abed's father, began planning the now familiar train journey with his family from Baniachong to the capital for the wedding. Siddique went first, on his own, staying at the judge's home. Early one morning, before the rest of the family arrived, Nayeemul, the judge's son, recalled hearing "a great hue and cry" in the house. Siddique Hasan had suffered a stroke, leaving much of his left side paralyzed. Abed, his mother, and his siblings boarded the next train to Calcutta. The wedding went ahead as planned, and Baiju soon became the darling of Sayeedul Hasan's crowd of literati in Calcutta as well as Abed's friend, for they were close in age. But his father was never the same again, and the aftermath of this event profoundly altered the trajectory of Abed's life.

⋆ ⋆ ⋆

Far greater changes were afoot. The British Raj dissolved in August 1947. Even for young Abed, the end of colonial rule was an exhilarating moment. But in the major cities, Hindus and Muslims fought one another in waves of brutal violence and communal rioting, extinguishing the fleeting jubilation of freedom. When Pakistan split from India, Bengal itself was split into east and west, putting Calcutta and Baniachong in two separate countries. The Muslim areas of Bengal were now East Pakistan, part of a new country, Pakistan, whose troubles seemed ordained from the start, its two sections separated by a thousand miles. Many relatives left Calcutta or would do so in the coming years. Sought after by both India and Pakistan, Abed's uncle Rashidul opted to join the judiciary of Pakistan and received a posting as a district judge in the city of Comilla, a hundred miles south of Baniachong.

Abed never sensed a sharp divide between the religions near his home, and he saw no communal fighting in Baniachong. Temples and shrines to gods in the Hindu pantheon stood close to the mosque outside the Hasan compound. People's shared language seemed to transcend religion, and every schoolchild, Muslim and Hindu alike, recognized the iconic, white-bearded face of the revered Tagore, a Hindu with a universal religious outlook. Those who had never gone to school seemed more concerned with the rising and ebbing of the water governing the rice harvest than which god or gods they worshiped. Nevertheless, the region's partition had a profound effect on local life. Many of Abed's Hindu schoolmates abruptly left for India, never to be seen again. Their parents may well have feared for their safety. The children of Muslims fleeing West Bengal for similar reasons replaced the familiar faces in the classroom. Abed already lacked many close friends his own age, and the sudden disappearance of Hindu classmates must have been a jarring experience for a young man just emerging from his shell.

Upheaval in the region and the classroom added to the upheaval at home caused by his father's stroke. Until now, the family had been living mainly at the house in nearby Habiganj. Abed, his sister, and his two younger brothers, all within five years of one another, attended an elite government school in the town while spending weekends on the Baniachong compound. Now, no longer able to work, his father had to retire early, and the family moved back to Baniachong to live there full time. This prompted one of the first major decisions Abed had to make on his own: he could stay in Baniachong and attend the local school, or he could live with his uncle Rashidul in Comilla and attend a much better school.

Leaving Baniachong would prove to be a permanent move. He was only twelve, but his parents insisted this decision be entirely his. He knew it would be hard to leave his immediate family, especially his mother and sister, but he viewed it as a challenge, as though he had something to prove. When he decided to move to Comilla, he took pride in the gesture of independence. "It was kind of a show-off thing," he said, many years later. It is hard not to see the influence of Sayeedul Hasan, who made Abed aware of a life more sophisticated than anything he would find within the walls of the rural compound and the surrounding thickets and wetlands.

In Comilla, Pakistan's fledgling government had given Rashidul Hasan a large house on a five-acre compound, where Abed would live well, surrounded by several older cousins, including Nayeemul. As a district judge, Rashidul was among the most distinguished men of the city. He owned a steel-blue 1934 Vauxhall, a car considered an antique even at the time, and when it came out, the town came to a standstill as people watched the judge go by. Disciplined and religious, he was fluent in Arabic and wrote commentary on the Koran in his spare time. To the children, he was a distant figure with a magisterial beard reminiscent of Tagore himself. The judge's house was like a museum, for he had inherited much of the furniture from the nawab's Calcutta palace. The damp air of the drawing room held the odor of old things, like carved wooden furniture and upholstery that was not to be touched, including the throne-like chair of the late nawab himself. In this rarified environment, Abed stepped out into adolescence.

He spent his teenage years in the judge's household, following the family even when his uncle was reposted to Pabna, a city far to the west. In the Pabna compound, Abed lived in a detached house with Nayeemul. The youngest in the house, Abed did not labor over his schoolwork, but rather was "sharper and more intelligent" than others who studied harder, Nayeemul recalled. The judge was equally detached from everyone, sons and nephews alike, and did not stand over the children's shoulders to check on their school performance. "Nobody was monitoring anything," Nayeemul said.

Abed continued to visit Baniachong. Soon he was reading old adventure novels like *Robinson Crusoe* in English. During school breaks, he would sit for hours reading in the corner bedroom at the front of his father's house, the door to the veranda open and the windows letting in a cross breeze. But he never lived at home full time again.

* * *

In 1952, Abed graduated from secondary school and entered Dhaka College, an elite school for boys from well-off families. Dhaka was the largest city in what was now East Pakistan, but it was still a sleepy provincial capital at the time, home to about 360,000, less than 1 percent of the population of predominantly rural East Pakistan. The population of Calcutta, by comparison, was a teeming four million.

Abed initially boarded at a college hostel, but when his maternal grandfather, the former minister, visited and saw his accommodations, he immediately moved him to the house of a maternal uncle who, like Rashidul Hasan, served as a district judge. His grandfather, apparently, was concerned he might fall under the influence of disreputable boys. While he lived in the home of this uncle, a cousin named Sarwat was born. Abed had just turned eighteen and was asked to perform the honor of the ritual recitation of the *azan*, the Islamic call to prayer, in her ear. (He would marry Sarwat forty-six years later.)

When he graduated in 1954, Abed still had no idea what he wanted to do with his life. For a time, he thought he might study law and become a barrister or a judge, like two of his uncles, or perhaps enter government service, like his father and maternal grandfather. He had done well in science in school and considered studying physics at university, but none of these ideas seized him.

The problem was East Pakistan itself, which held few meaningful opportunities. Divided Pakistan's center of power lay in Urdu-speaking West Pakistan, and to a rising number of Bengalis, it seemed the government was treating the more populous East like a poor relation, continuing the neglect of the British. Language itself was becoming politically divisive. A Pakistani regime wary of separatism and Indian influence viewed the Bengali language with suspicion. When the father of Pakistan, Muhammad Ali Jinnah, visited East Pakistan in 1948 and declared, in English no less, that Urdu would be the nation's only official language, the Bengali intelligentsia did not take it well. Brought up on Tagore, Bengalis felt they spoke a noble language that defined them as a people, perhaps more so than religion. Having broken free from the English yoke, they were not inclined to accept yet another foreign language as the national tongue. In the universities, students began agitating for the recognition of Bengali as an official language. As the years passed, demands for East Pakistani autonomy became increasingly vocal.

Abed felt this Bengali pride. At the same time, his uncle Sayeedul had awakened a sense of cosmopolitanism that made East Pakistan seem backward. Peripatetic since the age of twelve, Abed felt no need to remain in such a country. The United Kingdom beckoned, for, as Commonwealth citizens, Bengalis could freely travel and settle there, and by the time Abed graduated in 1954, Sayeedul had moved to London to work as the trade commissioner for Pakistan. Abed needed a decent excuse to go abroad besides wanting to see the rest of the world, so he chose a course of study that he could never have pursued at home: naval architecture. At the time, the country made almost no vessels larger than the flat-bottomed wooden boats that plied the rivers and rural wetlands. There was no shipbuilding industry; in fact, there was no industry at all. With Sayeedul's encouragement, Abed flew to London. This was before long-haul jets, and the journey took thirty-six hours with seven layovers, on propeller planes. From London he took the train to Glasgow, one of the great shipbuilding centers of the world, to begin his studies at the Royal Technical College. It was his first trip outside East Pakistan.

Abed was never able to adequately explain this odd first choice for his career. He did not know anyone in the shipbuilding industry or any relatives who had studied naval architecture, and, despite his earlier reading of *Robinson Crusoe*, he did not profess any romantic draw to the sea. He only recalled being "fed up with East Pakistan."

4

THE SWINGING CITY

Abed did not know a soul in Glasgow when he moved there to study naval architecture in 1954. He was officially eighteen; in reality, he was a year older. Short in stature with a cherubic face, he actually looked no more than fifteen. Since it was obvious from his dark brown skin that he wasn't a local teenager, people would often ask him whether he was in Scotland to visit an older brother. He began smoking a pipe to make himself seem older than he appeared.

Through family connections, he met Humayun Kabir, a fellow Bengali four years his senior who was studying pharmacology at the University of Strathclyde. The pair would often hang out at the British Council, a meeting place for international students, where they would play table tennis. The two became lifelong friends. This was one of the few lasting marks that Glasgow made on his life.

Naval architecture seems a random choice in hindsight, for Abed had no abiding interest in the subject and he retained little about hydrostatics or propulsion. He found Glasgow cold and dreary, and he craved more than what it could offer, for it failed to meet the expectations of a cosmopolitan life built up by his conversations with his uncle. He realized that if he were to go into shipbuilding, not only would he never be able to move back to East Pakistan, but he would also have to live in Scotland or someplace similarly cold and, in his mind, provincial, like Norway. One of the few things he learned to do in Glasgow was drink beer, the first time in his life he consumed alcohol. Bored by his studies, he turned inward, and to pass the time, he began reading the great English poets—from Shakespeare, Milton, Marvell, and Pope to the later Romantics like Keats and Tennyson.

After eighteen months, he confessed his dissatisfaction with Glasgow and his area of study in letters to both his father and his uncle Sayeedul.

They gave him conflicting advice. Siddique Hasan wrote back that, having made the choice, he should stick to it until he earned his degree. His uncle encouraged him to pursue something he might enjoy. "It's up to you," Sayeedul told him. "If you don't like studying naval architecture, don't do it." Naturally, Abed opted to take his uncle's advice.

★ ★ ★

"In this century, every decade has had its city," wrote Piri Halasz in a 1966 *Time* magazine cover story, and in the 1960s, "a decade dominated by youth," the place to be was London.[1] When Abed arrived in 1956 at the age of twenty, London was still emerging from its postwar funk. By the time he left twelve years later, "Swinging London" had become a global epicenter of fashion, the arts, and political activism. Perhaps more than any other period, Abed's years in London shaped his worldview and consciousness. He gained a deeper appreciation for the arts and began to develop his ideas about what an ideal society should look like. He also fell in love for the first time.

Sayeedul had, by that time, left London for a posting with the foreign trade office in Colombo, Sri Lanka (then Ceylon), so Abed initially stayed with a family friend named Tassaduq Ahmed. A former journalist in Dhaka, Ahmed would go on to become a political activist and a Soho restaurateur in the 1960s. His restaurant, the Ganges, was one of the first in London to feature a tandoori oven, and it would become a meeting point for Bangladesh liberation activists. In the late 1950s, however, Abed primarily remembered Tassaduq feeding him and his London friends a steady diet of Karl Marx.

In early 1957, Abed moved into the Pakistan Students Federation, a government-run student hostel for Pakistani nationals. Located amid the embassies in Belgravia, the hostel was a meeting place for young Pakistanis in London. Abed immediately gravitated toward the Bengali guests there, including Zakaria Khan, a wiry, garrulous law student. Though they had never before met, Abed and Zakaria turned out to have family connections: Zakaria's father, a civil servant in the provincial health ministry, was a friend of one of Abed's uncles. By this time, Abed had picked up other Anglophile affectations in addition to pipe smoking. Zakaria recalled him appearing "very much an Englishman, with a three-piece suit and an umbrella."

Abed fell in with a tight-knit group of young Bengalis, most of whom would remain lifelong friends. Besides Zakaria, this included Viquar Choudhury, who had also come to London for his studies. Viquar had initially chosen engineering but turned to law, drawn by an interest in leftist politics.

His gentle, philosophical persona matched Abed's, and the two became close friends. A third friend, Fazle Ali, studied accountancy and entertained the group with a dry, deadpan sense of humor. A fourth, Faruq Choudhury, slightly older than the others, already had a proper job, having come to London to train as a foreign-service officer for the Pakistan government.

To other young Bengalis in London, these four became known as an intellectual clique. None were opposed to the pleasures of drink. They would often meet at the pub and, as Zakaria put it, "discuss everything under the sun, starting from philosophy, to politics, to relationships and sex." They set up a Marxist study circle, which they dubbed the "College of Cardinals." Zakaria was tightly wound, with vehemently hard-left political views, and he got drunk faster than the others. He would frequently get into arguments, sometimes to the point of violence. Both Abed and Viquar recalled him getting so agitated that he once threw a chair across the room. As Zakaria put it, "I was a party-minded person."

When they started looking for longer-term accommodation, Zakaria's temperament gave Abed and Viquar pause. "Viquar and I decided that if we were to take Zakaria, we would not be able to study much," Abed said. "We would rather take a flat for just the two of us and leave Zakaria to his own devices. Zakaria was a little unhappy, because the three of us were close." Abed and Viquar soon found a cheap flat in Highbury, where they shared a single bedroom.

Abed initially considered studying law, until he looked closely at what that would entail: years of study with no income and a struggle to establish a practice back in East Pakistan. He enrolled instead in a five-year course at the Chartered Institute of Management Accountants. As part of the certification requirements, the institute required work in various firms to gain practical experience while studying for examinations on evenings and weekends. This would give Abed an immediate source of income. It would also give him a grounding in finance that would prove invaluable throughout his life.

One day in 1957, a telegram arrived from home, informing Abed that his mother, Syeda, had died of diabetes. Though he knew she had been diabetic for years, the news came as a complete shock. She was only forty-four. Shortly before he had left the country, his youngest brother had started giving her insulin shots before meals. "I didn't even understand in those days that it was a bad illness," he said. In the Muslim tradition, death rituals take place immediately, so there was no question of going home for the funeral.

Though he never shared her piety, Abed always cited his mother as his greatest teacher. He said the twin gifts of attention and affection had given him confidence and, therefore, the capacity to learn on his own. Many years later, Faruq Choudhury would comment on Abed's "amazing capacity to absorb shock." This was the first of many.

Abed took what little comfort he could in surrounding himself with people whose company he enjoyed. He also became, as he said, "a dilettante," further cultivating an air of culture. He began frequenting the theater and expanded his reading of literature into modernism. He tore through James Joyce's *Ulysses* in a matter of days.

Abed and Viquar found larger accommodations, joining Fazle Ali in a three-bedroom flat in Golders Green in the north of the city, just past Hampstead. Abed got a job in the office of a nearby meat-processing plant. In the evenings he'd experiment over the stove, making curries for Viquar and Fazle using English sausages from the plant. Their watering hole was the Old Bull and Bush, a centuries-old pub near Hampstead Heath.

Laila Kabir, the sister of Abed's aunt Baiju, recalled visiting him around this time. Though he had an upcoming accountancy exam, Laila noticed he did not seem to be studying for it, likely knowing he could take it again if he failed. After the exam, she asked him how it went. Abed blithely replied that instead of answering the questions on the exam, he had transcribed Edward FitzGerald's translation of *The Rubáiyát of Omar Khayyam* onto the paper. Abed remembered telling her this but insisted he was joking. "I wasn't that stupid," he said. He did not pass this exam, however, and it took him seven years to complete the five-year accountancy course. "That was the dilettante part of me."

While living in Golders Green, the young men paid frequent visits to the home of Roshanara Ismail and her two daughters, Runi and Putul. Roshanara's husband, Mohammed Ismail, had been Sayeedul Hasan's best friend and former business partner in Calcutta. By the 1950s, Mohammed Ismail had risen to become one of the top executives in the Pakistani industrial conglomerate Dawood Group. He had sent his wife and children to live in London for his children's education while he stayed behind in Pakistan, where he would reside until his death in a Pakistan International Airlines crash in Cairo in 1965.

Mrs. Ismail, or Ismail *chachi*, took it upon herself to look after Abed and his new friends, and they became a surrogate family. Fazle Ali declared that he loved her sponge cakes, so every time he visited, she gave him a dozen. Runi once visited the flat in Golders Green and found a smelly drawer filled with moldy sponge cakes. "He couldn't say no to my mother," she said.

Mrs. Ismail was described by all who knew her as a force of nature. Though her political sympathies lay firmly to the left, she could be as stern as Queen Victoria in her sense of propriety. She was also a phenomenal cook, and the scents of coriander and cumin filled the house. Abed, Viquar, and Fazle would visit for comfort food reminiscent of home. Years later, her daughter Putul recalled Abed bringing the choicest cuts from the meat-processing plant, which her mother would make into curries and kebabs. The uneaten sponge cakes notwithstanding, Mrs. Ismail's desserts were sublime. For instance, she had perfected a concoction of condensed milk encased in eggshells. She would painstakingly empty the contents of eggs before cleaning out the shells with pipe-cleaners and then fill each with condensed milk and, through a marble-sized opening that had been cut into the top with a needle, drop in balls of saffron-flavored kheer, a milk-based confection with the consistency of fudge. When the whole thing set, the saffron balls would sit suspended, like yellow yolks, within a custard-like white, surrounded by an unbroken shell. Breaking open the eggs, guests would wonder how such a delectation was even physically possible. Runi, who described the process decades later, said nobody else had ever been able to make it successfully.

It eventually became clear that Viquar was no longer visiting Mrs. Ismail's just for the food. He married Runi, her oldest daughter, in 1961, shortly after she turned eighteen.

* * *

In the early 1960s, London was a cauldron of new ideas, a city where artists, thinkers, and activists mingled and made noise. In Abed's circle of friends, he would "listen more than talk," according to Faruq Choudhury. "He was the youngest in the group, and he was not the nodal point, but on the periphery." They became part of a widening circle for whom the idea of independent East Pakistan, called Bangla Desh ("Land of the Bengals"), was gaining traction.

In 1958, Field Marshal Ayub Khan had taken power in a coup, and Pakistanis had lived under a military dictatorship ever since. In London, progressive expatriates from both East and West Pakistan came together to form the Committee for the Restoration of Democracy in Pakistan to protest his rule. It was not long, however, before the Easterners and Westerners began to realize that their interests were not aligned. Even with the restoration of democracy, all the centers of power in Pakistani society—the banks, the bureaucracy, the military—would remain dominated by the West. Young Bengali expatriates began to question the idea of a united Pakistan. They started raising money from Bengali-owned businesses in London to form an association devoted solely to the interests of East Pakistan, eventually gathering enough to purchase a house in Highbury, which they called the East Pakistan House. Three floors were used as a hostel for young Bengali travelers who needed a friendly place to stay. On the other floor, they hosted meetings and published magazines.

Zakaria helped organize the publication of a booklet titled *Unhappy East Pakistan*, which argued for the economic and geopolitical viability of Bangladesh as an independent country. "We had some difficulty publishing it, since it amounted to treason," he recalled. They published it under the incongruous pseudonym David Feldman, but the primary author was Kabiruddin Ahmed, a fellow activist so enamored of Marxism-Leninism that Abed and his friends nicknamed him "Kabiravosky."

What they wanted—autonomy, independence, or socialist revolution—depended on whom you asked. Some were committed to the democratic process, even though Pakistan had not had an election since its foundation in 1947. Many on the hard left argued that independence was an American plot to weaken Pakistan, but Zakaria Khan argued for independence via armed struggle first, then socialism. Zakaria recalled a private meeting at a South Asian restaurant in London in 1963 with an influential Bengali politician named Sheikh Mujibur ("Mujib") Rahman, who had been friendly with his father at the health ministry. Sheikh Mujib opposed Ayub Khan's dictatorship but was not yet openly advocating for independence. "I knew about him from the newspaper, but I had never met with him. I was a bit skeptical and suspicious about discussing [politics] with him openly," said Zakaria, since Sheikh Mujib was far to his right on the political spectrum. During this meeting, Zakaria stated plainly that he favored independence. He realized he could make common cause with those who favored politics over open rebellion when Sheikh Mujib "looked right at me and said, 'I agree with you.'"

Others in Abed's group were less convinced that full independence was the solution. Faruq Choudhury, who worked for the Pakistan foreign service, favored autonomy, a stance that did not change until the Bhola cyclone in 1970. Abed kept his opinions to himself and, according to Zakaria, was "neither yes or no" on the question of independence. Though he had nationalist sympathies, Abed, like many others, was likely never fully certain how strongly he felt until circumstances forced him to take a stand. That said, all of them were united in their dissatisfaction with the deprivation and exploitation of their Bengali countrymen and women.

Abed, Viquar, and Fazle Ali eventually decided they should no longer live together, since their socializing was hampering their studies. Over the next few years, Abed lived in a series of apartments. In 1962, he was alone in one of these when he received another telegram bearing bad news from home. His sister Nurani, to whom he had been closest, had fallen while pregnant, and both she and the unborn baby had died from massive internal bleeding. Abed sat alone with the telegram for some time until the phone rang. It was Fazle Ali, asking whether he would join them for drinks. "I lost my sister," Abed replied. Fazle immediately mobilized their friends to join him in mourning.

Yet another lifeline to home had been severed. Though he had friends to lean on during difficult times, Abed was essentially alone. His friends had been falling in love and even marrying. Viquar was now with Runi, and Zakaria had moved in with a woman named Diane, whom he would eventually marry. They had a tumultuous relationship, for Diane was one of the few people who could match Zakaria's energy. They also had a tolerant landlady who allowed them to throw parties in their Highgate flat. Zakaria recalled a typical Saturday. "We used to have parties all night," Zakaria said. "Then on Sunday mornings, Abed, Viquar, and I would go to the pub." They were not smitten with the new rock and pop music coming out at the time. Abed never had any interest in Bob Dylan or the other lyrical troubadours of the age. For him, T. S. Eliot was the greatest modern master of language. According to Runi, the soundtrack in the Highgate flat was diverse, including Miles Davis, whose landmark *Kind of Blue* came out in 1959; Brahms and other classical music; and, to the delight of their English friends, the songs of Rabindranath Tagore.

In 1962, at one of these parties, Abed met a woman named Marietta Procopé. She was dark haired, pale, and thin, perpetually wreathed in Gauloises cigarette smoke. Marietta was a ferociously intelligent twenty-year-old, six years younger than Abed, pursuing an undergraduate degree at University College London. She came from a wealthy family, the daughter of the former Finnish foreign minister and an upper-class woman from Yorkshire. Those who knew her said she had a light, ethereal quality, although this concealed an interior darkness, as she later became prone to periods of depression.

They quickly fell in love. With Marietta, Abed's lonely and humdrum life was suddenly filled with vitality. He found her generous and spirited, a companion for London's cultural explosion. They absorbed the films of Michelangelo Antonioni and Ingmar Bergman. She introduced him to opera. Other things began falling into place for Abed. He had received his British passport the previous year—as a Commonwealth citizen, he qualified after two years' residence—which allowed him to visit the European continent without the hassle of applying for a visa. In 1963, he finally received his certification as a chartered accountant, which meant he could get a proper job at a higher salary. He took a position as an accountant for an engineering firm, and he and Marietta began traveling together. They visited Faruq Choudhury, now stationed in Amsterdam with the foreign service, and hopped around to other European capitals.

Marietta was an ardent leftist and a fan of underdogs. She and Abed once went house to house handing out leaflets for the local Communist Party candidate, knowing he was unlikely to get more than a few hundred votes. "This was more sympathy for the underdog than support of the Communist Party," Abed said. The East Pakistanis were underdogs personified, and Abed introduced Marietta to his Bengali friends just as they were becoming increasingly politicized. Though she appreciated the East Pakistani ideals, she had a caustic wit and little patience for pretention and would say things others would typically keep to themselves, once referring to Kabiravosky as "a man educated beyond his intelligence."

Through Marietta's brother, John, Abed became acquainted with E. M. Forster, the writer who had mocked and memorialized the customs of British colonialists. Forster, then in his eighties, lived at King's College, Cambridge. Marietta, John, and Abed would visit his apartment for lunch. His quarters were small—a spartan bedroom and a sitting room with a dining table and a coal stove. Surrounded by old portraits of his relatives, he would take lunches of lamb chops and sherry. Abed loved perusing his bookshelves, filled with treasured volumes of Dickens and Tolstoy. Forster told Abed and his friends that he enjoyed being around young people because they made him forget his age. Abed recalled thinking he was a lonely man.

For Abed, Forster was a freethinker from a bygone era, who had ridden the streetcars of Alexandria during World War I and had worked for a minor raja in British India. He remained a keen observer of encounters between cultures and classes. He commented on how the character of King's College had changed over the years. In the old days, when he had studied there, only the upper classes attended Cambridge; now it was a mix of upper-, middle-, and even a few working-class students. On one occasion, at John's house, Abed cooked *rezala*, a Bengali chicken-yogurt curry, for Forster, who said it took him back to India.

In 1964, Abed and Marietta purchased a narrow four-story row house in Camden, a north London hotbed of fringe artists and intellectuals. Friends mockingly called him "Lord of Camden," joking that he would not take breakfast there without a three-piece suit and Beethoven. Cohabitation before marriage in those days was uncommon, even in British society, let alone for Bengalis, for whom arranged marriage was still the norm. "As far as I recall, even the English people wouldn't dare live together in those days," said Zakaria, who lived with Diane but did not marry her until 1967. "The idea of living together came in the 1970s."

Abed soon switched jobs, moving to AMP Incorporated, an American firm that manufactured electronics, including parts for the supersonic Concorde, which was in development at the time. Abed loved numbers nearly as much as he did poetry, and he enjoyed traveling throughout Europe for AMP, doing budgets and reconciling the accounts for their factories.

* * *

By 1965, Abed had been in the United Kingdom for more than a decade and hadn't visited home once during that time. He always knew he would eventually return to South Asia, and he was equally certain that he was in love with Marietta. According to Putul, it was the insistence of her mother, Mrs. Ismail, that finally led him to propose, though Abed claimed this had nothing to do with it. In any case, Marietta accepted, and they began making arrangements to visit East Pakistan. If they were to marry, she thought she should visit his homeland to see what it would be like to live there.

Abed planned a grand tour of the country for Marietta and her brother John. He flew home first and met them at the airport when they arrived, together with his cousin Sarwat, into whose ear he had recited the *azan* prayer after her birth, just before he left for Glasgow. She was now eleven and excited to meet the visiting foreigners. From the airport, he took Marietta and John to meet Sayeedul and Baiju, in whose home they stayed. John and Abed shared a room, and Marietta had her own.

They traveled the entire country. They went down to Chittagong to visit Abed's older brother, Zahed, who lived in a grand house provided by a local jute mill, where he worked as general manager. En route, they climbed to the top of the Chandranath Temple in Sitakunda, a Hindu pilgrimage site where the right arm of the goddess Sati is said to have fallen to earth. They went south to Cox's Bazar, which boasts the longest unbroken sand beach in the world, and inland to Kaptai Lake in the Chittagong Hill Tracts. They woke up in the morning mist of the rolling tea gardens of Sylhet, on an estate managed by the son-in-law of Rashidul Hasan, the judge uncle. Finally, they drove to Habiganj, the nearest town to Baniachong, where Abed's father came to meet them for lunch. After so much travel, they had run out of time to visit the family compound in Baniachong.

It was a wonderful trip, save for one problem: Marietta told Abed she couldn't imagine living in East Pakistan. As much as she enjoyed the country, she thought she would have trouble learning the language and adapting to the customs of Bengali society. She was worried about finding a social circle in which she could feel comfortable. The kind of life she would have there was not for her, she told Abed, and there was little he could say to persuade her otherwise.

They were at an impasse. Abed knew he did not want to live in London forever, but Marietta could never see herself moving to East Pakistan. They returned to London and remained a couple but agreed to put their engagement on hold. Slowly, a gap began to open between them. Increasingly, Marietta began experiencing bouts of depression. Much later, in hindsight, Abed realized she was experiencing a genuine disorder, as opposed to mood swings brought about by their fraying relationship. "I didn't realize what was happening to her," he said. "I didn't realize it was the kind of depression that needed treatment."

Abed stayed in London for three more years, during which Marietta enrolled in a postgraduate philosophy program at Oxford. He recalled driving her to Oxford. Thinking it would be an enjoyable day trip, they brought along Putul, Mrs. Ismail's youngest daughter, who was twenty at the time. But it was not a joyful occasion. Marietta was feeling low that day, and on their return to Camden, Abed remembered wondering whether she would last even a year at the university.

In the summer of 1968, Abed and Marietta visited Cologne, West Germany, where John was living. From there, they drove John's Volvo through Italy to Lake Ohrid, on the border of what was then Yugoslavia and Albania, and back again. By now, Abed was actively planning his move back to East Pakistan. "We didn't think we would get married, but we still liked each other, and we were still friends," he recalled. Their long road trip to Ohrid was their last significant time together as a couple. For Abed, their relationship had run its course, and it was time to move on with his life. Both understood that it was over, and each declared the other free to develop other relationships.

Abed did not regret the years he spent in London, which he viewed as exploring "consciousness of different kinds." In many respects, those years defined him, for he was barely out of adolescence when he arrived. But after fourteen years in the United Kingdom, it was time to go home. He kept his stake in the Camden house, for he thought it would be good to own property in London, but found renters for two of the floors and began scouting for jobs in East Pakistan. He found one that seemed promising: a position in the accounting department of Shell Pakistan, a subsidiary of the oil company Royal Dutch Shell, in the East Pakistan port city of Chittagong.

5

THOSE WHO HAVE SEEN DEATH

If Abed wanted a change of scenery after his breakup with Marietta, Chittagong certainly provided it. The East Pakistan port city was small and sleepy compared to London, and there wasn't much to do except work and hang out at the Chittagong Club. Abed excelled at both. Shell Pakistan hired Abed in 1968 as the number-three person in the finance department, where he supervised junior accountants. Within two years he would rise to become head of finance, a strategic role that had him overseeing the company's ten-year plan.

This job put him in an odd position, for he remained sympathetic to both nationalist and leftist causes, at least in the abstract. While he no longer thought Marxist ideals were attainable, and "what was attained by countries like Russia was not very palatable," as he put it years later, he still believed in a society where the poor and landless would have equal opportunities and feel empowered as individuals. This certainly did not describe East Pakistan.

He remained close to his uncle Sayeedul, who had left his career in the foreign service to enter the increasingly complex politics of Bengali nationalism. Sayeedul was treasurer of the party of Mawlana Bhashani, a leftist leader who favored greater autonomy for East Pakistan, the empowerment of the rural poor, and stronger ties with Mao's China. Meanwhile, Abed's job at a multinational oil company, in a subsidiary largely controlled by West Pakistanis, epitomized the bourgeois capitalist establishment.

Abed lived exceedingly well by local standards. About ten years earlier, Shell had moved its Pakistan headquarters to Chittagong to tap the region's oil and gas reserves after failing to strike oil in the West. Most senior Pakistani staff were from the West, and by law all Pakistanis, local or otherwise, were given the same perks as expatriate employees. The company therefore provided Abed with a whole floor of a two-family house in the upmarket Nasirabad neighborhood. He had four bedrooms, plus a cook, a gardener, and a remarkably capable butler or housekeeper (called a "bearer") named Mohammad Ali.

Enrollment in the club was part of the package. According to Juned Choudhury, who handled human resources for Shell Pakistan at the time, upon joining the company, senior executive staff received two pieces of paper: an appointment letter from Shell and an application to join the Chittagong Club. Muslims could drink alcohol freely at the club, provided they had a doctor's certificate stating they needed to drink for health reasons. The staff could provide one for a small fee; seeing an actual doctor was not required.

Had circumstances been different, Abed might have continued down this path. Within three years of arriving at Shell, the world around him would unravel instead.

★ ★ ★

Chittagong was socially unsatisfying. Abed knew hardly anyone there except a few colleagues. He did host an exhibition of a noted Bengali painter in his own home, and he became friendly with the upstairs neighbors, a couple with two daughters in their early teens. Apart from that, though, he spent his free time at the club. On weekends, he would often hop on a propeller flight to Dhaka, where most of his friends lived.

In Dhaka, Abed's social scene centered on the home of Viquar and Runi, who had moved back from London and now lived in the spacious tree-lined suburb of Gulshan. The provincial capital was expanding outward from the narrow lanes of Old Dhaka, which was crammed with crumbling bazaars, merchants, and traffic jams of cycle rickshaws. The sprawl had yet to reach Gulshan, where meadows still separated the homes and snakes hid in the grass. Like her mother, Runi delighted in cooking and entertaining, sometimes waking at 4 a.m. to buy fish directly from the ghat, the broad flight of steps leading to the water. Viquar was now a barrister with his own law practice. At their home, French doors opened onto a garden of jasmine vines and eucalyptus trees.

Bengalis and expatriates alike recall this period with nostalgia, as often happens when lifelong relationships are forged in times of change. Viquar and Runi had a tight circle of friends with diverse interests, who would call upon one another without phoning ahead. Gulshan was home to the Pakistan-SEATO Cholera Research Laboratory, funded by the US government, and Viquar and Runi were friends with many of the lab's young

American doctors and their spouses. In 1968, two researchers from the lab, Richard Cash and David Nalin, had established the effectiveness of using a simple mixture of water, sugar, and salt to treat children's diarrhea, an often-fatal condition. It was a breakthrough discovery in global public health.

According to Jon Rohde, one of the doctors at the lab, "There wasn't anything to do in Dhaka those days but visit friends." Described by those who knew him as a brash American with a competitive streak, Jon had attended Amherst as an undergraduate, followed by Harvard Medical School. He had come to East Pakistan with his wife, Cornelia ("Candy"), primarily to avoid being drafted and sent to Vietnam.

When Abed visited Dhaka, he made a strong impression on the Americans in this circle, with his pipe, ascot, and smoking jacket. Jon was struck by Abed's erudition. "Whenever Abed came up from Chittagong, we'd always have an evening talk, and it was almost always talk about politics," he said. "That was the reigning concern for the whole group of us, about what was going to happen to East Pakistan. Abed was always one of the most facile conversationalists, and he also was one of the broadest in his thinking. I never knew anything about what an accountant did, and it didn't matter, because he could quote Shakespeare, and he'd read many books from English literature that I had never read. He was just fun to talk with."

★ ★ ★

The Dhaka skies darkened on Thursday, November 12, 1970, the night of the Bhola cyclone. Al Sommer, another American doctor at the cholera lab, recalled a dinner party where people joked about "whitecaps on Gulshan Lake," a local pond that was normally a placid puddle. As in Chittagong, people of means slept soundly.

The next day, Abed received a phone call from Runi. She, her sister Putul, and Candy Rohde were in Runi's study in Gulshan, reading the reports in Friday's papers of scores of people having died in the storm the previous night.[1] The numbers would rise to tens of thousands on Saturday and hundreds of thousands on Sunday, although even a week later, the official government figures would remain "only" forty thousand. As early as the day after the storm, having read the initial reports of the dead and hungry, the three women had decided to do something to help. Chittagong was only a few miles away from some of the hardest-hit areas, and with its three extra bedrooms, Abed's house there would make a suitable hub for relief efforts.

Runi recalled that first phone call—and Abed's initial reluctance. "When I called Abed *Bhai* to ask if we could use his house as a base to get relief out to Manpura, his first response was that it may be difficult, as his house was a company property," she said. Abed said he did not recall having any such reluctance, but, in any case, he eventually agreed that since everything in the house was paid for by Shell anyway, it would hardly matter if people sullied the carpets. He opened his house, including the three extra bedrooms, to the nascent project, and before long he was as committed to the cause as Candy, Putul, and Runi.

The Shell job might not have been a perfect match for his ideals, but Abed appreciated aspects of it that others never would have. Where some might have viewed the large, faceless organization as an inherently ugly entity, he had seen the efficiency with which Shell managed large operations and recognized that it had its own kind of beauty. What if this managerial efficiency could be put to good ends? He told Putul and Candy to come down to Chittagong while he pulled other resources together. He began by convening colleagues, friends, and the local representatives of the Rotary and Lions clubs. Kaiser Zaman, a junior colleague at Shell, worked one floor above Abed. He recalled Abed poking his head into his office and saying, "Some of my friends from Dhaka are coming. Would you mind putting a few up?"

Kaiser stood out from the crowd because he had lost an arm in an accident in his youth, but, as Abed put it, "He was one of those people who could do many things with one hand that most people could not do with two." Abed remembered an earlier, work-related episode in which they were caught in a car in a rainstorm. Uncertain the driver could handle the road, Kaiser took the wheel, having recently participated in a car rally in his Volkswagen Beetle. "He drove with one hand while lighting a cigarette with a matchstick," Abed said.

As news came in that survivors of the cyclone lacked basic provisions like food and water, many middle-class Chittagonians began loading up their cars with essentials and driving to the affected coastal areas. Hardly anyone was thinking about survivors on more remote offshore islands. Candy attended a meeting in Abed's drawing room, surrounded by gold-framed reproductions of old masters, on November 18, the day after she arrived in Chittagong, six days after the cyclone. She had raised about 5,000 rupees (just over $1,000 at the time) from Dhaka friends and expressed her desire that it go directly to cyclone victims, without the risk of it being appropriated and misused. A Rotarian suggested contributing to a worthy project on the mainland, in an area that had hardly been affected.

Kaiser Zaman pushed back, suggesting a greater effort to reach those who truly needed help. "I immediately feel that he and I are on the same wavelength," Candy wrote in her account of the episode.[2] A core group began to emerge, including another American couple, a doctor at the cholera lab named Lincoln Chen and his wife, Martha ("Marty").

As the relief project grew, Abed would oversee it as administrator, never quitting his day job, going to work at Shell every day and coming home to the chaos enveloping his home. He did not, therefore, have a firsthand view of most of the heroics that followed; yet, without those heroics, it is likely that Abed's life would have taken an altogether different course.

The group soon found that boats were indeed going to nearby islands—nearly empty. Candy reported back to Dhaka on the need for more relief supplies: "The last ship that left Chittagong had one hundred tons of a six-hundred-ton capacity filled."[3] Using Abed's house as a base of operations, they began loading the next boat with essential relief goods, including tinned milk, water, oil lamps, matches, clothing, and even Abed's old curtains, which would serve as blankets. The house began attracting a crowd of volunteers. Mohammad Ali, Abed's bearer, kept things running smoothly while Abed was at work. "Throughout the day, students would come with relief, and they were novices," he recalled. "They didn't know how to get about the area, so I would organize and direct them."

The problem, they soon discovered, was that large boats could not ply the shallow waters surrounding the densely populated coastal *chars*, the silt islands at the mouth of the Meghna River. They needed more people, doctors especially, and smaller boats. Jon, still at his job at the Cholera Research Laboratory, recalled getting a phone call from his wife, who said, "What are you doing? You came out here to help people. Why don't you get down here and help us where help is really needed?" According to Candy's recollection, she simply said, "Jon! Bring an outdoor motor and ask everyone you know to give you at least a hundred dollars."[4]

The Rohdes and Chens put their names on an appeal they circulated to a wider group of friends and acquaintances in Dhaka. "Please give generously to make this program a success," they wrote. "We will give you a regular progress report and perhaps ask you for specific things (old bed sheets, pots, etc.) if the program succeeds. If it is apparent to us that the money is not being well-utilized, we will turn it over entirely to the government relief funds."[5] They soon found that their efforts exceeded anything the army or government was doing.

Jon acceded to his wife's demands and boarded a commercial flight to Chittagong, carrying a nine-horsepower outboard engine, borrowed from the lab, on his shoulder. On the tarmac, he approached two crop-duster pilots to ask if they would help him perform reconnaissance on the islands offshore. It turned out the pilots had already convinced their employer, a Swiss firm, to abort dusting crops in the delta to make supply drops from their plane. The next morning, Jon went up in the plane and had his first look at the devastated islands. As they swooped to within twenty feet of the ground, he saw "scores of hopeful gaunt arms" reaching toward them. The pilots had removed the doors and hatches, and Jon kicked burlap sacks of relief supplies out the doorway. Later, Kaiser would make the same run and described "hands raised toward the sky like praying to a distant god."

In reality, the airdrops were of limited use without a distribution team on the ground. Only a few people ate because only the strongest could reach the burlap bags; as would often happen with aid and relief efforts, local power relations, even at the most basic level, determined who got what. Meanwhile, the crowd at Abed's house continued to grow. The upstairs neighbors and their teenage daughters got involved, and even Mrs. Ismail came from Dhaka to join the effort. An assembly line on the veranda packed food into bags for the airdrops. Mohammad Ali made sure the cook had a steady supply of *kala bhuna*, a Chittagonian beef curry, feeding up to twenty people a day.

Ten days after the cyclone, another group from Dhaka arrived, including Viquar, Al Sommer, Lincoln Chen, and Abed's old friend Zakaria Khan, the London activist, known to his American friends as "Jack." They understood the need for boots on the ground. The majority of them joined Jon for an eight-hour journey to an island called Hatiya, in the middle of the Meghna estuary, on a WWII-era landing craft of the type seen at the Normandy landings. On board was a twelve-foot aluminum dinghy that Abed had requisitioned from Shell, the outboard motor from the cholera lab, and more relief supplies. On Hatiya, they found government relief efforts moderately well established, but, in the early hours of that night, Jon learned of a place called Manpura, to the west, where relief had yet to reach any of the survivors. After a sleepless night on a mud embankment, watching their supplies and fending off mosquitoes, Jon and Viquar set off the next day in the Shell dinghy.

"We were out of sight of land just heading west," Jon recalled. "Somebody told us Manpura was out there. We didn't know where it was. We just headed to where the sun was going down." The smell of decaying corpses came first. The tops of coconut palms soon appeared on the horizon. Bodies filled the muddy shallows surrounding the islands, the countless dead blocking access to the land, so they had to follow the shoreline for a mile before they found a spot to land. It was the eleventh day after the storm.

After they landed, surviving islanders began to emerge, almost all of them men. In addition to hunger, the first major medical problem they faced was what Jon called "palm tree syndrome"—the severe maceration of the chest, inner arms, and thighs, which the men had suffered as they clung for hours to the coarse tops of palm trees, fighting the tidal surge. Jon wrote in his report to the mainland, "Sinewy men sobbed as they recounted the loss of entire families, one by one picked off the treetops and swallowed in the maelstrom."[6]

As word spread that help had finally arrived, the gathering people, though desperately weak, threatened to overwhelm the small team. Viquar drew a line in the mud with a stick and shouted, "Form a queue behind this line! Anyone stepping over that mark will not be given any food." The islanders remained calm and formed a line. In four hours, Jon and Viquar distributed rations to 1,400 people. A photograph, taken either that day or the next, shows lines of survivors waiting for their rations, segregated by sex. The line of men stretches toward the horizon. The other has just four women and a child.

The first night, after a day without eating, the team cooked themselves stew and rice, but, as Jon wrote, "The stench of death defied the strongest appetite. I carried the cooking pot into the inky night beyond the ring of our small lantern to find two naked boys huddled against the chest of their father, clad only in a tattered waistcloth. Placing the food before them, they looked at me with blank fear. 'Here, it's for you. Go ahead. Eat,' I implored. No response. 'They've not eaten in twelve days, Sahib. They don't believe it's really for them.' The father coaxed and they dug their hands into the pot. They ate in the frantic silence of those who have seen death. I slipped back into the well of blackness, lay on my back looking at the riotous heavens above with the Milky Way coursing down the center, and wept."[7]

★ ★ ★

Abed heard these stories but lacked a visceral understanding of what was happening on Manpura. West German aid soon arrived in the form of helicopters, giving the crop dusters a rest. Abed went along in one of these helicopters, and at least one fellow passenger recalled him wearing a smoking jacket on board. The image of the dead in the shallows changed his life forever.

What had begun as a spontaneous gathering soon turned into a professional effort. By Christmas, Jon had to either go back to his job at the

Cholera Research Laboratory or likely lose it. They had bootstrapped the relief operations in the early stages, but the efficiency of the program on Manpura soon attracted foreign press, including Sydney Schanberg of the *New York Times*, who wrote that "amid the chaos of the relief effort" after the cyclone, "one fairly smooth operation stood out."[8] It also attracted major donors. The largest of these, the German charity Bread for the World, donated $1 million. Knowing he needed somebody with good business sense to run the field operations, Abed convinced Kaiser Zaman, who had decided to quit his job at Shell, to take over as full-time chief field coordinator on Manpura. The organization was registered under the name HELP, for Heartland Emergency Lifesaving Project, the word *manpura* meaning "heartland" in Bengali. Abed was board chair, and among the other full-time employees was Akbar Kabir, a retired government official and the father-in-law of Fazle Ali, Abed's former London flatmate.

Unfortunately, HELP would not last long as an organization, for despite the good intentions of its leadership, graft and corruption would eventually take over. It did not help that Abed, Candy, Jon, and millions of others would soon be forced to flee the country, and few trustworthy people would stay behind. Heroics matter; so does good administration. The initiative led Abed to begin questioning the life he had built for himself, but there was little time to make choices about the future. Events beyond his control began to make the choices for him.

6

CATALYST FOR REVOLUTION

The Pakistani government's inept response to the cyclone outraged the people of East Pakistan. The regime was so accustomed to neglecting the East that even a disaster of this magnitude failed to shake it into action. Pakistan had scheduled a general election, its first since the end of colonial rule, for December 7, 1970, just weeks after the cyclone. By now, Sheikh Mujibur Rahman, the politician whom Zakaria Khan had met in the London restaurant in 1963, had risen in stature, thanks to his charisma and an appeal to Bengali nationalist sentiment. He was now the leading political figure in East Pakistan. When the votes of the national election were counted, the split between East and West was laid bare for all to see. Sheikh Mujib's party, the Awami League, won 160 of 162 seats being contested in the province of East Pakistan, giving it an absolute majority in Pakistan's 300-seat National Assembly. It won zero seats in the West. The major party in the West, the Pakistan Peoples Party, headed by Zulfikar Ali Bhutto, won 81 seats, none of them in the East.

In a truly democratic system, the Bengalis should have formed the next government of Pakistan under the leadership of Prime Minister Sheikh Mujibur Rahman. Yet, despite a clear victory, the Urdu-speaking political and military establishment in West Pakistan refused to yield. Months of negotiation followed, but while the politicians were negotiating, the Pakistan Army was preparing for action.

On the night of March 25, 1971, West Pakistani troops launched a coordinated attack on Bengali regiments and police units in Dhaka. The crackdown was brutal, designed to crush Bengali nationalism with overwhelming force. Sheikh Mujib, who had already called for Bengalis to prepare to fight for their freedom, was arrested. That night, the army declared martial law and began indiscriminately killing anyone suspected of being an Awami League supporter, a Bengali nationalist, a Hindu, or merely a sympathizer. Students and professors at Dhaka University, which the army knew would be a hub of resistance, were massacred by the hundreds. Over the next forty-eight hours, radio stations still controlled by nationalists broadcast declarations of independence and a call to arms from Bengali political and military leaders alike, including a statement from Major Ziaur Rahman of the East Bengal Regiment, which pledged its allegiance to Bangladesh under the leadership of Sheikh Mujib. The war for independence had begun.

Indiscriminate killing continued in the weeks and months to come. The war affected nearly all seventy million people in the former East Pakistan, and for many it was complete upheaval. The Pakistani authorities were initially surprised that so many Bengalis heeded the call to rise up and fight. University students and others under the age of twenty-five fled the cities, joining defecting Bengali army officers to form a new liberation army. Millions left overland to India, traveling by foot, vehicle, rickshaw, and bullock cart. Many of the nation's elite in Abed's generation or older escaped to join the provisional government of Bangladesh at its new capital-in-exile, Calcutta, where they could organize support from abroad.

Abed was in a precarious position. Nobody was safe from suspicion, not even an accountant at a multinational oil company. Yet his bosses at Shell had no idea of his activist past in London, and he continued to show up for work for the next several weeks. In April, when his friends in the United States began lobbying for an end to American support for Pakistan, he knew it was time to go. The Nixon administration had sided with the Pakistanis, downplaying reports of Pakistan Army atrocities even from its own diplomats, who protested that in the case of "the Awami conflict," as they called it, "unfortunately the overworked term genocide is applicable."[1] Nixon and Kissinger believed that good relations with Pakistan were key to their overtures to China and a counterbalance to Soviet influence. After American personnel, including the doctors at the Cholera Research Laboratory, were finally evacuated, Jon Rohde testified in front of a US congressional committee on the unreported news of atrocities committed by the Pakistan Army. Jon and Candy had themselves visited the site of a mass killing of Hindus at a Dhaka temple complex and saw the bodies littering the ground. The Rohdes, Lincoln Chen, and others had begun lobbying for recognition of Bangladesh, and news of Jon's testimony was broadcast on Voice of America.

It was only a matter of time before the authorities linked Abed to his friends. He considered his options. With the country under martial law, air travel was prohibited for most, even those who could afford it. He could have tried crossing into India overland, but the army was terrorizing the countryside, shooting people for the merest hint of subversion, which included being an able-bodied person who could potentially join the resistance. He decided to keep his head down until he had a chance to flee safely.

An opportunity soon materialized. In the second week of April, the chairman of Shell Pakistan, a retired Pakistani major general, requested a lunch meeting with Abed at the Inter-Continental Hotel in Dhaka. "I have just been to see the chief martial-law administrator," the chairman told him. "They have requested somebody from the oil industry to be the liaison officer at the martial-law headquarters. They need somebody to ensure the security of the wells and pipelines." Abed chewed his food and nodded. The chairman continued, "I was thinking you might be able to do the job."

Abed had no wish to collaborate with the regime but did not feel he had much choice: rejecting the job on grounds of conscience could mean a death sentence. A plan began forming in his head even before the bill was paid. If he accepted a job at the martial-law headquarters, Abed would almost certainly be cleared for air travel—if not to any place he chose, then at least to West Pakistan. If he could get to West Pakistan without arousing suspicion, he would likely be able to slip over the Khyber Pass, the overland crossing to Afghanistan. "Of course I'll take the job," he told the chairman.

He received a martial-law identity card, which gave him permission to travel. Flying back to Chittagong, he gathered a few things from his house. He did not want to make any moves to suggest he was leaving for good, so he bought a round-trip ticket to Karachi and scheduled a short holiday from work. He did not make a large bank withdrawal, since being caught with a big sum of cash would call his "holiday" ruse into question. Somehow, he would need to pick up more money along the way. He knew someone, a Shell colleague in Islamabad, whom he thought might be willing to help.

Abed landed in Karachi, connected to another flight to Islamabad, and called the colleague as soon as he arrived. "I'm in town and thought I might pay you a visit at the office tomorrow," he said. It was a mistake that could have proved fatal. The friend had no idea what he was up to, and Abed was not about to tell him over the phone. Soon afterward, the colleague innocently mentioned to the chairman himself, the retired major general, that Abed was in town. The chairman immediately pieced things together and alerted Inter-Services Intelligence (ISI), the dreaded Pakistan intelligence agency.

When Abed arrived at the Shell office in Islamabad, ISI agents were waiting for him. "We'd like to have word with you, Mr. Abed," one of the officers said. They were polite, but their tone brooked no dissent. He was being placed under arrest.

ISI interrogated him at the Shell offices. The story of being on holiday in Islamabad was flimsy, yet plausible. Abed stuck to his story, telling them he was there for pleasure and had nothing to hide. "Where is your luggage?" they asked. He told them the truth: that it was with a friend—not the Shell colleague—with whom he was staying. They sent for it.

An ISI colonel oversaw a thorough search of Abed's bags, looking for papers or correspondence that might link him to the Bengali nationalist movement or reveal his sympathies. They found nothing except his clothes and a Shell Oil pay stub. Abed saw the shock on the colonel's face when he saw the pay stub. Abed's salary was 4,900 rupees ($1,029) a month. An executive at a local firm might be expected to make about half that, a colonel maybe a quarter or a third. "Why would a man of your means be involved in activities against Pakistan?" he asked.

"I told you, I'm not involved in any activities against Pakistan," Abed replied.

The pay stub helped, though probably not as much as his British passport. It would have been difficult for them to hold a British national indefinitely without hard evidence, and their search of his luggage had turned up nothing. If he had been traveling on a Pakistani passport, the military would have likely kept him under arrest. Given the number of people being "disappeared," he might never have been heard from again. Instead, the colonel held him overnight in a comfortable guest room at his home. The next day, Abed was told to take his passport and return to East Pakistan.

Abed's colleague from Shell came to pick him up. Abed was worried he'd put his friend in danger and no longer wanted to ask him for any favors. But by now the colleague suspected what was happening. "You must leave the country immediately," he said. "I'll tell them you've gone back to East Pakistan. Just find a taxi and get out."

A taxi got Abed as far as Peshawar, about thirty miles from the Afghan border. To keep up the pretense of being on holiday and minimize suspicion, he spent the night in the city's most expensive hotel. The next morning, his heart pounding, he boarded the first bus bound for Jalalabad, Afghanistan. He crossed the Khyber Pass into Afghanistan on his British passport without incident. He recalled a celebratory lunch in Jalalabad, at a filthy place near the bus depot with flies on the bread. It was hardly the style of travel he was accustomed to, but at least he was safe. Back home, people were being shot on the roadways where they stood.

When Abed rolled into Kabul on that bus in 1971, it was quite a different city than what it became in the years to follow. Ruled by a modernizing king, Afghanistan was a constitutional monarchy enacting democratic reforms, and Kabul was known as the Paris of Central Asia, with a cosmopolitan urban elite. Women attended Kabul University in miniskirts, not burqas, and shirtless hippies stopped there to smoke hashish en route to India.

But Abed was not here as a tourist and saw little of Kabul, for he had almost no money. He checked into the cheapest guesthouse he could find. Knowing that flights were uncertain, he was prepared to hunker down in Kabul for some time. Most of his Bengali friends were dealing with their own worries, including escape plans of their own. There was one person he knew he could still rely on, however. Abed telegrammed Marietta in London, explaining that he was stranded and asking her to send him a ticket.

He ended up staying two weeks in Kabul. His only excursion was a local bus ride to the Gardens of Babur, the final resting place of the first Mughal emperor. After receiving his telegram, Marietta arranged an Ariana Airlines flight to Istanbul and, from there, to London.

In London, war brought the old gang back together. Viquar and Runi had escaped by pretending to be going on a pilgrimage to Mecca and then flying from Jeddah to London. Zakaria, who had long dreamed of being part of a violent revolution, went underground in Bangladesh and tried to join the rebel army. They told him, to his disappointment, that he would be far more useful raising funds from abroad than actually fighting. He flew to London from Calcutta.

Liberation was no longer a theoretical concept to argue about at the pub. With Bangladesh in a state of all-out war, those in exile threw themselves into the liberation struggle, working the embassy circuits, lobbying foreign governments to recognize Bangladesh, and publicizing the ongoing atrocities of the Pakistan Army. Together with fellow activists from the old East Pakistan house, they raised money from Bengali expatriates in London. In the United States, Kaiser Zaman and Lincoln Chen helped secure a $25,000 donation, their largest, from a sympathetic Indian American businessman from Michigan named Shrikumar Poddar.

Though Abed took up residence on his own floor of the Camden house, he and Marietta never got back together. During the cyclone relief effort, Abed and one of the American volunteers had fallen in love, a relationship that would not survive the disruption of war. Marietta had a new boyfriend as well, though Abed never met him.

* * *

Back home, the Pakistan Army's ongoing atrocities against civilians angered and mobilized the population. Resistance grew stronger. Bolstered by defecting soldiers, the ranks of the freedom fighters, known as the Mukti Bahini or Liberation Army, had swelled, but the forces were still vastly outnumbered by the Pakistan Army. By the summer of 1971, the liberation forces had regrouped and divided the country into eleven sectors, each under a commander, to conduct guerrilla warfare backed by supplies from India. The liberation movement prepared itself for a war that they thought might go on for a decade or more.

Among foreigners, an international campaign for Bangladesh was gaining force through a disparate set of largely uncoordinated efforts. Marietta threw her weight behind the formation of a group called Action Bangladesh, along with two veteran activists, Paul and Ellen Connett. The Connetts had previously formed an international coalition in support of the separatist African state of Biafra, which had declared independence from Nigeria in 1967, leading to a civil war Biafra ultimately lost. Bangladesh may have seemed like a similarly ill-fated idea at the time.

According to Paul Connett, Marietta donated money, the use of her olive-green Mini Cooper, and the Camden house to serve as the headquarters of Action Bangladesh. The house (still co-owned by Abed) became a hub of campaign activity, the floors and furniture covered in pamphlets and posters. The injustice taking place in a faraway land stirred foreigners to action. Action Bangladesh organized marches in front of the US Embassy and lobbied members of British Parliament. Eventually, it led a massive rally in Trafalgar Square, where twenty-five thousand people came out to support Bangladesh on August 1.

In New York, on the same day as the Trafalgar Square rally, Madison Square Garden hosted the Concert for Bangladesh, organized by the Indian sitarist and composer Ravi Shankar and Beatles guitarist George Harrison and featuring a rare appearance by Bob Dylan. The event drew forty thousand people, raising awareness of Bangladesh and relief funds for UNICEF. Meanwhile, Quakers in Baltimore risked their lives to prevent a Pakistani navy ship from docking at the port. In "September on Jessore Road," the beat poet Allen Ginsberg, having visited a refugee camp in India, wrote of a million "starving black angels in human disguise" on the road to Calcutta. A word previously unknown to the world, Bangladesh was now a global cause.

★ ★ ★

Abed and Viquar wanted to use some of the money they raised to fund the liberation movement directly rather than just for advocacy and lobbying, as Marietta and others in Action Bangladesh were doing. They soon had a chance to do so. In July, Abed received a mysterious phone call from a man representing a group of British and American mercenaries who had fought in Vietnam. "We've got a plan for you," he said. "Can we talk?"

They received the mercenaries in Camden. Action Bangladesh had taken over the whole house, so they met in Abed's bedroom, the only place they could have privacy. Abed and Viquar never learned how the mercenaries had heard about them, but their guests seemed to know they were exploring options for furthering the cause, including military ones. They had a proposal: an attack on the Pakistan Navy at its fleet base in Karachi. Until then, the Bengali rebels had fought entirely in East Pakistan. An attack on the well-defended headquarters of the Pakistan Navy in its main port city would take things to a new level. "We'll go out of Gujarat on fishing boats," one of them explained. "We'll sail directly into Karachi harbor, and once we're there, we'll plant bombs under some of the Pakistani ships." The cost, including fishing boats, bombs, and divers, would be 16,000 pounds (about $38,400 at the time).

The plan sounded daring and feasible. The military value of an attack on Karachi, thousands of miles from home territory, would be limited, but it would provide a huge morale boost to the freedom fighters in Bangladesh. It would mean liberation forces were taking the fight directly to the enemy. Abed and Viquar agreed to the plan on one condition. Neither had been in direct contact with the Bangladeshi government-in-exile in Calcutta. They thought they should at least get its consent.

In September, they both flew to Calcutta, where they visited the house that served as the provisional government's headquarters. They met with the prime minister, Tajuddin Ahmad, who was leading the wartime government while Sheikh Mujib was in jail. He was not impressed with the plan. "We have no interest in symbolic victories," he said, according to Abed. "We could use this money to carry out our struggle here." Winter was coming, and, despite aid from India, the freedom fighters were still vastly underfunded. He also wasn't keen on the idea of working with mercenaries. "We want to fight this war ourselves," he said. "If you have this money, please send it to us."

Viquar and Abed called off the attack. The money they had raised instead provided much-needed clothing and material to the Bangladeshi forces. Shortly after their meeting with the prime minister, Abed recalled sector commander Major Ziaur Rahman coming to their hotel room. A future president of Bangladesh, Zia (as he was known) was the same age as Abed. They had mutual friends and had been neighbors in Chittagong. Zia was in a state of high anxiety. His wife, Khaleda, had just been arrested, and her fate was uncertain. They asked what he needed. "What I would really like is a new pair of binoculars," he said. "It's difficult to spot enemy positions."

Abed and Viquar resolved that Viquar would stay in Calcutta and set up a base of operations for their own organization, called Help Bangladesh (unrelated to HELP on Manpura), while Abed would go back to Europe to raise money and rally support in London, Paris, Bonn, and Rome. Over the next several months, Abed traveled the continent, speaking to members of parliament and giving media interviews. As winter set in, their small stream of funding would provide things like sweaters for the freedom fighters and binoculars for Major Zia. They also began channeling funding to relief efforts for refugees, for an estimated ten million Bangladeshis had fled the country and were living in squalid camps on the Indian border.

★ ★ ★

Expectations of a long war did not come to pass. On December 3, fearing India's growing involvement, Pakistan launched a preemptive attack on Indian air bases. This miscalculation cost them the war. India responded with a full-fledged invasion of East Pakistan and an attack on the West, including a missile assault on the Pakistan Navy in Karachi Harbour. Using missiles instead of fishing vessels, these attacks did a great deal more damage than the mercenaries would have, crippling Pakistan's naval capacity.

The momentum was finally on the side of freedom. Abed continued to travel to European capitals to press the case to governments and the media. On December 6, India officially recognized the independence of Bangladesh and the government-in-exile as the legitimate representative of the Bangladeshi people. At the time, Abed happened to be in Copenhagen giving an interview to a television station, urging the Danish and other foreign governments to do the same. The next day, he and a fellow activist thought they might take a chance and visit the Danish Foreign Ministry unannounced. As soon as the minister saw the slips of paper saying they had come from Bangladesh, he came out to greet them. "I saw you on TV last night," he said. "We are indeed sympathetic to your cause and plan to recognize Bangladesh soon."

What had once seemed impossible now appeared inevitable. Indian infantry divisions joined Bangladeshi guerrillas and swept through the country. One by one, the cities fell. On December 16, combined Indian-Bangladeshi forces entered Dhaka. Under the terms of the Geneva Convention, the Pakistan Army surrendered all its forces in Bangladesh, more than ninety thousand soldiers, one of the largest military surrenders in history. The war was over.

Liberation came so suddenly that Abed was initially unsure what to do. He knew the task of rebuilding would be massive. He awaited word from Viquar, who had been visiting refugee camps on the northern India-Bangladesh border during the last weeks of fighting. On the day of surrender, Viquar was in Assam, north of Sylhet on the Indian side. He followed the refugees as they began streaming southward across the border on foot. He wrote to Abed from Sylhet, in a letter that arrived in London four days later. The report was grim. Refugees from the surrounding countryside had returned to find nothing left of their homes. The Pakistan Army had targeted poor Hindu communities, though the destruction was often indiscriminate, with entire villages looted and razed. "He asked me to come home as quickly as possible and to bring as much money as I could," Abed recalled.

A little more than a year had passed since the Bhola cyclone. In that time, Abed's entire outlook on life had changed. For much of that year, Bangladesh had been a place of death. Under such circumstances, it had been hard to give much thought to career, possessions, or what might happen in five years' time. Everything was framed in terms of survival.

The only thing of value that Abed owned at this point was his half of the house in Camden, which he had purchased with Marietta in 1964. Marietta agreed to buy the rest of it, leaving Abed with about 8,000 pounds ($19,200) after he paid off the mortgage. He and Viquar would use this to supplement what remained of the money they had raised in London to try to make life a little better for refugees returning to liberated Bangladesh.

Abed packed up his few belongings. In London, he had kept a large collection of ties he no longer wanted. He left these for anyone to take. He recalled thinking he no longer needed material things, that he would live simply from then on. "I was quite ready to forgo everything and work with the people," he said. "I had just one suitcase and I didn't need all this stuff, I thought. No suits, some books, I think—probably my copy of Shakespeare and the complete works of George Bernard Shaw. That was it."

* * *

Nobody knows how many civilians were killed during the nine months of the 1971 Bangladesh Liberation War. Estimates range from three hundred thousand to three million.

Many of Abed's family members, including his uncle Sayeedul Hasan, who had illuminated his life with books and poetry, had stayed in Dhaka when the war broke out. According to Abed, Sayeedul had tried to arrange the release of R. P. Saha, an imprisoned Bengali industrialist and philanthropist. Laila Kabir, the sister of Sayeedul's wife, Baiju, said he also tried to intervene after the father of two Hindu girls, who were being harbored by friends, had gone missing. "After the father was abducted, Sayeedul went looking for him," she recalled. "On May 18, my brother-in-law said, 'Do you have money?' I gave him a blank check." Sayeedul told her he was going to meet a major in the Pakistan Army at the Inter-Continental Hotel and expected he could arrange the father's release by paying a bribe. "I said, 'Don't go!' But how could he not?"

Sayeedul Hasan never returned from that meeting. The family's contacts in the Pakistani government confirmed that the army had arrested and killed him, likely burying him in a mass grave. He was fifty-nine.

7

A SMOLDERING RUIN

Sarabala had not yet finished cooking breakfast when the Pakistan Army arrived to burn her village, Anandapur, to the ground.

Anandapur, a predominantly Hindu community in an area called Sulla (pronounced "shallah"), sat on a hillock deep in the *haor*, the lowland of northeast Bengal. During the summer monsoon, the villages here turn into islands on a vast inland sea. Until that gray morning in June 1971, the saddest moment of Sarabala's life had probably been her wedding day, four years earlier, when she learned she was moving here. She had cried when her parents told her she was getting married and would soon belong to another family. "I didn't know who these people were, how they were going to treat me, or where I was going to live," she recalled. It was a monsoon wedding, and the bridegroom traveled two hours by boat to reach her parents' village. Candles and lanterns lit the ceremony, and the night air was filled with the sound of flutes and the *dhol*, a traditional drum that hangs from the player's neck. She wept throughout.

When she moved to Anandapur, her days consisted largely of chopping chilies and cooking for her husband's family. Sarabala's husband was simpleminded and easily manipulated by others, but at least he and his family did not abuse her, as happened to many new wives. Within a year they had a daughter, Shujila.

In the summer of 1971, when Shujila was three, the residents of Anandapur began to hear gunfire in the distance. The Pakistan Army had a reputation for brutality, especially against Hindus, but the other villagers assured Sarabala there was nothing to fear, since the soldiers had no reason to come to such a remote place. The gunfire grew closer day by day, until one morning it was upon them. As Sarabala was cooking the first meal of the day, panic set in. There were about ten flat-bottomed rowboats on the shore. The villagers rushed to these without stopping to gather any possessions. Sarabala, Shujila, her husband, and two other families boarded one of the boats and began rowing, leaving with nothing more than the clothes they wore.

Out on the water, Sarabala clung to her daughter. Looking back, she saw her home in flames. The army had torched the village. Around her, a flotilla of wooden skiffs from surrounding villages joined them, carrying thousands of people north as plumes of smoke filled the sky all around.

They rowed for three days, eating little and sleeping rough on the shore, before reaching the Indian border. At a town called Balat, the refugees settled on a wooded hill. They cut the trees to make shelter, eating the leaves and whatever else they could find. In the days and months to come, tens of thousands of others joined them, until not a patch of spare ground remained. They depended on charity for food.

Locals would occasionally set fire to the camps to try to drive them out, burning the refugees alive. Cholera broke out, and death was common. Pregnant women and young children were especially vulnerable. In Sarabala's section of the camp, one doctor cared for three thousand people. They grew accustomed to digging graves in the sand. One day, Shujila turned to her mother and said, "You are going to put me in the sand like that."

Sarabala said she cannot remember the exact day she realized Bangladesh had won the war. She began to see small rallies, groups of people running with the flag used by liberation forces—a yellow shape of Bangladesh in a red disc, surrounded by green field—shouting, "Joy Bangla!" (roughly, "Victory to Bengal"). She continued hearing this Liberation Army war cry for more than a week. "I kept hearing it, but I didn't believe it until I saw the people close to me heading back," she said. They set off on foot and eventually reached the hillock where Anandapur had once stood. The family had survived, three of ten million returning refugees.

* * *

Bangladesh was born a smoldering ruin. In the first year of his country's existence, Abed looked at a list of countries ranked by wealth and saw Bangladesh second from bottom, above only Upper Volta (now Burkina Faso). One in four children died before the age of five. Much of the world had washed its hands of Bangladesh and its population of seventy million. In an oft-repeated phrase, an official with the Nixon administration remarked that the country, if it became independent, would be a hopeless basket case. "But not our basket case," replied Henry Kissinger.

Abed arrived in Dhaka on January 17, on the same flight as Zakaria. He was uncertain what he should be doing—where to go, how to start, how to live a life that had been completely upended. Those who survived the war navigated complex emotions and stark, inalterable facts. Though the war had been shorter than expected, so many had been lost that it was hard to grieve properly. They went directly from the airport to Zakaria's parents' house for a meal, where Abed likely met several members of Zakaria's family, including a younger sister, Bahar. Abed then paid a painful visit to his Baiju *chachi*, who had married his uncle, Sayeedul, as a coy teenager in 1947. It was hard to imagine her now living as a widow.

Viquar soon arrived from the north. He told Abed in person what he had described in his letter from Sylhet, of the harrowing journeys people had endured. He had followed one group of returning refugees to their villages in Sulla, a predominantly Hindu area only sixteen miles north of Baniachong, where Abed had grown up. Sarabala was among that group.

Sulla had been decimated. In village after village, the army had looted, burned the homes to ashes, killed the people's livestock, and destroyed their farm tools. The area was a geographical oddity, with its inland sea filling up and emptying yearly. In the hills to the north, in India's Meghalaya State, it can rain as much as fifteen inches in a single day in the summer, more than any other place on earth. The rainwater coming off these hills creates a depression, often described as a giant saucer or bowl, which fills every summer until it overflows onto the surrounding land. Rice cultivation and fishing are the main livelihoods here. During the monsoon season when the villages become islands, goats and cows stay close to the homestead and get leaner. In the winter, the waters subside, the grasses reappear, and the animals grow fat again. Subsistence was the norm at the best of times, the land yielding one annual rice harvest in April. It was a preindustrial land with neither motors nor electricity, and it took about twenty-four hours to reach it overland by rail, road, and boat from Dhaka. It seemed unlikely that anyone else would venture so far to help, so Abed and Viquar resolved to focus their efforts there.

★ ★ ★

Before returning to Dhaka, Viquar had established a makeshift center of operations in the market town of Derai, located in the center of Sulla. The only place available had been an empty store owned by a regime loyalist killed in the fighting. Viquar had already hired three people, but they needed guidance, especially because, as Abed later described it, Viquar was a good litigator but a bad manager. Abed would go there to pick up where he had left off, the first step on a lifelong journey, for this first trip to the north constituted the inaugural activities of what would soon become BRAC.

Abed would first need to assess people's needs and then figure out how to organize people to meet those needs. To do that, he combined and applied much of his previous experience, including the accountancy skills he learned in London, the managerial acumen he developed at Shell, and the modest expertise gained by administering a cyclone relief operation on Manpura. He went first to Shillong, across the northern border, to get permission from the Indian authorities to buy and ship bamboo stalks and wood to Bangladesh. From there he traveled south to Sylhet, the nearest city to Derai, where he spent the night in the Gulshan Hotel, a cheap guest-house, where he was repulsed by the state of the room and the dirty sheets. The journey to Derai by road and river took up most of the next day.

A local doctor, Manoranjan Sarkar, happened to witness Abed's arrival in Derai. The doctor had been shopping in Derai and wanted to return to his village by boat that evening, but the locals told him it was too late, so they invited him to sleep in the dilapidated store Viquar had rented. "Around dusk, a gentleman wearing an overcoat with suit, tie, and boots showed up, accompanied by an elderly local man," Dr. Sarkar said. "Not a sight you see every day." Recalling the incident years later, Abed said he was wearing the only warm clothes he possessed.

A group of locals gathered that evening, as Abed explained that he would need people to conduct a survey, distribute goods, and offer medical care. Most had lived in the refugee camps in India; they were eager to help and needed work, and many of them had no homes. That night, Abed climbed a rickety ladder to sleep in the dusty storage loft above the shop.

The sun blazed down on the paddy fields the next day. It was the dry season, so one could only reach the surrounding villages on foot. About a dozen people, including Dr. Sarkar, walked with Abed for about four hours to the market village of Ghungiar Gaon, twelve miles away, where the doctor lived with his wife. The Pakistan Army had garrisoned itself there, so it was the only settlement left standing, but everything had been stolen, even the dishes in people's homes. Dr. Sarkar invited Abed to dine with him and his wife at his home. "How can I possibly serve guests?" his wife exclaimed. "We have no crockery!" Dr. Sarkar ran to a nearby tea stall in search of plates.

Knowing it would be good to have a doctor on board, Abed asked Dr. Sarkar to join the team. He selected about fifteen literate people from the area and hired them to conduct a survey of destroyed or severely damaged villages. He instructed them to go from household to household, recording answers to a precise set of questions: How many people remain in the family? How much land do they own, if any? How many rooms were in the houses they had had before the war? How many cows? How many boats? And, finally, how much had been destroyed? Abed gave them hours of detailed instructions on how to collect and record data, along with how to verify it by checking with the neighbors, so that people did not claim to have had more than they did. One of the locals had a master's degree, so he put him in charge. "Get the survey done," Abed told him. "Send me the completed survey sheets every two weeks by courier."

On the way back to Dhaka, Abed stayed again at the Gulshan Hotel in Sylhet. The conditions were exactly the same, but this time he reveled in the relative luxury.

* * *

Shortly after the war, Viquar decided to move back to London. He and Abed went to Calcutta to sign over the money in the Help Bangladesh account to Abed. For the next several years they would both formally be credited as cofounders of BRAC, though in reality it was Abed's organization. The two men would remain close throughout their lives, but in Abed's view, for all his legal acumen and the selfless bravery he showed on Manpura, his best friend lacked the skills needed to run a large operation. These skills included giving precise instructions, motivating people to do the work, and following up to make sure they performed.

Abed hired a group of students from Dhaka University to help him analyze the data arriving from Sulla. Ever the accountant, he showed them how to organize the information into tables indicating exactly how much the villagers had lost: how many cows, goats, houses, and so on. It was still a bootstrap setup, initially run out of Viquar's law chambers in Dhaka, which were themselves sublet from Fazle Ali's accountancy practice—the three roommates, together again.

Abed hired Khushi Kabir, a young art-school graduate and Fazle Ali's sister-in-law, as BRAC's first executive assistant. She set up the first standalone office. "We went and foraged, taking furniture from people who were throwing things away," she recalled. They moved into a brick house on a main road in the Maghbazar neighborhood, within earshot of blaring horns at the nearby intersection and vegetable sellers shouting the price of potatoes. Khushi recalled finding a narrow, lumpy bed for Abed to sleep on, along with other pieces of used and broken furniture. Abed also located and rehired Mohammad Ali, his bearer from Chittagong, who had kept the house running during the cyclone relief efforts. Abed slept in the apartment upstairs, Mohammad Ali in a room above the garage.

The organization still didn't have an official name, but it presented a good face to the world. Abed was executive director. It looked good to have a trained accountant who had left his job at a multinational oil company and put his own savings into the effort. For the board of directors, he and Viquar recruited a group of eminent Bangladeshis with impeccable reputations. The poet and social activist Begum Sufia Kamal, an icon of the nationalist movement and beloved by all of its factions, served as board chair. Along with Abed and Viquar, other board members included Akbar Kabir, Fazle Ali's father-in-law (and Khushi's father), a retired government official whom Abed had hired for the cyclone relief project; Abdur Razzaq, a distinguished professor of political science; S. R. Hussain, a former executive with Esso, the oil company; and Kazi Fazlur Rahman, formerly of Burma Oil Company. They called themselves the Bangladesh Rehabilitation Assistance Committee.

Abed still had the 8,000 British pounds ($19,200) from the sale of his half of the London house. Closing the Calcutta account of Help Bangladesh gave him an additional $6,000. But it would take a lot more than that to make a substantial difference in people's lives. In the days after liberation, Dhaka saw an influx of foreign charities looking for ways to help, so Abed thought he might be able to tap their generosity. In March he received, through a friend, a dinner invitation from a French Canadian named Raymond Cournoyer. Cournoyer had been a Catholic brother with the Congregation of the Holy Cross and a principal at Saint Placid's, a Benedictine high school in Chittagong. He had lived in East Pakistan before and knew the country well, speaking fluent Bengali. He had returned as the local field director of Oxfam, the British humanitarian group, where he was pushing internally for more assistance to local organizations. "We might be able to support you," he told Abed over dinner.

Using the Sulla survey data, Abed drafted a funding proposal to rebuild about 6,500 houses using corrugated iron and bamboo, set up health clinics, build boats for fishermen, and more. Cournoyer was impressed enough to bring in the overseas aid director, Ken Bennett, who visited in March. The pair came to Viquar's law office and heard the pitch. Bennett, in an internal Oxfam report dated March 16, 1972, wrote, "It is difficult to take an optimistic view of Bangladesh's future," but nonetheless recorded his "favorable impression" of Abed and BRAC, which was "in the course of being registered" as a nonprofit organization.[1] He recommended the approval of a grant of $430,000, enough to fund not only the material but also a meager wage for BRAC's first office and field workers. Days later, on March 21, the Bangladesh Rehabilitation Assistance Committee received its official registration.

★ ★ ★

For the duration of the war, Bangladesh's political classes were united in the liberation struggle. However, infighting began as soon as the war ended, and Abed's project nearly fell victim to it. Shortly after receiving the Oxfam funding, Abed woke up to find his picture on the front page of a Dhaka newspaper, next to a headline calling him a CIA agent. The article maintained that BRAC was a front for American intelligence. Since the Americans had backed the wrong side in the war, the charge was damaging, even though it was patently false.

The background follows a twisted logic: Abed's uncle Sayeedul, prior to his death at the hands of the Pakistanis, had become a senior official in the leftist party of Abdul Hamid Khan Bhashani, known as "Maulana," the title for a Muslim religious scholar. Though he had supported the liberation movement, Sheikh Mujib's allies in the Awami League now viewed Maulana Bhashani as a political opponent, since he was the only other plausible claimant to leadership of the Bangladeshi people. Favoring closer ties with China, "the Red Maulana" (as he was known) was no friend to the United States, but as he was a rival to Sheikh Mujib, Awami League loyalists were suspicious of anyone linked to him. Abed's friendships with Americans, combined with his late uncle's association with Maulana Bhashani, were enough to hang a conspiracy on. The article claimed BRAC had been created to channel CIA funding to Bhashani.

Abed went to the office of the newspaper editor, Sheikh Fazlul Huq Moni, a powerful nephew of Sheikh Mujib, and confronted him. The conversation that followed was civil—even somewhat anticlimactic, given the severity of the charge. Abed explained BRAC's purpose and produced the Oxfam funding proposal and grant letter. "The CIA was against our liberation war," Abed told him. "Why would we work for them?" A long, wide-ranging conversation ensued. According to Abed, Sheikh Moni was convinced. "What's done is done," he said. "We won't write any more regarding this."

Though the damage had been contained, the accusation had some fallout. One of the original board members, Kazi Fazlur Rahman, resigned, saying, "My wife just doesn't want me to be involved in this." He was soon replaced by Humayun Kabir—the first friend Abed had made in Glasgow, where they had played table tennis at the British Council. Abed and Kabir had recently reestablished contact after losing touch for many years. He was now the Bangladesh resident director of Pfizer, the pharmaceutical company.

The CIA affair got people talking, even those who didn't take the charge seriously. The local head of CARE, the private American charity, saw Abed the next day. He was used to hearing the same accusation directed at him. "I hear we have the same employer!" he joked.

* * *

In May, Abed visited Shillong again to negotiate for bamboo, which was roped together, made into rafts, and sent down the river in a flotilla several miles long, all the way to Derai. In a donor report, Abed wrote of the "slow and perilous journey on bamboo and timber rafts down the River Kushiyara," and he commended the perseverance of BRAC staff "exposed to the ravages of the monsoon and the mosquitos." They also bought eight hundred tons of corrugated iron sheets from Japan and, in a pleasant surprise, received an additional two hundred tons as a government donation. They distributed 4,500 pounds of nylon twine so that fishermen could weave new nets. They set up health clinics and hired doctors to treat two hundred patients daily, fed fifteen thousand malnourished children with corn-soya meals from UNICEF, and organized fifty-two fishing and agricultural cooperatives. Through the latter, they distributed fifty thousand pounds of seed, two hundred sets of tools for carpenters and boat builders, and 125 handlooms for weavers.

The cyclone and the war had shaken Abed's priorities. This massive relief effort offered a way for him to ground himself. The new Abed was uncertain about many things—even, it seems, whether to continue to dress like a London accountant. He had left his tie collection behind, but he continued to feel more comfortable wearing more formal attire. He came to realize that he could never be an effective development professional by trying to live or look like a poor person. For him, thinking one could help those in poverty by imitating them was itself a form of vanity.

There was also something deeper at work, however. The physical transportation of thousands of tons of materials was "no mean achievement," as Abed wrote in his first donor report. As the year went on, he began to question whether this relief work was really making a difference. Part of him thought BRAC would be a temporary effort and that, after playing a small part in helping to rebuild the country, he would return to a comfortable life in the private sector, perhaps as an accountant or an executive at another multinational company. He was still young, with "time yet for a hundred indecisions and for a hundred visions and revisions," in the words of Eliot's "Prufrock," one of his favorite poems. But did it truly make a difference that some people received bamboo and tin for their houses, and new fishing nets and farming tools? Would their lives be any different from before the war? Would it break the cycle of poverty for future generations? The hard work was fueled by the idealism of university students from the cities, but when the project was done, they could always return to their lives of relative privilege. The people of Sulla would remain there, life going on as it had for centuries, the landless tilling others' soil with little to show for their efforts. What could the promise of liberation really mean to them? Theirs was not just a poverty of means but also a poverty of freedom, opportunity, and self-worth. Relief work almost seemed futile in the face of it.

⋆ ⋆ ⋆

After Oxfam accepted his proposal, Abed changed his plan for distributing the housing materials. He realized they could reach more people by asking for partial contributions from those who could afford to pay. Not everybody in the area was in the same financial boat. For instance, an educated and literate man like Dr. Sarkar may have been poor by the standards of the urban middle class, but compared to his neighbors, he was part of the village elite. Some were landowners; others worked as sharecroppers or tenant farmers. Many had no land or assets and relied on manual labor to survive.

Abed looked at the initial survey results and decided to classify people into four categories. The first, Category A, were the better-off landowners. He thought if BRAC could ask them to shoulder a portion of the costs—say, half the price of each sheet of corrugated iron—BRAC could reach a great many more people. Categories B and C were poorer and would pay token amounts. Category D, constituting about a third of the population, could not afford to pay anything and would not be asked to contribute. Largely thanks to this scheme, at the end of six months Abed found they had underspent and overdelivered. Where he had initially budgeted to rebuild 6,500 homes, they ended up building 10,200 and repairing 3,900 more, with 16,000 British pounds left over.

Abed wrote to Oxfam and explained the situation, offering to repay the unspent remainder of their grant. Oxfam was taken aback. Nobody at the organization could remember a time when a project had done more than promised while finishing under budget. They asked Abed to keep the money and apply the leftover funds to his next project.

Part of BRAC's genesis myth is that Oxfam's offer convinced Abed to continue. In reality, by then he had already made up his mind that BRAC would be a lifelong effort. Years later, he admitted he didn't really want to give Oxfam back the money, but he made the offer anyway, hoping it would convince them to give him another grant. It worked.

★ ★ ★

In June 1972, shortly after BRAC received that initial Oxfam grant, another event ruptured the connection between Abed and his earlier life. Abed and Marietta had remained good friends. In fact, many people thought they were still together, though they had broken up four years earlier. When Abed returned to London during the war, she seemed happy. Both of them had moved on and were seeing new people. Marietta had thrown herself into the liberation movement and knew all its key figures, so when independence came, it made sense that she should visit the country she had fought for. She had not seen Bengal since 1965, during her engagement to Abed.

Something fell short for Marietta on this visit. Those close to her said she found it a disheartening place, given the destruction, mourning, and infighting that was already plaguing the country's nascent politics. She stayed with Baiju *chachi*. "She stayed for two weeks and then left," Abed said. "She said, 'I'm going home,' and I said, 'Fine. I'll get my driver to take you to the airport.'"

During their years together, Marietta had often told Abed, "There's no life after thirty." Abed never knew how seriously he should take that. On June 6, 1972, days after her thirtieth birthday, Marietta Procopé committed suicide at her house in London by overdosing on sleeping pills and drowning herself in her bathtub.

Marietta left a note asking that the Camden house go to International Neighbors Housing, an organization that provided shelter for the homeless, and that a portion of her assets go to Gonoshasthaya Kendra, a Bangladeshi health-care organization launched by a British-trained doctor named Zafrullah Chowdhury, with whom Marietta had become close during her wartime activism. According to Abed, she also wrote, "Abed has enough money for BRAC, so no money needed."

It is hard, if not impossible, to know whether that is what the note really said. Paul Connett, who led Action Bangladesh, was living in the Camden house at the time and found Marietta's body. He heard the water running for far too long, knocked on the bathroom door, and eventually broke it down. The police found the suicide note in her bedroom and showed it to Connett. "It was striking and painful to read," he said. According to Connett, she had written, "I'm no loss to the world. I'm a shit and I want to rid the world of this shit." He does not remember the rest but said it may well have contained the passage Abed mentioned.

Zafrullah Chowdhury never received the money. According to Zafrullah, who went on to become a figure of renown in Bangladesh due to his work and activism on behalf of health care for the poor, Marietta's brother John argued that she was not of sound mind when she wrote that note and, therefore, it did not legally constitute a proper bequest. Not wanting a dispute but feeling the need to defend Marietta, Zafrullah said he went to Oxford to meet John, relinquishing any claim to the money in return for a written statement that Marietta was in a rational and lucid state of mind until the end.

The disjunction between the depth with which Marietta was loved by others and her self-loathing was jarring, according to Connett. "There is nothing I would not have done for her," he said. "I would have walked a hundred miles if she had asked me to. She could have asked me for anything. But she kept it to herself." Abed immediately flew to London. At the request of the family, Faruq Choudhury delivered the eulogy at a funeral attended by many members of the Bengali expat community, all of whom were in shock.

Abed said many people assumed their breakup and her suicide were linked. He insisted they were not and was convinced that Marietta suffered from clinical depression. "This remains in people's memories: that she was my girlfriend and I left her, and she committed suicide," he said. "It was not like that."

He also maintained that Marietta's departure from Bangladesh and her subsequent death were unrelated to the accusation that he was working for the CIA, even though others, including her own family, were led to believe they were connected. Ann Wigram, who went on to become Ann Procopé, was engaged to Marietta's brother Fredrik at the time and knew Marietta well. "Fredrik and I always understood that she was more or less sent back from Bangladesh—something about them thinking she was a CIA agent," she said. "She was certainly very upset by it all and it was one of the reasons why she committed suicide."

Marietta had been Abed's soulmate during some of his most formative years. With compassion and verve, she had also played a significant role in the Bangladesh liberation movement. Though Abed seldom displayed sentiment, he would profess, in an unguarded moment late in life, that he missed Marietta. In mid-1972, just as Abed was arriving at the purpose that would define the rest of his life, she had abandoned the world. That chapter was now closed and could never be reopened.

8

VISIONS AND REVISIONS

When Abed first arrived in Sulla, he had the idea of redesigning, in a more orderly and efficient manner, two villages the Pakistan Army had razed. He even brought architects from Dhaka to help him. "Nothing existed, so we thought we might as well build the houses in a straight line and run a road through the center," he recalled. "The people were not interested and built their houses right where they previously had been." Ideas like "local ownership" and "community buy-in" were not as prevalent in development circles then as they are now, but this was an obvious early lesson in the folly of paternalism. There would be many more.

As the summer floodwaters receded, Abed began to see the contours of a long-term development project. BRAC's first employees had thrown themselves into the work, enduring hardships for little pay to help the villagers rebuild their homes and livelihoods. Even though the project had surpassed its stated goals, it was not nearly enough for Abed. Poverty was too deeply entrenched to be affected by such short-term measures. The personal transformation that had begun in the helicopter above Manpura Island was now complete. Having found his calling, Abed resolved to dedicate the rest of his life to eradicating poverty.

In October 1972, Abed sat down at his desk in Dhaka to write a new proposal for Oxfam. He was not content to merely change the material conditions of people's lives. He wanted to change their outlook on life itself, to deliver on the promise of liberation by showing that a world of personal dignity and freedom, long denied to the landless and illiterate classes, was possible. To do that, he would need to confront or maneuver around the corruption endemic to life in rural areas. Abed had seen that a cruel and exploitative power structure held sway in the villages of Sulla, a net of economic forces, social customs, naked ignorance, and outright bribery that nearly always worked against the poor. One of BRAC's surveys found that 60 percent of the area's tube wells—steel pipes driven into an aquifer to provide the cheapest source of drinking water—were broken, and those that worked were often inaccessible. Abed discovered that many village leaders had used government funding to install wells in their own homes, barring others' access. Moneylenders, meanwhile, held the poorest under their thumbs, routinely charging interest rates of 200 percent when families needed short-term cash and often acting in concert with landlords, the police, and other elites. When families failed to pay back the loans, they faced forfeiting their land, their daughters, or both.

In his proposal for what he called "Phase II of the Sulla Project," Abed wrote, "Rural Bangladesh, with slight regional variation, remains wedded to her primitive ways. But the struggle for liberation has brought about a new climate, a new awareness, and a desire for change. The corrupt and exploitative rural leadership is being constantly challenged, and a new and forward-looking potential leadership awaits on the sidelines to be inducted into their future roles. The people, so long grasping in ignorance and mistrust, are now receptive to new ideas and institutions which would help them to break away from a centuries-old subsistence economy."

The language sounds outdated today, but it captures Abed's view on the widespread cruelty and oppression that held Bangladesh back and the potential he saw for upending the balance of power in the villages.

Education was of paramount importance. In Phase II, BRAC would avoid intensive capital investments such as agricultural mechanization, for this "would lead to wastage, dependence on the existing corrupt leadership, and would require prolonged BRAC presence in the project area." Major capital investments could take place in Phase III, but first they needed to tackle "the more difficult and challenging task of developing human resources to participate, guide, and manage" development projects without outside help. To make any activity "self-generating and self-sustaining," the key would be "awareness and participation of its beneficiaries."

His long-term targets were audacious, to say the least. Of the project area's population of 125,000, 90 percent were illiterate. He aimed for the "total eradication" of adult illiteracy within three years and a tripling of rice yields within five years.

* * *

Abed felt he had good reason to be optimistic. These were still the early days of the Green Revolution, the name given to the spectacular gains in agricultural productivity seen in other parts of South Asia in the late 1960s.

Farmers in India and Pakistan were now using high-yielding wheat seeds developed at agriculture research institutes in Mexico and the Philippines, and by 1970, India's wheat harvest had risen 63 percent from five years earlier. That year, the American biologist Norman Borlaug had won the Nobel Peace Prize for his contribution to the Green Revolution. In Abed's view, the Green Revolution's advances, along with concurrent progress in health, including immunizations for smallpox and other diseases, were a triumph of science and progress over fatalism and superstition. Humanity, it seemed to him, had finally called into question the belief that widespread human misery was somehow ordained by a higher power.

Though Bangladesh lagged behind its neighbors, Abed saw no reason it could not see similar gains. Farmers who still relied on rain-fed agriculture could learn how to irrigate their fields, employ better agricultural practices, and gain access to higher-yielding seeds and fertilizers. To do that, they needed to be educated. He sketched out a plan for what he called "integrated development," which would combine adult education, agriculture, fisheries, vocational training for women, health, and family planning. The latter was especially important, for most women had six or more children, far more than they could afford. Due to a combination of stigma, sexism, and low awareness, use of birth control was just 5 percent, with ominous implications for land use and overcrowding in a country that was already one of the world's most densely populated. At the current rate of growth, the population would double in less than thirty years.

Where a critic might see a hodgepodge of activities, Abed saw a holistic set of solutions that, delivered together, would give people the boost they needed to emancipate themselves from millennia of suffering and exploitation. They would form agricultural cooperatives to increase the amount of irrigated land, while training farmers on practices like line sowing, correct water usage, and the proper amount of fertilizer to put in their fields. They would train local health workers to diagnose and treat common ailments, encourage discussions about family planning, give women access to contraceptives, and drill tube wells for access to clean water. If they could show this process worked in Sulla, Abed saw it catalyzing advances that would spread nationwide. "It is hoped that the results of the concentrated attention being given to the area does not remain confined within its boundaries but would generate a rippling effect, gradually making itself felt all over Bangladesh," he wrote.

Literacy was the first and paramount concern. "An illiterate man can neither be aware of his rights nor conscious of his duties," Abed wrote. As he saw it, most development projects left out the education component, and, as a result, they "consistently show poor performance and fail to achieve what is supposed to be the major purpose of development—higher income." Without basic literacy and numeracy, people would have limited capacity for learning new things and could therefore never really take control of their lives. Literacy would boost self-confidence, open avenues to new knowledge, and prevent them, for instance, from signing over their land to a moneylender in ignorance of what the contract actually said. Knowledge of fundamental arithmetic would stop them from getting shortchanged by vendors and might even help them succeed in their own small enterprises.

Abed devised a plan to offer basic education to adults for reading, writing, and simple math through local "community centers." The community centers would be tin sheds where people in the village could meet in the evening to receive literacy and numeracy classes. This was the centerpiece of the entire program, with one community center planned in each of 175 out of the 220 villages in the project. Since every village had at least one person with enough schooling to teach others the basics, BRAC would recruit the more educated villagers to lead the classes. The teachers would receive a small payment for their work, with half coming from attendees and the other half from BRAC. The centers would also host discussions among women on family-planning matters, provide meeting places to plan collective farming activity, and serve any other use the villagers saw fit.

Impressed by BRAC's track record and ambition, Oxfam agencies in the United Kingdom, United States, and Canada joined forces to fund the project, with contributions from the Canadian aid agency and Community Aid Abroad in Australia. BRAC started work on Sulla Phase II in December 1972. Reflecting the shift from "rehabilitation assistance" to long-term development, the board changed the name of the organization to "Bangladesh Rural Advancement Committee," a name it would keep until the 1990s, when it formally became just BRAC.

* * *

In December and January, at the end of a riverside bazaar in Sulla called Markuli, BRAC built a small complex of mud-plaster buildings to serve as its field headquarters for the region. Field motivators, as the front-line staff were called, fanned out into the countryside to oversee construction of the community centers. Dry land was precious, but in each of the villages, the field staff found someone with a small amount of it to spare. Soon a team of about one hundred full-time staff was working in ten field offices, or camps, across the Sulla region.

Communication between Dhaka and the field headquarters was difficult, since there were neither electricity nor telephones. Abed spent one week of every month in the field, often continuing meetings all night to track progress before catching the morning motor launch to start the trip back to Dhaka. During these visits, he would gather the entire staff in the largest building in Markuli, where they would sit for long hours with no fans, baking under the tin roof. At night, they would work by the light of hurricane lamps.

By the end of 1973, they began to see the fruits of their efforts. Some of the agricultural cooperatives seemed to be working well, and by bringing doctors to Sulla and training locals to act as basic paramedics, they began delivering health care of a quality not seen before in the region. BRAC's demonstration plots, which showcased the advantages of using improved seeds and farming techniques, caused a sensation. The sight of educated city people working the soil brought sarcastic jabs and howls of laughter from the Sulla residents. But, as Abed wrote in an interim donor report, "the seriousness and persistence of our workers soon changed the villagers' attitude to one of respect." Once the crops came up, the plants stood out as among the best in the area, and farmers began asking BRAC to come to their fields and advise them.

By late 1973, a generator arrived at Markuli so they could work more easily at night. It was the first time anyone in the area had seen electric lights. People for miles around talked about this "company" called BRAC, lighting up the darkness in the middle of nowhere.

There was one huge problem: The community centers were a complete flop. Initially, about five thousand people had signed up for the literacy classes and attendance rates exceeded 90 percent, for nobody had ever offered anything like this in the area. After a year and a half, only 5 percent were still attending.

The issues were legion. The field staff had rushed to meet the construction targets Abed had set, and, as a result, they selected many sites without regard for the daily lives of the villagers. Many stopped going simply because the location was too inconvenient. Because the community centers were built on private land, the landowner often commandeered the structure for his own needs, like storage of grain or livestock. With so many community centers to oversee, BRAC did not have enough workers to stop this problem from happening.

Building quality was another issue. About a third of the structures fell into disrepair, unable to withstand the wind and the rain, and nobody cared enough to repair them. Worse, the teachers would often claim the classes were continuing even when they had stopped completely. When people stopped attending, they stopped paying their share and the teachers stopped teaching, but the teachers were perfectly happy to keep receiving the other half of their fees from BRAC—half being better than nothing—so they lied and said the classes were still taking place.

Abed had to step back and take a hard look at what was happening. Like redesigning the layout of the villages, the literacy classes had been entirely his idea. Most of the problems cascaded from the inescapable reality that the intended beneficiaries perceived little benefit from the skills he considered so fundamental to being an empowered human being. After a hard day's work, who wanted to go to a community center to learn to read and write? These skills, which seemed so valuable to Abed, were irrelevant to the daily struggles of the villagers and would not, in their view, ever be of any use to them.

Abed's goal of eradicating illiteracy in the project area within three years was obviously not going to happen. While they might see some modest increases in crop yields, it was also clear they would not triple within five years, as he had predicted. Farmers' habits were deeply ingrained and would not change so quickly. Abed's idea that concentrated attention across multiple sectors would transform life in Sulla within a few years, let alone have a ripple effect and spread throughout Bangladesh, had been naïve, to say the least.

Halfway through the three-year grant, Abed sent a sobering assessment to Oxfam. He came clean, putting into BRAC's first interim project report everything that had gone wrong. Despite the adult education classes being a huge part of BRAC's work, Abed wrote, with dry understatement, "the achievement of the programs was not commensurate with the effort."

Abed felt foolish. In hindsight, he was still learning the importance of participatory decision-making. Reading and writing were simply not at the top of people's list of felt needs, no matter how much he thought they should be. The top-down approach he had used as a manager at Shell would not work here. "I was still struggling to understand," he said. "As a manager in a corporation, you take pride in making decisions yourself, but here you are asked not to make decisions yourself but to consult people who, in many cases, are less educated than you are." It was BRAC's first major failure. In time, he would learn that lack of formal education, even illiteracy, did not make people ignorant of the ways of the world—nor powerless to change it.

9

SPEAK A TRUE WORD

In early 1973, Raymond Cournoyer handed Abed a slim volume and told him, without further comment, "You should read this." The book was Paulo Freire's *Pedagogy of the Oppressed*, and Cournoyer, a former Catholic brother and high school principal, thought it might resonate with Abed. He was right. It would be hard to overestimate the influence of this book, and Freire's ideas in general, on Abed and BRAC.

The failure of the adult education classes in the Sulla community centers was a setback, but Abed remained convinced that genuine human empowerment required an end to illiteracy. He had already immersed himself in leftist writing and asked his staff to do the same. "First he made me read *Wretched of the Earth*," said Khushi Kabir, referring to Frantz Fanon's 1961 anti-colonial manifesto. "Then Ivan Illich. He made us read all these Marxist books to understand what actually had to change in society." Abed was looking for a development model attuned to the felt needs of participants—their psychological and educational needs, as they perceived them, as well as the more obvious material needs. Freire, a Brazilian activist and educator, gave him what he sought.

Now considered a classic of pedagogical theory, *Pedagogy of the Oppressed* had been published in English only three years earlier. Freire went on to become an intellectual superstar of the 1970s. The son of middle-class Brazilian parents who had fallen into poverty during his childhood, he had launched an innovative adult-education program in northern Brazil in the early 1960s, teaching literacy to small groups of sugarcane farmworkers. Working in a remote, impoverished area, he had achieved the remarkable feat of teaching three hundred workers to read in just forty-five days. The program gained recognition and was poised to expand nationwide when a military coup interrupted the work. Freire, an ardent leftist, was accused of subversion, jailed, and later exiled to Chile, where he continued to refine his techniques. *Pedagogy of the Oppressed* was a crystallization of his approach.

Abed and Freire were separated by chasms of culture, religion, and geography. Born and raised Muslim in the upper classes of British India, Abed essentially had no religion at this point, and he certainly had no background in education. Freire was a Roman Catholic educator who subscribed to what others have called an unorthodox version of Latin American liberation theology. However, these were surface-level differences. In Freire, Abed found the breakthrough he was looking for.

Pedagogy of the Oppressed describes an approach to education that seeks to empower oppressed people by inculcating both literacy and social activism. It is not an easy read—ironic considering that it is, at least in part, a book about teaching people to read. The first chapter begins, "While the problem of humanization has always, from an axiological point of view, been humankind's central problem, it now takes on the character of an inescapable concern." Freire published it in 1968, the year of global rebellion and discontent, when students took to the streets of Paris, Chicago, Prague, Rio de Janeiro, and elsewhere. As Abed saw it, "the problem of humanization" referred to oppressed people everywhere, throughout history, whose basic humanity had been denied by vested interests. Behind obtuse language filled with post-Marxist terminology, Abed found powerful ideas at work and, more important, a practical way to put them into action.

Freire believed that in order to free themselves from poverty and oppression, people needed to go through a process of what he called *conscientizao*—"conscientization" or critical consciousness, perhaps best defined as an awareness of oppression, an understanding of what causes it, and an ability to act against it. Abed also must have recognized Freire's description of people like him, who had inherited the role of the dominating class and wanted to change an unjust system but did not always know how. "Those who authentically commit themselves to the people must re-examine themselves constantly," Freire writes, going on to mention "certain members of the oppressor class [who] join the oppressed in their struggle for liberation." These "heirs of exploitation" have an important role to play, but the problem is that "they almost always bring with them the marks of their origin: their prejudices and their deformations, which include a lack of confidence in the people's ability to think, to want, and to know." The oppressed must fight for their own liberation, and the conviction that they must do so "cannot be packaged and sold."[1]

This situation puts well-intentioned proponents of human development like Abed in a bind, since, according to this view, most attempts to educate the poor fall into a trap of ineffectual paternalism. Freire rails against a "banking concept" of education, which treats the minds of docile students as empty bank accounts that need to be filled with knowledge. Dominant elites, he says, have long used the banking concept of education to encourage passivity in the oppressed, often by encouraging learning by rote memorization instead of strengthening the capacity for critical thinking.

This point hit home for Abed. He was guilty as charged. He thought back to his failure with the community centers. The teachers had bored the villagers with lessons on basic reading and math, a system of one-way teaching in which the students were supposed to sit and passively receive information. Exhausted from the day's work, many of them probably fell asleep, and eventually they stopped attending entirely. In Freire's words, this situation epitomizes the "false generosity of paternalism," which purports to do good but instead encourages inaction.[2]

In the 1960s, Abed's group in London had dabbled in Marxist-Leninist ideology, dubbing their reading circle the "College of Cardinals," but most of them found the real-world implications of a communist revolution hard to stomach. In Freire, Abed found a Marxist-leaning leftist who seemed to truly believe in individual empowerment, as opposed to the empowerment of masses or groups, which was so often used as a pretext for empowering oneself as the self-styled vanguard of the proletariat. "He is talking about individuals and individual self-worth," said Abed. "He is not talking about masses. He is not talking about class. He talks about how to get individuals to build their own self-worth." He added, "I looked at BRAC's way of working and began to think about more sustainable changes in society than even the communist revolution" might provide.

Freire proposed that a true pedagogy of the oppressed be based on dialogue, whereby the student-learners come together and discuss among themselves the problems they face in common. For the sugarcane workers in Brazil, he created a space where students, working in small groups, not only learned how to read and write words but also discussed the true meanings of those words in the context of their own lives. Within this space, they began to come up with their own ways to confront the myriad injustices that held them back.

The centrality of language to Freire's approach must have appealed to Abed, who had long been a self-taught student of literature, dating back to the childhood recitations of poetry encouraged by his beloved uncle, Sayeedul Hasan. Essential to dialogue is "the word" itself, according to Freire.

Words deprived of their potential for social action and change are idle chatter at best—"an alienating and alienated 'blah'"—whereas "to speak a true word is to transform the world."[3]

Perhaps, Abed thought, he could do as Freire had done in Brazil and Chile, using literacy lessons as a platform for people to discuss the problems of rural Bangladesh and explore avenues for change—to help them speak a true word. He grew convinced of the importance of empowerment in the Freirean sense, the empowerment of individuals to learn and grow, to dream and plan for the future, to lead the lives they wanted instead of the lives prescribed for them. If they could do this while BRAC continued to provide basic services such as health care and economic support—providing small loans at low interest rates, for instance—they might make modest progress. And perhaps, in the end, the poor might have something to teach BRAC rather than vice versa.

★ ★ ★

By now, Abed had lost both his parents, his mother having died just after he moved to London and his father shortly before the war. It was left to his aunts, therefore, to remind him of the impropriety of still being single in his late thirties. As long as Marietta had been alive, many people, including his relatives, had persisted in believing they were still together. Abed did nothing to dissuade them, not necessarily because he was reserved in discussing his personal life—though he certainly was—but because staying quiet served a purpose. If they thought he and Marietta were still a couple, his aunts might leave him alone.

After Marietta died, people began to talk. One of his maternal aunts called him. "Abed, if your mother were alive to see you still unmarried, she would be terribly unhappy," she said. "I feel it is my duty to try and convince you to get married." BRAC was everything to Abed at this point. He felt he had little time for courtship or family life. The mention of his mother moved him, however, and he began to reconsider.

One day he received a call from Baiju, the aunt to whom he was closest. "We have somebody in mind," she said. Baiju's daughter, Sharmeen, who treated Abed like a brother, had been scheming to match him with a woman named Ayesha, whose older sister was married to a cousin on her mother's side. She had already been hounding Ayesha, who was known to everyone as Bahar. "Get ready," Sharmeen told Bahar. "You're going to marry my cousin-brother."

In the interconnected world of the Dhaka elite, Bahar also happened to be Zakaria Khan's sister. Abed almost certainly would have met her in

January 1971, the day of his return to newly liberated Bangladesh, when he and Zakaria went directly from the airport to Zakaria's parents' home for lunch. It had hardly been love at first sight. There was no romantic spark at that first meeting, according to Abed. "It didn't register," he said. "I was too busy with other things."

Entering into a traditional arranged marriage would be a departure for Abed. With Marietta, he'd fallen in love before moving in together, not after. He knew Bahar lectured in English at a girls' college and had heard she was a bookish type, but that was about all he knew. There also was the matter of potentially mismatched expectations. Her father, Yahya Khan Chowdhury, a prominent former member of parliament and a district magistrate, lived in a grand two-story house in Eskaton, one of Dhaka's affluent neighborhoods. Abed still lived above the BRAC office in the brick house in Maghbazar, a middle-class area that was fast becoming part of the urban sprawl. There was no yard and just enough space to park two cars inside the gate, and the windows let in the sounds of car horns, passing traffic, and rickshaw bells. The upstairs had a decent-sized living room and a guest bedroom for visitors and field staff, but it was hardly luxurious. Needless to say, BRAC's salaries were low compared to government jobs or the private sector.

If they were to get married, Abed needed to make sure Bahar understood that being his wife would not be easy, given his preoccupation with a cause that would not offer the comforts she grew up with. "I need to speak to Bahar about this directly," Abed told Baiju.

In Bangladeshi custom, men and women did not meet together before they got engaged. However, Abed could not envision getting engaged to a woman he hadn't spoken with, and he arranged to spend some time alone with Bahar at Baiju's house. Bahar was in many ways the opposite of Marietta, who was sharp tongued, thin, and often chain smoking. She was gentle, with soft features in a heart-shaped face. They spoke for several hours and found they shared the same outlook. Abed was pleased to find that she had an intellectual side, but he warned Bahar that his ideals and aspirations would not give her the lifestyle she might be hoping for. "If we get married, you'll have to accept the hardships that may lie ahead," he told her. "If you want to live a comfortable life, you shouldn't marry me."

She laughed and replied, "I will be comfortable with whatever you are comfortable with."

To be sure, they did not fall for one another instantaneously. "I was not in love with her," Abed recalled. "But I could get engaged to her. I could, over time, even love her."

Abed reported back to Baiju that the match was suitable, and Bahar evidently agreed. On behalf of the family, Abed's aunts paid a formal visit to Bahar's home to make the proposal and fix the date. After that, Abed could visit Bahar openly, though they never left the house together. Abed and Bahar had several versions of the same conversation before they married. "We might have to live in a village," he warned her. "This is not going to be what you're used to."

"If you choose to live in a village, I will live there with you," she replied. "If you're going to work hard, I'm going to look after you."

The wedding took place on Saturday, April 7, 1973, at Dhaka Ladies Club in Eskaton. About seven hundred people attended, not an unusual number for an upper-class Bangladeshi wedding. The guests included the president of Bangladesh, Abu Sayeed Chowdhury, plus a cabinet minister and future president, Khondakar Mushtaque Ahmad, both of whom sat at the groom's table as guests of honor.

A traditional Bangladeshi wedding is an elaborate affair, signifying the departure of the bride from one family, often with accompanying tears, and her entry into another. Abed and Bahar followed the traditions, minus the tears, and photos show them alternating between stone-faced seriousness and restrained laughter. After the guests ate, the garlanded couple moved from the main banquet hall to a smaller room, and there, on a raised platform in front of their families, they performed the *rusmat*, the ceremonial unveiling of the bride to the groom through a handheld mirror. This is intended to be the man's first glimpse of his wife's face as she lifts her veil and holds the mirror before her to show the groom her reflection. Abed and Bahar then took *sharbat*, a fruit-juice-based drink, from a shared goblet, symbolizing their and their families' union, before rejoining the crowd as husband and wife.

* * *

"What's this you're reading?" Bahar asked the day after their wedding. She must have noticed the book on his pillow the night before. It was their first day of married life together. Abed had taken just a single day off work following the wedding. "That's *Pedagogy of the Oppressed*," he replied. "You should read it." She did, cover to cover. An educator herself, Bahar took to Freire's ideas and soon became a champion of his dialogue-based teaching methods.

Abed and Bahar did not, in the end, live in a village, as he had warned her they might. As Abed tells it, his thinking shifted. When he had left London, he was prepared to endure deprivations for the cause.

Even when he married Bahar, part of him was still entertaining the idea of living with Gandhian, or at least quasi-Gandhian, simplicity. "I was ready to forgo everything and work with the people," he said. He took inspiration from Albert Schweitzer, the great French-German humanitarian who died in 1965. Schweitzer would have left an admirable legacy as a theologian and musicologist, including a monumental study of Johann Sebastian Bach, had that work not been overshadowed by his last fifty years spent caring for the sick in Lambaréné, a river town in French Equatorial Africa, now Gabon. He had often said, "Everyone must find their own Lambaréné."

Perhaps Abed thought he would find his own Lambaréné in Sulla, serving the poor and forgoing urban luxuries, reading the classics in his spare time, surrounded by a library like E. M. Forster's at Cambridge. The idea proved short-lived. He realized the last thing people in Sulla needed was someone living among them for the sake of quaintness. If he were to put his skills to the best possible use, he would need to live a city life, in Dhaka, overseeing BRAC's finances and administration, building an institution that would last, and being visible to potential donors. To make a difference, he would need to raise a lot more money, which meant going to meetings, dinners, and receptions of foreign donors and diplomatic missions in the capital.

Bahar moved in with Abed above the BRAC office. They made a concession to austerity by limiting their personal use of the air conditioner. From March to October, Dhaka suffers from stifling humidity and heat. Abed ran the air conditioner in the downstairs office, knowing he would work better if he was comfortable. But in the upstairs bedroom, even on Dhaka's hottest evenings, Abed and Bahar slept without it. If they got used to cool air at night, they thought, they would never be able to sleep when they spent time in the field.

Bahar became an essential part of the organization. One of the first things she did was make the BRAC house in Maghbazar look decent, putting pictures on the walls and discarding the broken furniture. The office no longer had the feel of an underfunded start-up. They replaced the narrow, lumpy bed in the upstairs apartment, and the food improved dramatically after Bahar arrived, according to Khushi Kabir, the first office assistant. Since there were few dining options nearby, they hired a cook to prepare a simple lunch of mixed-vegetable curry and roti. The staff would set up a table on the front veranda and eat together next to the road. That house became their hub, with the charged atmosphere of people who felt they were making a difference in the world.

From the start of their marriage, Bahar joined Abed's monthly visits to Sulla, sleeping at the compound at Markuli, riding country boats across the inland sea that summer, and participating in meetings with staff and villagers. Abed recalled her first visit to Markuli. "She was asked to speak by the staff, and everybody was delighted by what she had to say," he said. "She became very popular right from the start. She became the *bhabi*" (the respectful term for one's older brother's wife). She also became the listening post for those who felt they were unable to confide in or confront Abed.

The latrines in Markuli were poorly made and the hygiene was terrible, but Bahar never complained, according to Geespati Roy, one of BRAC's first employees, who confirmed Abed's account of her first speech to the staff. According to Roy, she introduced herself by saying, "He whose soul is BRAC—I'm his other half." She then pledged to be with them every step of the way.

Abed's circle of new acquaintances in Dhaka included S. K. Dey, an Indian Bengali who had served in the cabinet of Jawaharlal Nehru, India's first prime minister. Dey had championed rural development as a way to strengthen India's emerging democracy. Now in his sixties, he had moved to Dhaka after the liberation war and told Abed that he reminded him of a younger version of himself. Dey had nearly thrown up his hands in resignation when Abed told him about his upcoming wedding. "You will become a family man if you get married," he tutted. "And when that happens, your whole ethos changes." He was wrong, according to Abed, because Bahar's commitment rivaled his own, and in time, BRAC began to seem like a joint project of the two of them.

On March 27, 1974, Bahar gave birth to a girl, Tamara, who began joining them on their trips to Sulla when she was about eight months old. Abed had thought he had little time for family life, but BRAC was now a family affair.

10

CAN A TIGER BUILD A HOUSE?

An American named Leon Clark arrived in Bangladesh in July 1974, not long after Abed's daughter Tamara was born. Abed immediately sent him to the field offices in Sulla, in the far north of the country, to get a feel for the place at the peak of flood season. Abed had hired him to help BRAC revamp its adult-education course, but to do that he would need to understand the realities of life for participants. "Arrived at the base camp in Markuli," Clark wrote in his journal. "Everything flooded. Water thigh-high inside BRAC headquarters. Obvious to everyone that disaster had hit once again. Conversations fluctuated between the crisis at hand and ideas for the functional literacy classes. Water only four inches from my mattress and filled with fish, frogs, and snakes. Frogs would jump on the bed at night; fortunately, no snakes followed."[1]

Although BRAC prided itself on being a homegrown organization, Abed wanted an outsider and an expert on the work of Paulo Freire to offer a new perspective. His first choice was Paulo Freire himself, but the Brazilian did not answer his letter. He then came across a US-based organization, World Education, that had begun using Freirean techniques in rural education programs in a number of countries, most successfully in Thailand. World Education had been founded in the 1950s by Welthy Honsinger Fisher, the elderly widow of an American Methodist bishop with a mission to improve literacy around the world. In the early 1970s, the organization was making its name in "functional education," the name it used for its adaptation of Freirean technique.

With funding from Oxfam, Abed hired World Education to send a consultant. That consultant was Leon Clark. A former high school teacher and journalist with a master's in English literature from Yale, Clark had already worked on literacy projects in India and Ghana, and by the time he arrived in Bangladesh, he was in the midst of his PhD studies at the Center for International Education at the University of Massachusetts Amherst, a center for critical pedagogy, the name given to the emerging field of studies based on Freire's work.

The day after Clark's night with the frogs, the BRAC staff took him on a tour of Sulla. Clark was seeking a mental and emotional landscape—what mattered to people and what was preventing them from achieving their dreams. Afterward, the staff gathered in his room in Markuli, where they "perched on bedstead and windowsills" to discuss the project while the rain came down in sheets and "the wind pushed waves four to five feet high against the tin walls of the house."

When he returned to Dhaka, Leon dried off and slept in the spare bedroom above the cramped office in Maghbazar. In the coming weeks, he would encourage the BRAC staff to be as methodical as possible in the way they shaped the curriculum. Leon and several staff members—mostly male, at first—selected key words from people's common vocabulary that related to their struggles, goals, and aspirations. Freire called these "generative words," because when discussed in small groups, they tended to generate new words and ideas that induced further learning.

Abed took a back seat during this process. Khushi, his executive assistant, impressed Clark. The staff assigned to curriculum development was all male, and they would take turns playing the roles of learner and facilitator. Khushi would offer her input from behind her typewriter. "Khushi, the secretary in our office, is now participating more and more in our discussions, and her contributions are always superb, always on the mark," Clark wrote.

Suspecting BRAC staff were imposing their urban culture on the villagers, Clark would interrogate their assumptions, asking whether the needs were truly felt by the villagers and eliminating those that were not. "In the end, the list of felt needs was very short indeed, consisting of only four items: land ownership, housing, price of commodities and food. With these needs in mind, we began selecting topics for the individual lessons."

They worked late hours. "Khushi ran upstairs at one point to call the director's wife to join us," Clark wrote, referring to Bahar. "She was enormously helpful, especially with family planning, nutrition, and cookery. With Khushi and Bahar working together, they were in a much stronger position to have their ideas accepted. Both are bright, responsive, flexible, and always positive in their thinking."

Weeks of dialogue-based teaching techniques and curriculum development followed, during which Abed released Khushi from her secretarial duties to join the project team full time. Clark's daily journal entries follow BRAC staff as they embraced a teaching philosophy based on "human beings as free, creative, transforming beings, not merely reactors to the world." He records one major relapse in which, after Clark was certain they had already embraced the philosophy, Khushi reported to him that the group had reservations about discarding the top-down, didactic teaching methods of the past.

Clark called the group together and asked how they truly felt about having an open-ended dialogue with the unschooled poor. "What I heard then was not just frank, it was downright shocking. Everyone seemed to think the teachers should give lectures to the villagers and that the classes should focus on literacy almost exclusively; that the learners should be taught ABCs first before confronting words. In effect, the group wanted to go back to the old method used last year." The people of Sulla, after all, were still "grasping in ignorance," in the words of Abed's earlier proposal; one could not expect them to teach themselves. Clark called in Abed, who encouraged the staff to go along with the new approach, assuring them that they planned to pilot it with illiterate test learners in the BRAC office before taking it to Sulla.

After several more days of lesson development, they brought in their first test learners—a group of women from a nearby slum, who had been promised a lunch of rice and fish in exchange for sitting through their lessons. Bahar taught the first test class while Khushi sat in and observed. They were worried the women would feel inhibited around men, especially a foreigner, so for two hours the men waited outside expectantly, "like fathers in a maternity ward," Clark wrote.

The results were mixed. They had based the first lessons on two-dimensional drawings sketched out on poster board. The slum dwellers were migrants from the countryside, and the instructors assumed they would relate to pictures of rural life. But some of the images meant nothing to them. What the instructors thought was an obvious drawing of a house with chickens outside it looked like nothing but scratches to them. The educators realized they would have to find images that were unequivocal in their meaning.

Clark and the other curriculum planners eventually identified a list of one hundred generative words around which the teachers based their lessons. The result was a set of one hundred posters, each based on a single word with a representational drawing. During the lessons, students would not just learn to read and write the words but also discuss the words' significance in the context of their lives. BRAC would no longer treat people as passive receivers of knowledge but as co-investigators discussing a new issue.

Abed said Clark had a strong influence on the young organization, but the two men eventually lost touch with one another. After his brief consultancy with BRAC, Clark went on to become an accomplished scholar, author, and professor of international education. He died in 2003. The Leon E. Clark Fellowship at American University, where he taught for many years, is given annually to graduate students in international development.

The stories Clark told after returning from Bangladesh made a powerful impression on his wife, Maria Donoso Clark. "I think what impressed me the most was the unbelievable odds," she said. "The weather, the lack of transportation, the risks. I think he was inspired to see Abed's commitment. If it weren't for Abed and the kind of leadership he provided, it would have been a waste of labor." She added that Clark shared memories of sitting on the rooftop in Sulla at night, after the rain had stopped, as the BRAC staff sang songs and recited Bengali poetry into the darkness.

Abed recalled that Clark felt his managerial style could be domineering. "He had ideas that I was a dictator, telling people what to do," Abed said. "But he could never really get that out of BRAC staff."

In fact, what Clark had written in his journal was "Abed, without actually telling the people what to do, is extremely persuasive."

* * *

They restarted the classes in Sulla. The students gathered in an open space in the village, often outside. The first poster was based on the word "home," *bari* in Bengali.

"Why is the home important?" the teacher would ask, pointing to the image. The villagers pointed out that the word signified more than just a dwelling. It included children, spouses, livestock, and the patch of land surrounding the hut.

Once the discussion got underway, the classes would often get animated. "Some people's homes are better than others," one person might say.

"During stormy nights, it rains right through my roof," another would chip in.

"Why don't you fix it?" the teacher asked.

"Because I am poor," he would say. "I can't afford to."

Next came *bagh*, the word for "tiger." Every Bengali knows what a tiger is and what it represents: fierceness, wildness, the untamed state of nature. The teacher, now acting more like a facilitator, would ask, "Can a tiger build a house?"

Of course not, the people in the group replied. A tiger cannot build a house. If it rains, he runs under a tree. He does not have the ability to change his environment. He can only adapt himself to whatever happens.

"Can you build a house?" the facilitator asked.

Of course, the villagers replied. They discussed it among themselves. If we had access to the tools and the materials, we could all build homes for ourselves.

"Human beings are therefore different from the tiger, because we can adapt nature to suit our needs, whereas the tiger can only adapt himself to nature," the teacher would say. "We do not go from place to place in search of food but choose to plant seeds and till the soil so we can stay put. That is our choice. This process of changing nature to suit the needs of human beings through their own creative activities is called the process of civilization, and it is humans alone who engage in it."

The tiger cannot plan ahead. He cannot build a boat to go from one village to the next when the floods come. In the words of Freire, the tiger exists in an "overwhelming present," with no history, no development, and little concept of today or tomorrow.[2] Nor can a tiger do much to help another tiger. A hundred tigers cooperating could still not build a house. But men and women acting together can do many things.

"Can each of you discuss what creative activities you have done today?" the facilitator would then ask.

Somebody might volunteer that he had planted seeds or harvested rice. Another might have repaired the thatch on the roof. Perhaps somebody worked on a floodwall to direct the flow of water so it would irrigate the fields properly.

The point started to become clear. They had already contributed to the building of civilized life. Society was theirs to own and to shape, not something given to them. Acting collectively, they could do many more things. Poverty had been made by humans; it could be unmade by them, too. This was the most basic lesson for human consciousness.

Another word was *upash* ("hunger"). Everyone who has ever been hungry will recall the discomfort, but for the participants in Sulla, it was sometimes overwhelming. They said hunger was like being in a cage, cut off from others, unable to communicate except with those who were equally hungry and helpless.

They went on to discuss why some people were hungry and others were not. Some people worked hard, but they remained hungry because their wages were so low. Why should people work hard and remain poor? Who decides your wages? Soon the villagers were discussing the nature of poverty itself, along with the many injustices they faced and how they might act together to confront them.

Some people, especially the local political bosses who had an interest in keeping things as they were, thought BRAC was sowing the seeds of conflict within communities by raising provocative questions about wages, poverty, and exploitation. They said BRAC was fostering resentment toward the rich. This may have been true. Some of the staff even thought they would be arrested for subversion, as Freire had been in Brazil. But Abed, no doubt more confident in his safety given that he had sat next to the president at his own wedding, thought they could advance the cause by stealth. "I thought we could provide an umbrella over our revolutionary work because we were also doing health care, which the government wanted us to do," he said.

They also encouraged patience and wisdom when faced with injustice. Abed knew that if the people went into a fight immediately, "they would be decimated." He encouraged them to gather strength first. The staff also encouraged participants to think critically about their situation—to ask, for instance, whether exploiters emerged from their mothers' wombs as exploiters. Usurious moneylenders were not born; the system created them, and that system included the people who borrowed the money. Sometimes there were wiser alternatives to outright conflict.

The effect on the villagers was remarkable. They began to question their situation, imagine a better future for themselves, and think constructively about how they could work together to bring it about. It would not be enough to simply encourage critical thinking; access to essential services like credit, livelihood training, and health care would still be needed. But none of these would mean a thing if the people did not first believe in the possibility of change. The first sparks of self-worth had begun to flicker. Once lit, those flames would be hard to extinguish.

11

A DOWNWARD SPIRAL

In the summer of 1974, on a road between two villages, Abdul Kashem feared he had encountered a *pisach*, a flesh-eating demon with the ability to shapeshift into the form of a human. It was dusk, when the *pisach* is known to emerge from the overgrown ponds and wetlands, and the merchant farmer had spotted a female figure slowly approaching from a distance. He could think of no reason for a woman to be walking alone at this hour. According to Bengali folklore, a female *pisach* has no feet. She moves by floating just above the ground. From a distance, Abdul Kashem could see no feet beneath the billowing fabric of her clothes.

Abdul Kashem and Abdul Mojit are lifelong acquaintances from Rowmari, an isolated spit of northern Bangladesh wedged between the Brahmaputra River and the Indian border. The two farmers worked at a BRAC feeding center there in 1974, the organization's first expansion outside Sulla. In their eighties when interviewed in Rowmari in 2019, they shared their memories of the terrible famine that struck the area forty-five years earlier, including the spine-chilling encounter with the figure on the road.

As the figure drew closer, Abdul Kashem continued, he could make out the features of a young, gaunt face and saw, to his relief, that she had feet. But she was a walking skeleton. "I asked her what she was doing out at this hour," Abdul Kashem said. The young woman replied that her husband had left her, unable to provide food. The farmer asked why she hadn't gone back to her parents. She replied that her parents were also unable to feed her and had turned her away, so she was walking to the town in search of food.

"I took her home and told my wife to feed her," he recalled. "That night, she slept in our home. The next day I took her back to her village. I talked to some of the better-off people in the village, asking them, 'How do you live with yourselves, with a woman wandering off to the next village like this?' They acknowledged they should have done something." Both Abdul Kashem and Abdul Mojit expressed concern at the moral degradation, which in their view included women leaving their homes alone, caused by the impending famine as people struggled to survive. "Then I went to her parents, and I saw their situation was even worse," Abdul Kashem added. "Their physical condition was horrible. I could see their ribs. They could barely walk."

There was indeed a demon stalking the land in 1974—the specter of mass starvation, which tore apart social norms, marriages, and even the bonds between parents and children.

⋆ ⋆ ⋆

To understand the 1974 famine, it helps to know the context of the rapidly deteriorating state of Bangladesh itself. At the time of independence in December 1971, it would have been hard to imagine conditions getting worse in the country. At least the newly liberated people had hope and a sense of unity. These swiftly disappeared.

Asked to describe the difference between Bangladesh immediately after liberation and two years later, Kaiser Zaman, Abed's friend from Shell, said, "Did you ever see the YouTube video of the raccoon with the cotton candy?" A raccoon receives an incredible treat, but since raccoons habitually moisten their food before eating it, he dips the cotton candy in water. It dissolves instantly, leaving him grasping in dismay and confusion. "Independence was like that."

The country was in a downward spiral by the time Abed and Bahar's daughter, Tamara, was born in April 1974. Corruption pervaded all aspects of public life, from the village to the capital. Politics had turned violent and would soon grow more so. Sheikh Mujib, the wartime leader who was now the prime minister, struggled to maintain control in the face of open challenges from leftist parties. As the government nationalized major industries, those in the ruling party appointed relatives and cronies to lead the large companies. Rather than restructuring the enterprises to make them more productive, the new corporate leaders smuggled essential commodities like rice and jute to India to sell on the black market, where they fetched more than they would locally, due to an exchange rate that was artificially fixed to prop up the value of the new Bangladeshi currency, the taka. Direct foreign aid, relatively generous in the wake of liberation, began to dry up. By the time the United Nations wrapped up its major postwar relief program in late 1973, the government in Dhaka had done little to prepare the country to stand on its own. The price of basic foodstuffs began to skyrocket. By midyear, the economy was on the brink of collapse. Kissinger's "basket case" prediction seemed to be coming true.

★ ★ ★

The rise and fall of the mighty Brahmaputra was a seasonal clock that determined the timing of the planting and harvest. When that clock was off, the consequences could be devastating. The rains in the north came early and heavy in 1974, which is why Leon Clark had frogs jumping onto his mattress in Sulla when he arrived that summer. There, far from the banks of the Brahmaputra, BRAC was able to mobilize entire villages, which worked day and night to build dams and embankments to protect the rice fields from the rising waters. The area suffered "only" about 40 percent crop loss. To the west, though, the river overflowed into vast croplands, destroying successive harvests.

A properly functioning government might have averted disaster. Instead, the floods compounded the country's woes at the worst possible moment. In July, newspapers reported that people were starving to death in the north. In August, the river overflowed its banks yet again. In a cruel twist, the United States withheld food aid in response to the country's deepening relationship with Cuba. The Bangladesh government had signed a trade agreement with Cuba to export jute, one of its only cash crops.

Late that summer, Cole Dodge, the newly arrived Oxfam field director, showed up at BRAC's Maghbazar office on a day when "it was pissing down rain just after lunchtime." Cole was an American from the rural Pacific Northwest who had served in the Peace Corps prior to his arrival in Bangladesh. By now it was common for foreign aid workers to pay a visit to Abed to hear his views on the country's situation—often over a cigar, since Abed had given up pipe smoking due to the difficulty of finding pipe tobacco in Bangladesh. Abed was far more comfortable in face-to-face conversations than in addressing large crowds.

Abed's secretary, Mahera, was not at her desk, so, according to Cole, he poked his head into Abed's office and found the boss sitting behind his desk, which was always stacked with neatly arranged piles of correspondences, spreadsheets, and reading material. Abed knew the name "Cole Dodge" from one of Oxfam's grant letters but had never seen his face. "He looked up in surprise," Cole said. "I had a very huge beard and long hair, not a typical person Abed was expecting." Cole had the thoughtful intensity of a schoolmaster, but this concealed a softer side, both of which Abed would grow to appreciate.

Cole said that first meeting revolved around "a pointed set of questions from my side" about the number of indigent people in the city. He recalled asking, "Is it normal to see so many destitute people on the streets of Dhaka?" Since his arrival in Bangladesh three weeks earlier, he had learned the conventional wisdom in the capital was that, yes, visible poverty seemed to be on the rise, but this was more the product of the government's incompetence than of flooding in the north. Abed said he did not have a clear answer one way or another. Cole immediately went north to see for himself.

In Rowmari, one of the worst-hit areas, Cole found a full-blown famine underway. The government was setting up gruel kitchens, but these were overburdened. Crowds lined up for hours, sometimes for half a piece of unleavened flatbread. The army maintained control, often beating people back to keep them in line. Under Cole's direction, Oxfam began supplementing those meager efforts by setting up its own feeding centers for children under ten, many of whom were too weak to walk and, if they were able to get there at all, often fed last at the government feeding stations.

Nick Fogden, a British photographer who worked for Oxfam at the time, described the chaotic scene in Rowmari as he arrived by helicopter to take fundraising photos. "We hovered as people gathered below, and as we descended, we blew the people standing directly below us off their feet. On landing, people gathered around, and a local police officer came and attempted to keep people back, but as the two pilots came out, a man rushed forward and threw a dead child at their feet."

By now, many able-bodied people had left Rowmari, leaving behind their families, including the gaunt young woman Abdul Kashem had encountered on the roadway. Those who made it to the cities often fared little better. In a grim spectacle reminiscent of Calcutta in the 1943 Bengal famine, droves of migrants came to Dhaka in search of work or food. Finding neither, they began dying on the streets. The British documentary journalist John Pilger visited Dhaka and accompanied a truck that gathered the dead, showing British television viewers the body of an eleven-year-old girl named Hazana "who died in the gutter a few hours before we arrived." The truck normally collected a few dozen bodies of indigents per day, Pilger reported. Now it collected hundreds. He began the segment by imploring his viewers not to tune out, admitting that his producers, wary of Bangladesh misery fatigue, had told him, "Don't do Bangladesh. People won't watch it."

In Rowmari, Oxfam had initially partnered with a government-affiliated development group run by influential people from the area, including a local strongman who was a prominent member of the ruling

Awami League. This affiliation allowed relief operations to start up quickly and without hindrance from authorities. By the end of the year, however, Oxfam's surveys continued to show severe malnutrition among children, and the organization was starting to question the effectiveness of the partnership. The leadership in Oxford had a reflex response, which was to mobilize a British emergency medical team, including a doctor and four nurses, whom they would send immediately to run an expanded operation.

Cole, who was new to Oxfam, had a different idea: send BRAC. He visited Abed again. The two men agreed that sending a group of foreign medical experts, given the language and cultural barriers, would be neither wise nor necessary. "That's not the way you build capacity," Cole told Oxfam headquarters. The logic seems obvious today, and much later, in the 1990s, the idea of partnering with local institutions for "capacity building," or at least paying it lip service, would itself become a reflex response among Western donors and development agencies. At the time, "corporate Oxfam was not looking for local partners," said Cole. "But I was."

It helped that BRAC already had a reputation for efficient coordination of relief and development programs. Cole won the argument within Oxfam, which provided funding for a famine-relief project administered by BRAC. Terre des Hommes, a Swiss charity, also offered support, according to Abed, but the organization insisted on sending its own nurses to look after the malnourished children. Abed thought Bangladeshis were more than qualified to do this work and that the presence of well-intentioned foreigners would prove a bigger burden than the value they would add, so he politely said no—the first time he declined money from a donor.

In January 1975, Abed journeyed north to Rowmari to work out the logistics of a famine-relief program. By now, he had become friends with a handful of foreigners based in Dhaka, who had seen BRAC's Freirean classes and understood his aim of confronting the twin scourges of corruption and oppression. Among them was John Paul Kay, the local director of the American Friends Service Committee, who accompanied Abed on that first trip to Rowmari. John Paul was a tall American with Jesus-like long hair and a beard, but, unlike the reserved Cole, John Paul "was always laughing," according to Abed's secretary, Mahera Rahman. He had lived in the guest bedroom at Maghbazar for several months, including the night Tamara was born. Abed, who never had any compunction about hiring friends and family, said John Paul became "the first friend to work at BRAC" when he later hired him as a consultant in 1976.

In the town of Rowmari, Abed and John Paul found the markets filled with goods—kitchen utensils, furniture, and live goats—as people had sold what they could to survive. "I chalked out the exact program we wanted to do," Abed said, shifting staff from Sulla and sending doctors and supervisors from the Dhaka home office to get the program started. Procuring food and ensuring fair distribution at the feeding centers "was a logistical nightmare, but we managed it." BRAC contracted with local builders to erect twenty bamboo huts to serve as feeding centers, along with a makeshift hospital where severely malnourished children could receive treatment.

Abed returned about a month later, this time with Cole Dodge and David de Pury, Oxfam's field secretary for Asia, in an Oxfam-owned Land Rover nicknamed Samantha, which had previously worked in India, Iran, and Peru. They set off before dawn, stopping at a roadside stand in the market town of Jamalpur for a breakfast of omelets, parathas (pan-fried flatbread), and tea. Cole, an expert off-road driver, piloted Samantha straight through the river at one point. "We crossed and went on and on and on, Cole Dodge driving and his boss in the front seat," recalled Abed. Along the way, de Pury questioned Abed about the effectiveness of the BRAC program.

At the Rowmari feeding stations, lines of hungry people had emerged from the surrounding countryside. What struck Abed the most was that mothers, famished though they were, nevertheless insisted on giving all their food to their children. He also saw Cole's warmer side. "Cole had a wonderful quality," he said. "All these emaciated children with scabies—he would take them in his lap. I found it difficult, but he had no inhibitions." The two men became lifelong friends, and though Cole would spend most of his life in East Africa, he remained one of Abed's most trusted advisers outside BRAC.

In Rowmari, Abed intended to establish a foothold by providing emergency relief before pivoting to long-term development, just as BRAC had in Sulla. Backed by Oxfam, BRAC purchased a plot of land that would serve as field headquarters for an "integrated program," similar to the Sulla program, pursuing activities in functional education, agriculture, family planning, and health. Despite Oxfam headquarters' initial reluctance to give the relief work to BRAC, David de Pury "came away utterly impressed with the record keeping and efficiency of the program," according to Cole. It looked increasingly likely that BRAC would establish a permanent presence in Rowmari.

* * *

In Sulla, BRAC's work on raising "critical consciousness" (Freire's term) had met with resistance from village leaders. The solidarity that emerged from the discussion groups forced some changes. Geespati Roy, one of the first BRAC staffers in Sulla, shared several stories of BRAC participants who, following the discussions in the adult education classes, decided to stand up for their rights. Ansar Ali, a mullah at a mosque located near one of the camps, summoned men to the market one day and announced that women would no longer be allowed to work on the food-for-work project, one of the few government programs in the Sulla area. The project, which involved working on roads and embankments in exchange for wheat rations, required women to leave their homes. This, the mullah declared, was against the tenets of Islam.

The following week, about four hundred women—all of whom had participated in BRAC programs—showed up at the mullah's house, each carrying a spade. Some hadn't eaten in days. Their leader was Kadbanu, a fierce divorcee in her mid-thirties. Like the others, she was thin as a reed, almost skeletal. "Ansar Mullah!" she shouted. "We are hungry! If you do not allow us to work, then you yourself should feed us!"

Ansar Ali came out and told the women to go home. "If we can't work, then you will give us rice from your own store!" Kadbanu shouted back. Ansar Ali refused and again tried to order the group to disperse, but the women wouldn't budge. "If you can't feed us and you can't give us food to bring back to our homes, then what gives you the right to deny us a chance to work to feed our families?" Kadbanu asked.

Faced with four hundred angry women brandishing spades, the mullah realized he had lost the argument. The next day, he summoned the men to the market, withdrew his decree, and apologized.

In nearby Derai, the chairman of the Union Council, the most local unit of government, was known to have embezzled about eighteen tons of rice from the allocated rations for the food-for-work project. In such incidents, the culprits often made no attempt to hide the crime, so accustomed were they to getting away with it. In this case, as many as one thousand women, most of them from BRAC villages, surrounded a local government office and demanded they be paid within twenty-four hours for the rations they had already earned. The chairman returned the eighteen tons of rice, and the women received their rations the next day.

Many disputes involved land. In one area, local zamindars took over a plot the government had set aside for landless people to cultivate. When the time for harvest came, the landowners tried to intimidate the landless farmers to prevent them from taking the rice home, even calling the police to arrest them for so-called forceful seizure of the harvest. In other circumstances the landless farmers would likely have fled, but in this case BRAC had organized them to stand up for themselves. When the police arrived on the scene and saw their numbers, they took the farmers' side.

Having any chance of success in these areas required a bone-deep understanding of the dynamics of rural life, which most outsiders lacked. BRAC researchers would later conduct a series of in-depth studies, hiring anthropologists and ethnographers to investigate the myriad connections that made up the power structure in rural areas, including its rival factions, the network of protective patronage relationships, and how the elites enriched themselves through embezzlement, smuggling, cattle rustling, and other crimes. Food rations were nearly always siphoned off by local leaders, including Union Council members. Appropriately, the study was called "The Net," for it described a web of corruption that seemed to keep the landless trapped.

In one instance, a timber dealer and Union Council member named Kamal had a racket with the council chairman and the local rations dealer. The government had sanctioned the rations dealer to sell rice and wheat at an affordable price for a small commission, but, instead, he and Kamal sold it on the black market and split the profits between themselves, local clerks, and the nine other members of the Union Council. Kamal also happened to be secretary of the local primary school committee, allowing him to make extra money by offering jobs at the school in exchange for kickbacks. Through his influence, and by bribing local police, his brother Salehuddin and his friends got away with repeatedly stealing people's cows. Salehuddin had at least eleven cases filed against him and had been jailed and released multiple times. On the way back from an unsuccessful cross-border smuggling run, one of Salehuddin's friends, Humayun, himself a member of a notorious family of bandits, had attempted to rape three landless women but was instead beaten and captured by the women and their relatives, leading to a clash between Salehuddin's faction and the landless peasants. When the landless went to the police, they detained Salehuddin briefly and, after receiving their expected bribe, released him.[1]

It went on and on. These convoluted relationships between the elites cast a net that captured all the external resources meant to help the poor, including those from nongovernmental organizations (NGOs) and charities. Only by creating their own web of solidarity could the landless resist.

Outside Bangladesh, as Freire's star rose in the 1970s, some leftist critics took aim at World Education, which had helped BRAC develop its consciousness-raising curriculum in Sulla, and other purveyors of what they called "pseudo-Freirean adult education."[2] They claimed these education providers, who were often sponsored by governments, were watering down Freire's revolutionary aims by using his dialogue-based methods to teach them how to cope with poverty by working harder, while avoiding overt political action. They argued that any true Freirean education would name the real enemy—systematic oppression—and encourage the poor to take action against it.

Abed was walking a fine line in those early years, encouraging revolt on a local level while seeking a protective umbrella by working with the government on essential services like health—an umbrella strengthened, no doubt, by the respect he commanded in establishment circles in the capital. Clashes with the mullahs would persist and BRAC staff would occasionally be assaulted and even arrested—though, like the thief Salehuddin, they would always be released a few days later. As time went on, and as the organization began to scale up, BRAC would veer toward less confrontational approaches, including economic empowerment through skills training and microfinance. But as long as the poor had strength in numbers—that is, as long as they could win—BRAC would encourage them to stand up for themselves.

* * *

In March 1975, a young university graduate with a mop of shaggy hair walked into Abed's office in Dhaka. "My name is Aminul Alam," he said. "A family friend, Dr. Harun, told me you might have a job for me." The reference from Dr. Harun counted for something, for he was one of BRAC's best clinicians in Sulla, having been recommended to Abed by Zafrullah Chowdhury, the founder of Gonoshasthaya Kendra—the British-trained doctor whom Marietta had named in her suicide note and the only other Bangladeshi organization doing meaningful rural development work at the time.

"Let me see your CV," Abed said. Amin had received middling grades, but Abed later learned this was because he had spent most of his time at university immersed in leftist politics. In any case, grades didn't overly concern Abed, since he was hiring people mainly on the basis of values and by trying to assess their potential. His hires were based largely on gut feeling. He wanted honest people with a strong work ethic driven by an urge to change the country. Their commitment to those values could only be tested in the field. Amin came across as headstrong, perhaps even arrogant, but something about his attitude convinced Abed to give him a try.

"You can start with us on April 1," Abed told him. "We need help at our feeding program in Rowmari. Your starting salary will be five hundred taka per month." This was about $60 at the time.

Before his start date even arrived, Amin came back and tried to negotiate a higher salary. "*Bhai*," he said, "I think you should give me six hundred taka."

Abed laughed. "This is your first job out of university," he said. "You're here to negotiate a raise before you've even started? I have a man working for me who's had his master's degree since 1969, who's been a university professor for three years, and he's only getting six hundred taka per month. So, as I said earlier, your starting salary is five hundred taka." That was the end of the discussion.

Amin later admitted that he had applied for a job at BRAC because he thought he would be getting a car. Relief organizations, or "vol-ags" (for voluntary agencies), as they were then called, were known for their perks. This was not BRAC's style. Amin would find himself walking from one village to the next on foot or, at best, riding a bicycle or shared motorbike. Abed and Amin never argued about his salary again; indeed, Amin rarely questioned Abed about anything, even when, decades later, he had risen through the ranks to run almost all of BRAC.

Amin would later recount that his ideas about poverty were smashed to pieces in Rowmari. He had visited rural areas with Communist student groups to work with people he believed were poor. At the time, he thought that anyone who lived under a tin roof was poor. In reality, the Communists had been working with the rural middle class, who were often the exploiters of the poorest and most marginalized people in the village. In Rowmari, Amin would later say, he saw truly poor people for the first time in his life.[3]

Given Abed's plans to expand BRAC's footprint with a branch in Rowmari, it seemed likely Amin would stay there quite some time. There is one factor none of them had adequately considered, however.

* * *

Famished people continued to arrive in Rowmari from the outlying areas, especially the *chars* along the river. Abdul Mojit describes a man who arrived in the evening and died on his neighbor's property during the night. "We couldn't even find burial clothes," he said. "We had to use a *dhoti*" (a loincloth used by Hindus).

The landowners tended to survive, as did merchant-farmers like Abdul Mojit and Abdul Kashem. "We helped to the extent possible, but we had to make sure we had enough for our own families," Abdul Kashem said.

Another man, Abdur Razak, was a former activist and journalist who supervised one of the BRAC feeding centers in 1975. He recalled the background of the famine when interviewed in 2019 in Rowmari, where he was working as a homeopathic pharmacist, mixing vials with a dropper and dispensing compounds in a booth at the back of a narrow lane. "We had a good harvest that year, so it was surprising that it got so bad," he said. "The famine felt manmade." Everyone was affected, he added. The price of basic commodities like salt went up by a factor of sixty. The government's official death count eventually came to twenty-six thousand, although at least one scholar estimates as many as 1.5 million people died from starvation and its after-effects.[4]

One morning in April 1975, the BRAC team in Rowmari went to meet with the carpenters they had contracted to build the new field headquarters, intended to be the new hub of post-famine development activity once the feeding stations were no longer needed. But the carpenters didn't show up for the meeting. Surprised, members of the BRAC team went to their houses to ask why. Without explanation, the carpenters said they would no longer work on the project. The same day, the branch manager at the local bank in Rowmari refused to allow BRAC to withdraw money from its account, giving an excuse that made no sense to any of the BRAC people. BRAC also had an arrangement with local bullock cart drivers to deliver food to the feeding centers, and they, too, refused to work. The local firewood merchants, who provided the cooking fuel for the feeding centers, refused to sell BRAC any firewood.

That night, someone attacked a BRAC supervisor at one of the outlying feeding centers and beat him badly. The next day, the village leaders accused the same supervisor of rape. The accusations began piling up. One of the BRAC doctors at the feeding stations was accused of "womanizing," and a village court convicted another employee of stealing milk powder and smuggling it across the border to India, even though records showed he had been outside Rowmari when the alleged theft took place.[5]

It was obvious these incidents were related, so Abed alerted the authorities. A team of local officials investigated, including the Rowmari police chief, who offered to provide protection to BRAC staff. This turned out to be unnecessary, because the mastermind soon revealed himself. It was the local strongman and Awami Leaguer who chaired the Rowmari Central Cooperative Association, the government-sponsored entity Oxfam had initially partnered with to set up the children's feeding program. A wealthy landowner and jute exporter, the chairman had seen BRAC's arrival as an intrusion, especially when it began streamlining the distribution of food aid to ensure that it was both equitable and based on need.

The chairman was a character Abed knew all too well at this point, with one finger in politics, another in business, and a third in crime. In this case, his racket was smuggling grain across the border to India, where his wife's family had connections. A longtime member of the ruling party, he also had well-connected friends in the capital to protect him. After being reproached by the local police inspector, the chairman agreed to end his obstruction for the time being. The only immediate compromise was that henceforth BRAC would have to buy firewood from intermediaries rather than directly from the villagers. These intermediaries also turned out to be members of the Rowmari Central Cooperative Association. BRAC needed the firewood to continue cooking at the feeding stations, so Abed agreed.

Amin sat in on the negotiations with local authorities. As a new hire, he was reluctant to speak up. But he later said he was dumbfounded by the mendacity on display when the local strongman and his cronies made one patently false accusation after another. They were so accustomed to being the beneficiaries of aid programs that they considered it an entitlement, even in a famine.

The chairman had sent a clear message. If BRAC were to establish themselves in Rowmari for the long term, they would have to deal with him. Abed refused. In Sulla, BRAC might have taken care of this problem through patience and persuasion and, if need be, by mobilizing large numbers of the landless poor. But as newcomers, they were on shakier ground here. This was a battle Abed could not win—or, perhaps, did not want to risk losing. As soon as the child-feeding campaign was finished, BRAC pulled out of Rowmari, leaving all the assets they had gathered for the planned field headquarters, including corrugated iron sheets and other building materials, to local organizations.

By June 1975, the famine had ended. A survey showed that nutrition levels among the thirteen thousand children fed by BRAC had returned to roughly normal, with a majority now exceeding 90 percent of the international weight-for-height standard.[6] The BRAC staff went back to Sulla, and Amin returned to Dhaka to care for his father, who had fallen gravely ill. Amin told Abed he felt the burden of being the chief decision-maker for his family, so Abed told him to take as much time off as he needed.

There was still the matter of the plot of land that BRAC had purchased. When BRAC wrapped up the feeding program, the previous owner, a relative of the local strongman, tried to reclaim it by putting a fence around it, arguing that BRAC had abandoned it. Abed gave Abdur

Razak, the journalist-activist who ran one of the feeding centers, a certified copy of the property deed and told him to fight the matter in court if necessary. Deed in hand, Abdur Razak threatened the previous owner with legal action and convinced him to take the fence down. Abdur Razak then mobilized a group of landless people to occupy the property—and kept his eye on it for the next thirty years.

12

SMALL ISN'T BEAUTIFUL

There was a refrain popular among idealistic aid and development types in the 1970s—"small is beautiful," the title of a 1973 book by German-born economist E. F. Schumacher. If the Rowmari experience taught Abed anything, it was that his fledgling organization could not afford to remain small and beautiful. "A lot of people wanted us to be eliminated," he told an interviewer in 2014. "I decided at that point that I could not remain small and beautiful. The thing to do was to become large and powerful enough to be reckoned with."[1]

The "small is beautiful" thesis resonated with those who saw capitalism's relentless advance as an impediment to human progress. Schumacher criticized the reliance of poorer countries on "modern economists from so-called advanced countries," who offered ever more efficient economies of scale.[2] He instead encouraged the development of "self-sufficient local communities."[3] According to Schumacher, "Ever bigger machines, entailing ever bigger concentrations of economic power and exerting ever greater violence against the environment, do not represent progress: they are a denial of wisdom. Wisdom demands a new orientation of science and technology towards the organic, the gentle, the non-violent, the elegant, and beautiful."[4]

The idea of local self-sufficiency was appealing, but there was nothing "elegant and beautiful" about the Rowmari central cooperative, whose leader's thuggish motives and tactics kept food from hungry people during a famine, or the local Union Council members who embezzled grain rations allocated to the landless poor. Abed also reflected on his experience at Shell Oil. Was the corporation ugly merely because it was large? His view differed markedly from others in the nonprofit sector both then and now, for when Abed looked at the modern multinational corporation, he saw efficiency, not ugliness. Shell invested in its staff and developed their capacity, including by teaching them how to manage large operations effectively and at optimal cost—precisely the things he wanted to do for socially beneficial ends with BRAC.

Abed's worldview was falling into place, and it would shape the organization that BRAC would become. It was never really a "committee" to begin with; now it had just over a hundred employees. Abed saw that it would have to become much, much larger. To solve a problem as massive as human poverty, one would need to create solutions on the scale of the problem itself. And one would need to do so with the efficiency of the private sector, by training large numbers of people, minimizing unnecessary work, and routinizing essential tasks. The state might help where it could, but given the country's dysfunctional government, BRAC would have to do the bulk of the work itself. To people who preached the Schumacher mantra, Abed had a response: "small may be beautiful, but big is necessary."

⋆ ⋆ ⋆

Abed was always remarkably bad at marketing himself. BRAC had no communications department to speak of for the first twenty-five years of its existence. Equally remarkably, he rarely had a problem finding money for expansion, even in the organization's early years. This was in part due to his reputation and visibility in Dhaka, where as early as 1973 he was making a name for himself as an unlikely figure—the accountant turned revolutionary, the cigar-smoking former Shell executive who was now a devotee of Paulo Freire.

The only other homegrown organization doing significant rural development work at the time, Gonoshasthaya Kendra (People's Health Center), had a far more focused mission of providing health care and medicine to the masses. Led by Zafrullah Chowdhury, a charismatic British-trained surgeon, it was also born from the Liberation War. In the years to come, many civil society organizations would emerge, in part because successive Bangladeshi governments, to their credit, recognized they needed all the help they could get to provide basic services. Groups like Grameen Bank and the Association for Social Advancement would grow quickly, especially after the practice of microlending took off. But in the early years, there were few options, apart from Gonoshasthaya Kendra and BRAC, for those keen to support Bangladeshis with a long-term vision. "All the 'vol-ags' met monthly in Dhaka," Abed recalled. "I remember meeting Mother Teresa, who was also starting something here. All the agencies were foreigners.

Only two agencies were started by Bangladeshis at that time—me and Zafrullah Chowdhury. We were the two exceptions."

And it was impossible to confuse Abed and Zafrullah, since the latter had an unkempt look that almost seemed cultivated, with the clothes of a truck driver and Che Guevara–style long hair. Though the two men had great respect for one another, Abed's dapper image was the polar opposite, and he was one of a kind. Ian Smillie, who worked for the American organization CARE, one of the largest nongovernmental organizations (NGOs) active in Bangladesh at the time, recalled the first time he met Abed in 1973. It was at a small Christmas gathering hosted by the local representatives of the American Friends Service Committee, an international organization founded by Quakers. "I remember Abed came with Bahar," he said. "They were a good-looking couple, and I remember whispers going around: 'That's Abed.' They were whispering because he was kind of a phenomenon. Here's a guy who's a Bangladeshi, and he's got his own NGO and he's doing his own development work. He was an oddity—in a positive way."

Smillie later cofounded Inter Pares, a Canadian group dedicated to building up local organizations, which was still a new concept for most of the large international NGOs. By 1975, BRAC's donor list included Inter Pares, UNICEF, Bread for the World, the Dutch aid and development organization Novib, and various Oxfam affiliates in Australia, Britain, Canada, and the United States.

⋆ ⋆ ⋆

Abed had the vision, the drive, and the money, but he was still missing the crucial element of success. The gap between the expectations he had raised and ground realities continued to widen. By the end of the famine in 1975, BRAC had a fully-fledged program in just a single area, Sulla, and, notwithstanding the success of the rebooted adult-education classes, the Sulla program was not working especially well.

To be sure, the Freirean method changed people's attitudes. The classes developed people's confidence, built solidarity, and raised awareness of their rights. They cast aside fatalism and embraced a better future. None of these, however, would be enough to end poverty. Change would only materialize when an enabling environment existed where self-empowered people stood a chance against the forces aligned against them. This would require additional services such as livelihood support, vocational training, and access to credit and health care. These programs were not gaining the traction Abed had hoped for.

Enthusiasm buoyed the project during those early years, and, for a time, Sulla was a zone of experimentation. Any idea that might make people's lives easier—especially if it benefited women, who had little income of their own—was ripe for consideration. For instance, each village in the area stood ten to fifteen feet above the surrounding fields. This meant the fringes of the village always had uncultivated patches of land where the ground sloped down to meet the paddy fields. Land was in short supply, and Abed wondered if women could use this land to introduce vegetables into people's diets. Nearly every meal in Sulla consisted of rice with an occasional bit of fish for protein—hardly the most wholesome diet. BRAC imported vegetable seeds and, having caught farmers' attention with its demonstration plots, gave away the first batches free of charge, with instructions on how to prepare the seedbeds and care for the plants. Cultivating vegetable gardens could provide both cash and nutrition for the households. "It was the first time they had seen carrots and cauliflower," according to Abed.

Papaya had also never been a major crop here. Abed recalled walking around the villages, counting the number of papaya trees a woman could plant around her hut. He would calculate how much fruit these trees would yield and how much she could get for each. BRAC started growing papaya saplings for distribution to the women of the village, who planted them on their tiny homesteads. The 1974 flooding destroyed all the papaya trees. Abed might have blamed that on bad luck, but there would never be a shortage of bad luck in Sulla.

In any case, schemes for garden plots and papaya trees were just tinkering around the edges. To create large-scale change, growers of the main crop, rice, would need training in modern farming practices and access to the high-yield seeds and fertilizer that had boosted India's grain harvests so dramatically during the Green Revolution. Abed had sent twenty-two BRAC workers to India for agricultural training and recruited agronomists, including one from Germany, to supervise field activities. These experts made the rounds of local paddy fields, offering advice to farmers. Abed wanted communities to manage development activities on their own, rather than relying on outside experts. Through cooperatives of farmers, fishermen, and tradespeople, including some women-only groups, people would join forces and take collective action. They could take classes to learn more effective methods of cultivation, and they could pool their resources and take lines of credit to buy high-yield seeds and invest in new equipment. Fishermen, one of the most exploited segments of the community, would increase their bargaining power over landlords, who would otherwise extract a huge portion of their catch as royalties for fishing rights. The most active members of each cooperative would receive training from BRAC on how to manage the operation, making it self-governed and self-sustaining.

By concentrating on one geographic area, Abed had initially thought he could generate a ripple effect that would gradually make itself felt all over Bangladesh. If BRAC could make crop yields shoot up in one village, farmers in the next village would emulate the changes—and then the next village, and so on. With enough funding, they could spark a nationwide Green Revolution by opening a BRAC program in one subdistrict (the equivalent of a county) in each of Bangladesh's sixty-four districts, as though scattering stones in a pond.

These efforts were rarely as successful in practice as they seemed in theory. The problems were almost too numerous to count. To start, Abed had trouble finding and retaining staff with the right attitude and work ethic. Originally, he had only hired locally. That would be one of BRAC's calling cards, he had thought: when they went to work in a village, they recruited directly from the area. Even in Sulla, where the vast majority of the population was unschooled, they were initially able to find enough people with a high school education to create what Abed thought was a solid village-level cadre of development professionals, many of them born and raised within walking distance of the project sites.

The local hires had performed well in the immediate relief phase, but when he shifted to long-term development, many of the local staff did not work well with their less educated neighbors. He needed people who could be open-minded and patient; however, many of the local hires did not seem to understand the value of participatory decision-making. He had to lay off about twenty of the original local field workers "who were found wanting in leadership qualities and mental discipline to play this vital role effectively," as he wrote in his interim report to Oxfam.

To replace them, he recruited university graduates from Dhaka and other cities, but it was hard to convince such people to move to Sulla, especially at the wages BRAC was paying—and Abed firmly believed that the mission of helping the poor required paying low wages. Sukhendra Sarkar, a twenty-four-year-old schoolteacher from Jhenidah, a city in the southwest nearly two hundred miles from Sulla, was among the first batch of university recruits in 1973. With his bachelor's degree, Sukhen, as he was called, would likely have qualified for an entry-level position in the Bangladeshi civil service, which paid about 450 taka ($56 at the time) per month. Abed had interviewed Sukhen at the BRAC office in Dhaka and, impressed with his energy and understanding of the mission, asked him to go to Sulla at an initial salary of just 325 taka ($41) per month.

Sukhen described how he arrived at Markuli on a summer evening after a twenty-four-hour journey by train, bus, and boat. Eleven other recruits arrived the same day. It was the height of the monsoon, and Sulla was almost completely underwater. They spent the night, and "in the morning, we found that two or three staff had left already, after seeing the condition of the area." Sukhen stayed on, and within a few years he would be supervising the entire Sulla program.

Gaining people's trust remained a concern. During their long meetings under the tin roof at the Markuli field headquarters, the staff debated how to dress when visiting the villages. "We should not come to them in shirts and trousers," one staffer said. "We should wear a *lungi*." The *lungi* is the long traditional sarong worn by rural Bengali men, fashioned from a single piece of cloth and gathered at the waist.

"Let me ask you," Abed interjected. "The village moneylender—does he wear a *lungi*?" There were murmurs of assent. "The landlords, the corrupt village bosses—they, too, wear *lungis*, do they not?"

Abed reminded them that in the villages, people who looked poor to their eyes were often, in fact, the oppressors. "Dress as you feel comfortable," Abed said. "Don't worry about your appearance. People will judge you by what you do for them, not by how you look."

Lack of irrigation proved to be another major hurdle. Unlike in India, the vast majority of crops were entirely rain-fed. Only about 10 percent of all the cultivated land in the country was irrigated at the time of independence. Without irrigation, the Green Revolution's high-yield seeds and chemical fertilizers would have limited impact.

Inflation also wreaked havoc on their plans. By 1974, the price of essential commodities had tripled over the course of the previous two years, with no stability in sight. The community centers were supposed to have been built out of solid timber, but this option quickly became unaffordable. One staff member spent two months in New Delhi negotiating permission for duty-free exports of timber from India. They ended up building most of the community centers from cheaper bamboo and corrugated iron, which is one reason so many fell down. Even doing this often required BRAC to resolve age-old disputes between feuding factions within the village before they could begin.

Sulla was a difficult place to work even by Bangladeshi standards. The isolation was a blessing in some respects, because, apart from a few food-for-work programs, government influence was so weak that BRAC could do almost anything it wanted. But isolation was also a curse. There were occasional bouts of lawlessness. Criminals used the unrest surrounding the national elections in 1973 as an excuse to attack and loot entire villages. Dealing with corrupt village leaders was an expected challenge; roaming gangs of armed thugs were something else entirely. Furthermore, the total lack of infrastructure also meant that distributing items like vaccines—for both children and animals—was nearly impossible, since these required adequate cold-storage facilities.

After two seasons, Abed could see they were barely scratching the surface of people's problems. The timetable period for proposed activities in Sulla Phase II was just twenty months, taking them through mid-1974. By April of that year, Abed formally reported to Oxfam that they would not meet their targets. They had planned to form 220 cooperatives, but fewer than half that number existed. They had planned to open family planning clinics, training one "lady family planning officer" in each of the two hundred villages to organize and motivate women to use contraception. They had only trained thirty-eight. In order to provide clean drinking water, they had wanted to repair one hundred tube wells and drill two hundred new ones; they had repaired thirty and drilled none.

The success of the relief phase had made Abed overconfident in what he could achieve. It had indeed been "no mean achievement," as he had written, to move thousands of tons of building materials to one of the most remote regions of the country at minimal cost. Changing people's habits and mindsets was a much more difficult task. "The wider and deeper experience of the development process now convinces us that the time we allowed ourselves is too short for the far-reaching changes in ideas, attitudes and priorities we hoped to bring about in the project area," Abed reported to Oxfam. There would certainly be no ripple effect, and it would take years (decades, in some cases) to see the real impact of BRAC's work. Abed asked Oxfam for a grant extension of eighteen months and an additional $58,000 on top of the $510,000 they had already given BRAC for Phase II. Evidently still impressed with his earnestness and honesty, they agreed.

★ ★ ★

If BRAC were to ever become "large and powerful enough to be reckoned with," its programs would need to achieve some measure of success. Eventually, this came down to solving two problems.

The first was that the cooperative approach had inherent shortcomings. Abed had followed the dominant model of rural development in Pakistan and, later, Bangladesh, which sought to build small local institutions, or cooperatives, that brought together farmers and fishermen to plan and manage activity meant for the betterment of the whole community.

In trying to empower exploited groups, however, Abed found they were often simply enabling the exploitation of others down the line. Fishermen's cooperatives, for instance, had existed long before BRAC arrived, but they were financed and controlled by moneylenders, who charged usurious rates of interest and often acted in concert with the landowners, who charged exorbitant fees for fishing rights. The fishermen, in turn, would take advantage of the women in their community by paying them a pittance for endless hours of net making and fish drying. "Exploitation by an exploited group cannot be condoned," Abed wrote in his 1974 interim report. He described a complicated workaround, whereby BRAC developed women's cooperatives for net making, set a minimum payment to these women's cooperatives, charged the fishermen's cooperatives directly for the raw nylon twine, and then insisted the fishermen's cooperatives pay the minimum amount to the women's cooperatives for their net-making services before taking delivery of the nets.

This approach failed to address the fundamental problem—namely, that local groups, which would in theory have a better sense of how to allocate resources, were significantly more vulnerable to corruption, a phenomenon known by development scholars as "elite capture." No matter what BRAC did, the village elites always seemed to end up winning at the expense of the poorest.

The second problem was related to the geography of Sulla itself. In addition to the isolation and occasional lawlessness, the area was atypical of the rest of the country in terms of its economy, lifestyle, and geography, governed as it was by the great inland sea that rose and fell each year. The land gave just one harvest per year—not two or three, as in other areas—and that was almost entirely rice. Vegetables, lentils, mustard, jute, and sugarcane were options in the rest of Bangladesh; however, apart from a few isolated plots of land near people's houses, these would never catch on in Sulla. It was supposed to be the proving ground for poverty innovations, but for this reason alone, the Sulla zone of experimentation could never be the prototype for a nationwide program. BRAC would have to look elsewhere.

13

NAMES ON THE WALL

The house in Maghbazar was getting crowded. Abed, Bahar, and Tamara shared a single bedroom upstairs, often with a fourth person—a visitor, a field worker from Sulla, or John Paul Kay—using the guest bedroom, plus Mohammad Ali above the garage. On the ground floor, new donors and projects, including a monthly journal for newly literate readers funded by UNICEF and a research initiative funded by the Ford Foundation, meant additional staff. Abed and his secretary, Mahera Rahman, shared an office, while the other rooms, originally designed as bedrooms, each held five desks. According to Mahera, Abed, as a new father, would go upstairs every time he heard his daughter crying. Mahera lived next door, with only an alley separating the houses—close enough to be woken up by the baby at night. Visitors to the office also wanted to go upstairs to see the new addition to the BRAC family.

By 1975, Abed began to sense that Bahar wanted more privacy. Likely, he did too. According to Abed, Bahar complained just once during their time living there. The wife of one of the doctors sent to Sulla would visit the house and whine to Bahar about her husband being so far from home. "She used to come and badger her all the time," Abed recalled. "She thought she had full rights to come and hang out and be a pest." Ever the gracious hostess, Bahar was all smiles, but Abed knew the doctor's wife was getting on her nerves.

When Tamara was about a year old, Bahar's parents invited them to move into the first floor of their two-story house in Eskaton, where Abed had first met Bahar. The city's elite had their homes in Eskaton. One of Sheikh Mujib's sons lived there, and the chief of the air force lived right next door. Bahar's parents' whitewashed house was large and elegant by Dhaka's middle-class standards, set back from the road by a circular driveway, with verandas on the front and side. "It was a distinctive house," said Abed. "Everybody knew it." They would live on the ground floor, with the in-laws just above, so the arrangement would allow Tamara to grow up close to her grandparents. She could play in the yard of a three-quarter-acre lot with swings hanging from the trees. Mohammad Ali came with them, joined by a cook and a maid.

Even after they moved, nothing separated their personal and professional lives. Lincoln and Marty Chen had returned to Dhaka, Lincoln having been assigned by the Ford Foundation to work as the scientific director of the Cholera Research Laboratory. Both Marty and Bahar began formally working at BRAC, officially as Abed's "executive assistants," although their roles encompassed far more than that. They soon became best friends. Marty, having grown up in India as the daughter of Protestant missionaries, took great interest in rural issues, especially women's livelihood.

On evenings and weekends, the Abeds would host the Chens and others, including Putul (Mrs. Ismail's youngest daughter) and her husband, Monowar Hossain, an economist at the Bangladesh Institute for Development Studies. Both couples had children of their own. On the screened-in side veranda overlooking a small pond, an oasis within the chaos of the growing city, they would discuss BRAC for hours on end. "I remember Bahar serving high tea from a wooden cart on wheels with two shelves, which she would cover with linen and lace doilies, and a carved wooden handle," said Marty. "Bahar had an old-fashioned grace and elegance in all that she did." While the adults talked about work, the children clawed at their parents' legs and clambered on the porch's rattan swing chair. "We were so immersed," Marty added. "We called our kids the 'BRAC brats.' We would go to their house for lunch around the corner from the office and talk 'BRAC, BRAC, BRAC.' We thought we were the center of the universe. It was so new to all of us, and there was so much to be done."

"They definitely talked only about work," recalled Greg Chen, Lincoln and Marty's son, who turned six in 1975. "It was all-consuming for all of them. It was not small talk or gossip, but whether certain breeds of chickens might work well, or what kind of system might support chick rearing."

With the addition of Marty and Bahar, the BRAC headquarters grew to thirty staff and expanded to occupy the second floor of the Maghbazar house. Abed's old bedroom became his office. Despite the myriad problems in Sulla and the premature closure of the Rowmari program, by mid-1975 they were ready to try expanding again.

* * *

The Freirean classes, the most distinctive and powerful component of the work in Sulla, provided an obvious starting point for growth. Though it was hard to quantify the real impact of functional education, course-completion rates had shot up since the failure of the initial literacy classes. About 41 percent of the people who enrolled completed the first cycle of eighty classes, and when BRAC shortened and simplified the course in the next cycle, the number edged up to 54 percent—hardly a stellar result, but a far cry from the 95 percent drop-out rate of the original literacy program. Those who dropped out tended to do so for unavoidable reasons, such as having to work extra hours in the field during harvest time. Moreover, groups were emerging from the classes to pursue joint projects like cooperative farming. With affordable credit otherwise unavailable, BRAC began to give small loans to the groups for investments in seeds, plows, and bullocks. If the classes were successful elsewhere, they could jump-start a wider program of economic empowerment.

The curriculum developed for Sulla, however, was too context-specific for the rest of Bangladesh. Many of the "generative words" that made sense in Sulla—"flood," for instance—lacked the same force and meaning in places that were not regularly underwater. Bahar led the effort to rework the posters for more universal appeal. Abed asked Sukhendra ("Sukhen") Sarkar, who had arrived in Sulla the previous summer, to return to Dhaka to work under Bahar in a four-person materials development unit.

A former schoolteacher with a bookish demeanor, Sukhen was an obvious addition to Bahar's unit. Bahar began by asking the team to read *Pedagogy of the Oppressed*, but Freire wrote in such abstractions and the English of the translation was so impenetrable that they could hardly understand a word of it, according to Sukhen. "It was very difficult on our part to grasp," he said. "So our honorable *bhabi* told us to simply read it at night, and she would explain it in Bengali the next day. We couldn't digest it without her." They brainstormed new words and concepts to incorporate into their curriculum and ran test classes in several locations to gauge people's reactions. After six months of iteration, they landed on a set of words and concepts which they believed would be applicable across the country. These would be combined, when possible, with specific lessons tailored to the geography.

Their understanding of Freire shaped their whole outlook on the field of development. Decades later, Sukhen shared his understanding of the core Freirean philosophy in words that echo the lesson on whether a tiger can build a house. "If you are a development worker, first you have to believe there is a difference between man and animal," he said. "A man may be illiterate, but he is a man, and man can create. An animal cannot create but can only adapt. If you believe the poor are men, you must believe that they can create and are creating. They may be illiterate, they may not be as educated as you—but they are creating."

Sukhen added, "They know their problems better than you, even if you are a PhD holder, so it's better to listen than to try to educate them. And if you feel like your prescription would be better, then share it and find out whether it is acceptable to them or not. You should only be the catalyst. If you do not learn from the people, you are not a development worker at all." This philosophy was relatively new at the time but rapidly gaining traction in development circles worldwide. Based on it, BRAC began providing training sessions to about a dozen other organizations that wanted to offer functional education classes of their own. Soon they had trouble meeting the demand.

★ ★ ★

Khushi Kabir was now working in Sulla. It had proven impossible to keep her behind a desk in Dhaka. During one of Abed's monthly field visits, she showed up unannounced, having arranged a seat for herself on a UN plane to Sylhet. "The UN had a Cessna that they allowed for relief purposes, and I used to organize the plane," she recalled. "I decided I wanted to go see Sulla. I can't be sitting there doing nothing in Dhaka. Since I was writing the letters, I put my name on the list of passengers to bring Abed *Bhai* back. When I got there, he said, 'You're here. How did you get here?' I said, 'I got here.'" She returned on the flight with Abed, but he soon realized her value was in the field, not an office, and transferred her permanently to Sulla. Before long she was in charge of the entire program.

Among the many visitors to Abed's office in Dhaka was Stephen Minkin, a lanky American in his twenties. Having worked in famine relief in India in the 1960s, Minkin had been drawn into the Bangladesh movement in New York, where he worked as coordinator of the Bangladesh Action Coalition, an umbrella group of organizations supporting independence. He had first come to Bangladesh in December 1971, immediately after liberation, and traveled throughout the country, learning Bengali along the way. Though Minkin was a total outsider to the UN system, the local UNICEF office hired him largely on the strength of his familiarity with Bangladesh and eventually allowed him to start a nutrition program from scratch. Most of UNICEF's funds went directly to governments, but Minkin convinced his bosses to break with protocol and support local NGOs like BRAC. Part of UNICEF's contribution to BRAC was a white Volkswagen Beetle, which allowed the staff at the home office to move around the capital more easily.

Minkin, like others in Dhaka's foreign aid sector, enjoyed visiting Abed's office to hear his thoughts on the country's situation, which was increasingly dire even as the tenor in the BRAC house remained unyieldingly optimistic. "The BRAC office was an exciting place to be in," he said. "There was an enormous amount of innovation going on. Abed sat at his desk puffing away on his cigar, and people would come in and out to discuss ideas and for Abed to review expenditures. There was lots of laughter and confidence about changing the country for the better."

As the Rowmari program was winding down, Minkin told Abed of his visits to Jamalpur, a market town to the north on the eastern bank of the Brahmaputra. Abed knew Jamalpur, for it had been a stopping point on the long journey to Rowmari; he and Cole Dodge had eaten breakfast there during the road trip in Samantha, the Land Rover. Branches of the river marbled the surrounding land, which produced rice, lentils, mustard, sugarcane, and tobacco. In normal times, Jamalpur farmers would carry these goods to market over rickety bamboo bridges in giant bundles on their heads or in two baskets balanced on a shoulder yoke. But these were not normal times. As in Rowmari, the river had destroyed much of the cropland during the floods of 1974. A year later, people had not recovered. Most of the men had left, looking for work elsewhere, and many of their wives had given up on hearing or receiving anything from them ever again.

Earlier in the year, Minkin had witnessed a crowd of women surrounding a government office demanding food, a scene that seemed to be repeating itself with frequency all over the country. As in Sulla and elsewhere, the government had started a food-for-work program, distributing wheat rations to those who contributed their labor to public works projects. When women broke with cultural norms by showing up looking for work, the officials in charge, like the mullah Ansar Ali in Sulla, told them to go home.

Moved by what he had seen, Minkin had launched a UNICEF food-for-work project exclusively for women. He asked the World Food Program for a special allocation of wheat and received it over objections from those within the UN system who were skeptical of the notion of women growing crops. The women in this project began sowing and harvesting crops like sorghum and sunflowers along the riverbanks in exchange for wheat rations. Along with providing income to women in need, the project tested the viability of growing crops in sandy soil, something few had tried before. UNICEF had expected about one hundred women to join the program. More than eight hundred showed up, the famine having stripped away religious and cultural prohibitions.

Minkin shared this with Abed. He explained that the women's work on the sandy riverbanks had been more successful than the skeptics within the UN system had predicted. By June, the first harvest had seen good yields, and UNICEF wanted the program to continue. But the waters were rising again, and there would be nothing for the women to do until December, the start of the next planting period. Minkin had arranged for Gonoshasthaya Kendra to provide health care to the participants during the slack season; he asked Abed whether BRAC would be willing to offer functional-education courses until December. "We said, 'All right, we'll give them a meal, but we'll also give them a lesson,'" Abed recalled. Instead of food-for-work, it would be food-for-Freire.

When Abed visited Jamalpur in June, he asked the government administrators of the food-for-work scheme to identify thirty women they thought might make suitable teachers. When a BRAC team came back to interview the candidates, they found more than one hundred women waiting. Of these, about forty were obviously unqualified to be literacy teachers, since they themselves were illiterate. Of the sixty who remained, they chose fifteen who seemed receptive to nontraditional teaching methods. It was a young group, mostly between the ages of nineteen and twenty-three. Some had not even completed high school, but that did not matter. They wanted women with strong, warm personalities who could spark discussion among learners.

It made sense to choose a woman to supervise a women's empowerment project, so Abed turned to Khushi. She moved alone to Jamalpur, where most people had never seen a single adult woman living on her own, let alone one who wore jeans instead of a sari. She recalled forming strong connections with the fifteen teachers and others in the community: "I remember Bahar coming and saying, 'Khushi, all the rickshaw *wallahs* are your friends!'"

The fifteen teachers quickly latched on to basic Freirean principles, including the radical notion that every person, even a woman, is the foremost "expert" in his or her own life. The teachers understood they weren't just trying to get people to learn the alphabet. Together they set down a list of common objectives, including teaching literacy, raising awareness of family-planning methods, and providing skills training.

The rains began in July and came down hard for most of that month. For shelter, the women gathered under the seats of the local football stadium, where Khushi divided them into thirty groups. They would take their classes right in the stadium, receiving their wheat rations according to the number of classes they attended. Khushi may have been popular with the teachers and rickshaw drivers, but gaining the acceptance of the participants proved more difficult. Most of the 840 women were suspicious, even hostile. Many had to walk five miles in a torrential downpour to reach the stadium. Sometimes only three people in a class of twenty-five showed up. The concept of timing proved difficult to communicate. The teachers had to explain that if your class was scheduled for 12:30 p.m., it would not do to show up at 8:00 a.m. and demand that class be held immediately. Worse, for reasons outside BRAC's control, the local government's distribution of the wheat ration—the only income for most of the women—was delayed, and for several weeks they received nothing. They blamed the teachers for this, for as far as they were concerned, it was all one program.

Khushi persevered. In August, the skies cleared and the promised wheat rations finally arrived. By the end of September, the tenor of the classes had changed completely. The teachers and learners had built a rapport. Women began opening up about their problems, leading to a feeling of camaraderie and solidarity that many had never experienced before. Some had been abused and exploited by their husbands, in-laws, and landlords. And, until now, nobody had ever simply said to them, "We hear you, we understand, and we're on your side." Urged on by the teachers, they began to dig beneath the surface of their problems and come up with concrete solutions. They learned to write their names for the first time—a significant achievement. For a time, according to Minkin, the Jamalpur stadium had the buzz of a university campus.

* * *

Even as things were looking up for the women of Jamalpur, however, the country as a whole continued its slide into chaos. In an attempt to maintain control in the face of open challenges from both the right and the left, Sheikh Mujib had declared a one-party state. Though he had united the Bangladeshis, many thought he was an ineffectual administrator. Before dawn on August 15, 1975, a group of army majors attacked the presidential residence and other locations in the capital, killing Sheikh Mujib, along with his wife, senior ministers, party leaders, and every member of the president's extended family, including young children. The only members of his family who survived were two daughters who happened to be visiting West Germany at the time.

The brutality of the killings notwithstanding, some thought the end of Sheikh Mujib's rule might bring some stability to the country. This would not be the case. Khondakar Mushtaque Ahmed, the cabinet minister who had sat at the groom's table at Abed's wedding, declared martial law and assumed power immediately, ordering the imprisonment of several Awami League party leaders who refused to cooperate with the new regime. These included Tajuddin Ahmad, the former prime minister of the government-in-exile who had vetoed Abed and Viquar's plan to attack Karachi with mercenaries.

The new regime would be short-lived; after ordering and overseeing the execution of Tajuddin Ahmad and three others in November, Khondakar Mushtaque Ahmed was himself deposed in a countercoup. A wave of killings and further coups followed. The leader who finally emerged from the chaos was none other than Ziaur Rahman, the army major who had visited Abed's hotel room in Calcutta in late 1971 requesting a pair of binoculars.

The streets of Jamalpur, like almost everywhere else in the country, were eerily quiet after martial law was declared in the wake of Sheikh Mujib's assassination. But out of nowhere, Khushi recalled, strange new graffiti appeared on the walls. These were not political messages in any conventional sense. A few of the 840 women, having learned to read and write for the first time, had picked up charcoal and scrawled their names on the walls of the town. That was their statement.

⋆ ⋆ ⋆

The Jamalpur project was BRAC's first program to empower women exclusively. Although it was not founded explicitly as a women's empowerment organization, BRAC would, in effect, become one. Abed would often observe that women were the "managers of poverty," bearing the responsibility, fairly or unfairly, for allocating the household's scant resources. They performed this role remarkably well, given the circumstances. He came to believe that if they were the managers of poverty, they should also be the managers of development. Much later, in 2012, on the fortieth anniversary of BRAC's founding, Abed cast the issue more starkly in terms of social justice. He declared gender equality "the greatest unfinished agenda not only of my life's work but of our time," adding that he considered "the subjugation of half the world's population to be the greatest injustice in the history of humankind."

Per the agreement with UNICEF, BRAC had planned to discontinue the Jamalpur classes when the women went back to the fields in early December 1975. In Abed's mind, this had been a small experiment in using Freire's methods in a new part of the country. But when the women heard the classes were ending, they objected. BRAC had to make sure they understood that the wheat rations would no longer be offered as an incentive. That didn't matter. They wanted the classes to go on anyway. They felt their work was not yet finished.

14

THE PROVING GROUND

"You've come all the way to Sulla," Abed recalled one of his first BRAC employees telling him. "But there are places near Dhaka that are just as poor." The man had his home in mind, one of the closest rural districts on the way out of the capital—a place called Manikganj.

In the fall of 1975, BRAC was again on the verge of expansion. Khushi Kabir had just been posted to Jamalpur, the organization's second foray outside Sulla. Jamalpur was four hours north of Dhaka by road, far closer than the twenty-four-hour land-and-water journey to Sulla, but four hours each way still made for a tough day trip.

The need for a program with easy access to the home office, where BRAC could tinker and learn, was clear. Part of the reason Abed had launched the program in Sulla three years earlier had been its isolation. No other relief organization would likely venture to a location so hard to reach. Increasingly, the distance and isolation seemed more like a drawback. Deep in the *haor* area, Sulla was atypical of the rest of Bangladesh and limited in terms of its potential. No matter what BRAC did in agriculture, for instance, the land there would never yield more than one harvest per year, whereas, with the right investments, Abed knew other areas could begin yielding two or even three annual harvests. "As a place where you experiment with new development ideas, Sulla was not the best," said Abed. "You can't make three-crop lands. You can't experiment with new kinds of agriculture. If you want to educate a child, it's difficult to find a teacher in the village. Everything was difficult in Sulla, and sending people to run the program was also difficult. We wanted a more representative area."

They eventually chose Manikganj, close to where two of Bangladesh's great rivers, the Jamuna and Padma (the Bangladeshi names for the Brahmaputra and Ganges) have their confluence. Criss-crossed by at least five named waterways, the land flooded often during the wet months and stayed mostly fallow during the dry ones. With sandy loam soil that was difficult for rice cultivation, the people of Manikganj were among the poorest in Bangladesh.

In November, with funding from Bread for the World and Oxfam Canada, BRAC launched the preparatory phase of the Manikganj Integrated Project. Thanks to its proximity to the capital, activities as diverse as animal husbandry, child immunization, and chicken vaccination were now vastly more feasible. "It was near enough to Dhaka that we could keep track of things easily," said Abed. "Manikganj became the experimentation zone."

* * *

Months earlier, when Abed had pulled up stakes in Rowmari after his clash with the local boss, he had sent most of the BRAC staff who had worked on the famine-relief project back to Sulla, with one notable exception. Aminul ("Amin") Alam, the headstrong university graduate who had argued for a raise before his first day on the job, requested to return to Dhaka, where his father had fallen ill. Abed wanted to find a place for him to continue working at BRAC, but a series of family emergencies kept Amin away for several months. His father survived the illness, but on August 15, 1975, the same day as Sheikh Mujib's assassination, Amin's mother died.

As one of eleven siblings, Amin came from a large family even by the Bangladeshi standards of the time. His father, native to Gopalganj, southwest of Dhaka, had a job at Bangladesh Railways that moved the family around so much that Amin later found former schoolmates in every corner of the country. Much is expected of older brothers in Bangladeshi culture, including being a counselor to younger siblings in matters of education, marriage, and career. Amin was the third son, but his two older brothers already had families and jobs of their own, and he felt the pull of familial obligation. After his mother's death, he told Abed that if he were to continue to work at BRAC, he needed a job close to Dhaka. Abed sent him to Manikganj, just forty miles west of Dhaka.

Abed had recognized Amin as a hard worker as soon as he joined. He initially served as deputy to the program head, but before long Abed put Amin in charge of the whole Manikganj project. The location was ideal for Amin, since, in theory, he could visit his extended family, which he had professed to be so concerned about, every weekend. But he became so immersed that he tended to work through the weekends. As he said years later, "In six months, I never once came to Dhaka. It's a one- or one-and-a-half-hour drive, but I never came to Dhaka. My family was very upset."[1]

These were the type of people that Abed wanted, and it would be hard to overstate the impact Amin would go on to have within the organization. He was a hard taskmaster, both feared and revered by those who worked under him, and he rose through the ranks quickly. Stories are still told about his work ethic and the demands he made on staff—calling a branch manager at 6:00 a.m., for instance, to ask whether a task assigned the evening before had been started yet. Eating, sleeping, and other worldly obligations seemed to come second to work, and his commitment to both Abed and BRAC bordered on religious. Abed called him a "loyal disciple" whose "total devotion and faith" created the impression that, for Amin, "nothing matters other than BRAC."

Marty Chen, who became close to Amin in the 1970s, described the contrast between the styles of Abed and his chief acolyte. Abed visited the field reasonably often, especially in BRAC's early years, but he was an "armchair leader," according to Marty. His way of learning was receiving debriefs from the field, reflecting, and "putting the puzzle together" in his office. "Amin was his field marshal," she said. He enjoyed being on the front lines.

* * *

The Manikganj program broadly mimicked the design of the Sulla program but introduced several important changes. Chief among these was the manner in which BRAC selected its participants. When Abed launched the Sulla program, he had lacked a nuanced understanding of rural power dynamics. He thought if people could learn to work together effectively—by tilling the land as a cooperative, for instance, or pooling their resources to buy fertilizer—the whole community would rise from poverty. "In those days, community development was the thing, which means the entire village," Abed said. "It doesn't work in practice."

The problem was hard for city dwellers to grasp, since nearly everyone in the village seemed poor. By certain standards they were. The messier but more accurate truth was that enough heterogeneity existed within the crude category of "poor" to make the classification almost meaningless. The poor or near-poor would often exploit those poorer than themselves, sometimes ruthlessly. The early failures of the Sulla program led Abed to conclude that there was no point to "community development" as such, for the community itself was at best a fiction and at worst a tool of oppression. "There is no such thing as community," he told an interviewer once, in an unlikely echo of Margaret Thatcher.[2] "People who are landless and landed are not the same people," he later said. "Their interests are in conflict." In a rural setting where crude exploitation was the norm, a rising tide did not lift all boats.

This observation was rooted in experience, but it was also influenced by Abed's reading of *Pedagogy of the Oppressed*. "Paulo Freire wanted the landless, the poor people, the oppressed people, to be together, thinking and analyzing their situation," Abed said. "As soon as we started analyzing this, we saw that, in a classroom where you teach literacy, you wanted a homogenous group of people, not sharecroppers and landlords and landless people together. That was the first separating of the oppressed from the oppressors."

The thinking was further colored by BRAC's anthropological studies of village life. After the famine, BRAC's in-house research unit began a series of studies called "Peasant Perceptions." Through focus-group discussions and a series of open-ended questions, the researchers explored how people struggling with poverty viewed issues such as famine, credit, sanitation, and the law. These discussions revealed, among other things, the strategies of upwardly mobile people who were once poor.

The process begins by accumulating money. People usually then acquire some land. Since land by itself does not confer status, they try to leverage their landholding by marrying their daughter to a local government official, which brings not just wealth but also power. From these studies, Abed learned of an entire category of near-poor people, the upwardly mobile rural middle class, whom "you don't need to help at all. You don't need to touch them, and don't expect anything from them either. They are not going to be of great help to you in getting people out of poverty." The once-poor who have moved up through such machinations "are not to be trusted. They would sell their mothers to move up."

These people had to be excluded from the programs. Otherwise, even those with a small amount of land and power would somehow find a way to appropriate the gains of development for their own benefit. The solution was to bring together people who were all facing similar circumstances—landless women, for instance. "Unless you have homogenous people, they won't learn from each other," Abed said. It took several years for BRAC to bring this understanding to its logical conclusion, which was that it was a waste of precious resources to spend time or money on anyone but the poorest people. The result was the "target-group approach" inaugurated in Manikganj, which focused only on those without assets or land, with men and women grouped separately.

In Manikganj, the selection of participants began with a food-for-work program, similar to the government programs that had sprung up around the country in the famine's wake. Those who showed up for a day of work—usually moving earth by hand to build a road or embankment, or digging an irrigation canal—received three kilograms of unmilled wheat, which could be ground into flour or sold in the market. Those willing to work for three kilograms of wheat per day were, almost by definition, eligible BRAC participants, since only the poorest of the poor will sell their labor for survival. "Work was considered a lowly thing to do," said Abed. "A person who has some land will not offer himself as a manual worker." He added, "Manikganj started with a very concrete idea of what poverty was and what we were going to do. We didn't want anybody having land. Somebody poor enough to do manual labor—he or she was our target."

Food for work, though hardly the most innovative solution to poverty, was thus a cheap and effective way to identify the poorest people in any given community. It took advantage of the plenitude of donated wheat available in the post-famine period. Many American organizations, including the Mennonite Central Committee and CARE, had access to wheat, often from official US food aid, and would donate one hundred tons at a time to BRAC. "It was easy to get that food for organizations that were ready to do the hard work of distributing it through a project," said Abed.

To be sure, food-for-work schemes were neither an equitable solution nor a long-term strategy for breaking the poverty trap. For one thing, the infrastructure it created—mainly earthworks like roads, embankments, and canals—only tended to benefit those who owned land already, thus widening the divide between landed and landless. "The landless people got their wages, but the landed people had their land improved," said Abed. "One-crop land becomes three-crop land once you have a canal by the side of it." However, it was a short-term tactic to bring participants into a program that promoted other economic activities in which self-employed landless people would own the fruits of their labor. Once identified through the food-for-work scheme, landless people were organized into groups and went through functional-education classes. As in Sulla, the classes provided an initial forum for discussion.

Within two years, the target group approach became the new norm for BRAC, even when participants were selected through means other than food for work. The programs developed strict criteria for who could join. People had to be landless or very close to it (that is, without enough land to grow substantial crops), and they had to be engaged only in manual labor; a schoolteacher didn't count. Their labor also had to be sold to an unrelated party, as opposed to a man working for his brother's business. "A woman who is carrying bricks on her head from one place to another, or breaking bricks manually—we were going to work with her," said Abed. Few people, including Abed, can remember the details, but according to a donor report, senior staff decided at a three-day strategy meeting in November 1977 that henceforth BRAC would "work only with the landless or near landless (who sell their labor for survival)." Likely the decision was a foregone conclusion by then, since the founder had already made up his mind.

★ ★ ★

In Manikganj, many of the elements that would come to define BRAC began falling into place. Freirean education was the starting point for group-based empowerment, but BRAC was now large enough that it held a variety of views on whether this was enough. Amin, in particular, believed that if BRAC was not creating new opportunities for people to earn a living, the work they were doing, even if they were making people more hopeful about the future and giving them the confidence to stand up for their rights, was ultimately pointless.

Abed was inclined to agree. His early donor reports from Manikganj—he wrote nearly every BRAC donor report until about 1980—put it bluntly: "The first premise of human existence is that man must be in a position to live." Various economic support schemes took shape, including organizing landless laborers into groups of sharecroppers that would negotiate advantageous deals with landowners, leasing land for a portion of the yield. Such schemes included growing peanuts in previously fallow land on the sandy banks of the river and cultivating sugarcane by hand, without the use of costly plows or oxen. BRAC organized people to excavate ponds for fish cultivation, offered loans for the purchase of handlooms, and trained women in wooden block printing. The latter proved to be especially profitable: women printed patterns onto bedsheets and tablecloths, which BRAC sold in a handicraft shop it opened in Dhaka, called Aarong. The raising of silkworms and the spinning of silk, which women could do in their own homes, also began to look promising.

The groups that emerged would eventually be called "village organizations," or VOs, a term that would go on to denote the main locus of empowerment in the BRAC universe. In the BRAC archive of reports, the first appearance of that term comes in 1979, in a report on a pilot project for rural credit (later known as "microfinance"). But the essence of the idea—an organized group of landless villagers, who underwent training by BRAC for various roles and duties—probably existed in Manikganj as early as April 1976, when the preparatory food-for-work phase ended and the first formal phase of programming began.

By now the demand for training was constant. At any given time, new hires were going through orientation, old staff were learning new methods, and participants were receiving training; BRAC was even training staff at other nongovernmental organizations. Abed set up a separate training division, with training centers located close to the project areas. In fact, much of BRAC's budget went into training for village group members themselves, rather than staff. "We wanted to have poor people's leadership," said Abed. "A large amount of our time was capacity development. We used to call it 'institutional capacity development.' We were training our group members for capacity development more than anybody else. For the whole of the 1970s and 1980s—the early 1980s anyway, until about 1985—most of our trainees were in fact group members."

The training of landless people brought new insights. Among them was the observation that the most eloquent people were not always the best group leaders. "I've always doubted the really articulate people," said Abed. Outsiders would tend to seek out and trust those who could speak well, but Abed said they were often not the most trustworthy or capable people in the village, for they had a tendency to become "touts," or power brokers. "Let's say you are a poor man and you've got a problem, and you have to go to a police officer, but you feel shy," he said. "You feel too small to go talk to a police officer. So you get somebody who is articulate enough to talk on your behalf, and he will earn something from this. He will do it for you but for money." Meanwhile, there were others in the group who were quieter but more trusted. "They would speak less but people would respect their values and the way they handled things. I think villagers had fairly good ideas about who their leaders were, even if [other] people didn't."

⋆ ⋆ ⋆

In Manikganj, BRAC began to shift its attention to women's empowerment, which was not explicitly part of the original mission. Abed had seen the depredations of the famine tear families apart in Rowmari. "The mothers would bring their children, and they would be happy if their children could eat," he recalled. "I could see that the kind of sacrifice mothers make for their children is just phenomenal, and that's the kind of perception that drove me—that it's the women who need to be supported. They are able to sacrifice so much to keep their families together and alive."

The shift to women's groups was pragmatic as well as ideological, born from the observation that the men's groups were simply not as effective—and the staff only had so many hours in their days to support and administer the groups. The logic of the target-group approach, which sought to bring people with common concerns together, had meant convening women's and men's groups separately, since their needs were so different. The men worked in the fields during the day, while the women stayed close to home doing domestic work. BRAC therefore convened the women in the daytime and the men in the evening. "You could not have group meetings with the men before night, when everybody comes home from work," said Abed. "So our staff used to go at night to men's meetings, and this became too much of a problem. Our staff were working in the afternoon with women's groups, at night with the men's groups, going in the morning to collect money, and it became too much. When we started becoming larger, we decided these night meetings had to stop."

Men's groups were also hard to coalesce around collective enterprises. "Some were working very hard and complaining that 'I have to do all the work and the others are not working,'" Abed said. He added that "women, given the money individually, seemed to be working harder than three or four men working together."

This shift to women's groups is not highlighted in project reports, so it is hard to say when it took place. By the mid-1980s, men's village organizations still existed—in part because women did not work in the fields, and BRAC wanted to continue to have some impact on agriculture—but, according to Abed, "they were coming down gradually." In 1989, BRAC described its overall rural development strategy as targeting "the landless rural poor, with particular emphasis on women," marking the first time it used such language in a major proposal.

* * *

Melinda French Gates told the *New York Times* in 2012 that BRAC "pioneered the community health worker model,"[3] which is partially true, in the sense that BRAC popularized it and scaled it up. Many can lay claim to having "invented" the idea, which has its roots in the Chinese concept of the "barefoot doctor"—people from rural areas getting minimum basic medical training to serve their communities—which Mao Zedong institutionalized in the 1960s. As far as BRAC is concerned, the community "health worker" (or *shasthya shebika*) model had its genesis in Manikganj. The idea likely had more long-term impact than any other innovation piloted there.

In Sulla, BRAC had learned that about 95 percent of rural health problems were attributable to about a dozen diseases that could be treated without seeing a doctor. Provided there was a decent referral system for the remaining 5 percent, nearly all rural health needs could therefore be covered, in theory, with just a handful of doctors and clinics covering a large area. Initially, BRAC had trained a cadre of mostly male paramedics, who were assigned five to seven villages and expected to visit each village once a week. After four years of experimentation with different methods for recruiting, training, and incentivizing these traveling health workers, it finally became clear that they were ineffective. Having trained them, BRAC found it had trouble supervising them. To earn extra money, many began expanding the drugs and treatments they offered beyond what they were qualified to do, merely adding to the already large number of quacks masquerading as medical professionals.

They had also tried a more local model, training "lady family planning officers" (LFPOs), each serving no more than one hundred nearby families. For small monthly incentives, the LFPOs were trained to raise awareness of family planning and deliver contraceptives, and they did not have to travel far, mostly working in their own villages. This proved far more effective.

In Manikganj, BRAC began relying on trained volunteers from the village groups, who would do many of the tasks performed by paid staff in Sulla. In the project's first phase, from 1976 to 1979, Amin trained and supervised about four hundred volunteers from the area, called "education helpers" or *shikkha sheboks* (for men) and *shikkha shebikas* (for women), to conduct the functional-education classes. Volunteer *sheboks* and *shebikas* in other specialized areas would soon emerge.

In 1978, Amin began recruiting *shasthya shebikas*, which translates to female "health helpers" or "health volunteers." These community health workers were similar to the Sulla family-planning workers, except they catered to the village's general health needs. Rather than traveling from village to village, like the Sulla paramedics, they would serve only their own communities. That year, BRAC trained the first sixty-eight of these community health workers on basic care for ailments like diarrhea, dysentery, and worms, all of which were common in rural settings. They were self-employed in the sense that they took no salary from BRAC but made their income selling pills, condoms, and other goods at a small markup.

Initially there were both *shasthya sheboks* and *shebikas*, half male and half female. Over time, however, it emerged that training both male *sheboks* and female *shebikas* was less effective than having a single female *shebika* for the whole village. A woman might not want to discuss family planning or other women's issues with a man, especially if that man was a neighbor, whereas female health workers were acceptable to everyone. In time, the linchpin of the entire BRAC health system became the *shasthya shebika*—a local woman with basic training, traveling on foot like a door-to-door salesperson, serving the basic health needs of her neighbors. From that first batch of sixty-eight, the number would increase over the next thirty years to about eighty thousand.

★ ★ ★

There were many other aspects of its work that would not last, however. For instance, one of the conclusions of the November 1977 strategy meeting was that BRAC should work with landless people "not on an individual basis but as a homogenous group."

The concept of solidarity and group cohesion among landless people worked better on paper than in practice, especially as BRAC began making loans to the village groups to start their own livelihood projects. "We found that the group responsibilities did not work very well," said Abed. "Over a period, we found there were a lot of free riders. That doesn't work very well. Group cohesion doesn't develop. If you gave money to an individual, he would use it the way he wants and would probably pay back the loan much more responsibly. You can make him responsible for it."

Another concept that never took off was the federation of village organizations. Abed had envisioned the landless poor organizing themselves into a political force, which could exert influence on a national level. He admitted that this idea did not transpire the way he'd anticipated. "The village poor didn't really organize themselves into powerful groups and challenge the supremacy of the rich," he said, adding with a quiet laugh, "None of the proletarian revolution took place in our lifetime in Bangladesh." The essentials of life would have to come first. "It's too much to ask them to go and take on the bigger forces of people who are powerful, who gave them jobs, and fight it out without any income themselves, without having anything to eat."

He went on: "Groups never gelled to the extent that they would form federal-level organizations, like the trade union movement that happened in Europe and America," where unions organized themselves in the formal sector. "In Bangladesh's situation, it was peasants who were not formally working for anybody. There was no one employer that you could negotiate with."

It is hard to say when, or even if, the idea of federated organizations of the landless was completely abandoned. Even at the end of the eleven-year Manikganj project, there were still references in project reports to the amalgamation and federation of village organizations to exert political pressure at the level of the subdistrict. Even in 2022, a version of the idea still exists in one BRAC program, which promotes women's voices at a local level—by encouraging them to contest local elections, for example. But it long ago stopped being a core part of the organization's approach.

As far as Abed was concerned, Paulo Freire would always remain one of BRAC's intellectual godfathers. ("We were leftist then, and we are still leftist. Our ethos is leftist," he said in 2015.) In practical terms, however, BRAC gradually ceased to be an organization guided by an urge for revolutionary political change. As the 1970s came to an end, BRAC would increasingly focus on economic empowerment and especially on the provision of credit, the lack of which was one of the greatest constraints to rural livelihood development. The practice was becoming increasingly controversial within the growing organization.

* * *

Amin would spend eight years in Manikganj. While stationed there, he married Gulrana Haque, the daughter of a college principal from Kushtia, in an arranged marriage. Coming from an academically minded family, Gulrana had a master's degree in economics from Dhaka University and a full-time job at the state-owned Bangladesh Mineral Development Corporation in the capital. A soft-spoken woman, Gulrana clearly had an independent streak, as she was not put off by having to ride the bus from Dhaka to Manikganj, where her husband lived, in order to see him on the weekends. He would wait for her at the bus stand with his Honda motorcycle—in the early days, field staff pedaled around on bicycles, but by now BRAC had graduated to motorbikes—and drive her back to the branch office, where they would stay.

"His lifestyle was very different from the traditional lifestyle of other people back in those days," said Gulrana. "He was really into the programs, even on the weekends. I was working full-time, which was difficult, so I would visit him on the weekends. This was not a typical nine-to-five job. He would wake up very early in the morning and get ready for work, and I would have breakfast with him and the staff. At night we would go to the village meetings. He really used to love to show his work, so he would take me along on the back of a motorcycle." His faith in Abed was genuine, she added. "I never really saw Amin disagreeing with him, even privately."

According to Marty Chen, Amin "had a tenaciousness and a capacity to get to the heart of the issues that was quite extraordinary." She added that he had an uncanny ability to connect with people and a relentless drive to understand their problems down to the smallest detail, even if it took hours or days to get there. "I remember one time he was working in an area with a lot of difficulty with agriculture in the oxbows of the river," she said. He sat in these meetings with farmers for three days, shouting to his staff, "Bring cigarettes! Bring tea!"—even though he himself didn't smoke. "He was just trying to crack what it was, where the bottlenecks to viable agriculture were in these oxbow areas where the soil had a different type of salinity. He was tough on his fellow staff, but at the same time, he was the kind who remembered every village woman and would bring them saris. He had a real heart."

Abed agreed that Amin's qualities went beyond his loyalty, his work ethic, and the demands he made on subordinates. "He would come back at eight o'clock at night, and if there were [nearby] workers who hadn't eaten, he would invite them to eat with the staff. 'It is late and he shouldn't be eating alone,' he would say. He had a kind of empathy for everybody, so he earned a lot of loyalty."

He was notoriously hotheaded on the job, but according to Gulrana, he was a completely different person after hours. He never brought his temper home to his family. He simply wanted the work done well, she said. "He used to tell me that if you're running an operation, you have to be a bit strict. He would get angry, but the good thing is that he used to cool down quickly."

BRAC was looking more like a spring-loaded catapult, fully loaded and ready to release. Abed had spent years setting up the mechanisms and conditions for scaling up. These included programs that met participants' demands, efficient back-office functions and training centers, a solid reputation among donors, and a deputy who would go to the ends of the earth for him. Abed was finally ready to go big. Two events would nearly wreck all he had built, however—one a rupture with a trusted senior staffer, the other a shocking personal tragedy.

15

FALLING OUT

Khushi Kabir had become a force within BRAC, having risen from office assistant to education supervisor. As BRAC grew larger and expanded the suite of services it provided, including a growing portfolio of loans, she became uncomfortable with the direction the organization was heading. Abed had few qualms about offering "rural credit," or what later became known as "microfinance," provided the loans were offered at a reasonable interest rate, directed at those who were genuinely poor and coupled with training and other services. Khushi and others were deeply committed to the Freirean creed of self-empowerment and moving in a different direction.

Putting village moneylenders out of business had long been an essential part of Abed's plan. As early as 1974, BRAC had supported farmers in Sulla, where a survey found three-quarters of households were indebted, with loans repayable over two to three years. The villain here was the rural moneylender, who played an unsavory role in a story that repeated itself time and again. A landless person, or a collective of landless laborers, might gain some land, often by claiming government-owned fallow plots, which the law required be made available to the landless. Before this land would yield a single taka, however, they had to level it, buy seeds, plant, and harvest, all of which required significant capital. With no access to bank lending, this could only be financed by a local moneylender, often a landowner himself charging usurious rates. If the harvest fell short, the farmers defaulted and forfeited the land. The landowners thus increased their holdings, and the poor went back to being landless. The BRAC strategy of lending at reasonable rates disrupted this pattern. It also allowed BRAC to reach more people as it recirculated the money after the borrowers repaid.

By mid-1978, the organization had made about $100,000 in loans in Sulla, Jamalpur, and Manikganj.

Being a microfinance provider as well as an educator put Khushi in an uncomfortable position. She recalled visiting women who had "shared every bit of their lives and their problems with me," only to have them avoid her on repayment day. One woman sent her child to the door when Khushi called. "The little kid said, 'Ma is not at home.' I said, 'Of course your ma is home,' and I would go and say [to the mother], 'Why have you said that?'" The mother confessed it was because she did not have the money to make her scheduled loan repayment. "This happened a couple of times," Khushi said. "It's not just one story, but this is the one that really wrenched me. Here is a woman who, two nights back, had told me all her personal and marital problems. She suddenly felt that I have become, more than anything else, the collector."

In the decades to come, volumes would be written on microfinance, and debate would rage over whether it helps or hurts the poor. Research now tends to support the conclusion that microcredit has a modest positive impact in terms of income levels, but, by itself, it is seldom transformative. Khushi did not believe that putting poor people further into debt would help them. Moreover, there was a basic moral calculation: she could not be simultaneously a friend and a debt collector to women struggling with poverty.

Khushi was part of the inner circle of BRAC. She was there at the start and, though others can make the same claim, was often called "employee number one." Her father was also a board member. She had followed Abed in his embrace of Freirean activism and had proved an indefatigable field manager. But she never believed in the "big is necessary" mantra, and as the organization grew, so did the friction. Complicating matters, both Abed and Bahar considered Khushi a personal friend, and Bahar and Khushi had grown especially close. The dispute was based "not on personal differences but on ideological differences," according to Khushi, but as she became the leader of a small group of disaffected people within BRAC, the dispute would boil over into bitterness and recriminations at the highest level of the organization. In time, it would lead to BRAC's first major crisis, threatening to cripple the organization.

* * *

The late 1970s into the early 1980s was a period of intense activity and wrenching change that permeated all aspects of Abed's life, both personal and professional. It started with Abed's shift toward moneymaking ventures. Microfinance would eventually become BRAC's largest source of internally generated revenue, but long before that happened—and before it was even launched as a standalone program—Abed had already turned heads in the nonprofit world by creating several BRAC-owned money-making ventures. His aim was to chip away at the dependence on donor funding. "We have always thought that donor money is too fickle," he said. "It is here today, gone tomorrow."

In BRAC's first three years, all his letters of appointment to staff—the official document giving them a job—explicitly offered "temporary" appointments. "We were completely dependent on donor money, and if it stops, you have no job," he said. "So I used to give temporary appointments." This stopped in 1975, when he became more confident of the inflow of donor funding and began offering permanent positions. He seemed to have little difficulty raising money for expansion despite BRAC's often middling results.

Nevertheless, he wanted a more solid foundation. As he wrote in donor proposals, "uncertainty of a continuous flow of funds saps staff morale." Cole Dodge recalled when Abed raised the idea of a BRAC printing press, the first of BRAC's own enterprises. Functional education and other training programs always needed new posters and booklets, and they also published a magazine for the newly literate, so the organization had considerable printing needs. There were not many good printers in Dhaka. Rather than outsource the job, Abed thought he would be better off starting his own printing company, which could operate commercially after meeting BRAC's needs. Cole sensed that Abed's driving motive was the commercial objective. "There was a market niche in Dhaka, but in my mind, it was very clearly a money-earning operation," said Cole. "It had nothing to do with efficiency of programs."

Abed and Cole put together a short proposal that was flat-out rejected by Oxfam's overseas director, Michael Harris, who said, according to Cole, "We have never given money for an enterprise and have no intention of doing so. You should spend the money on social welfare and development. We should raise the money and BRAC should spend the money." Cole said he then "kicked it upstairs" to Guy Stringer, the deputy director. Like Abed, Stringer had experience in the business world and was interested in the printing press proposal. Cole invited him to see for himself, along with the top man at Oxfam, Brian Walker, who was relatively new on the job. According to Cole, Bangladesh was Walker's first overseas field visit, and he was impressed by BRAC's tight accounts, regular reports, and management structure. It would take Cole eighteen months to steer the proposal through the personalities, committees, and boards that made up Oxfam's internal management, but he was ultimately successful.

By then, another funder had appeared on the scene—a Dutch nongovernmental organization (NGO) called the Netherlands Organization for International Development Cooperation (Novib). Oxfam and Novib jointly funded the $210,000 start-up costs for BRAC Printers, including the purchase of a Heidelberg Press from West Germany, considered the Rolls-Royce of printing presses. Operations started in 1977 in Mohakhali, a relatively quiet area of the capital adjacent to Gulshan, the leafy suburb where most of Abed's friends had lived prior to the war. "The brilliance of it was buying the land in Mohakhali," said Cole. Above the printing press, BRAC went on to build a five-story building, which in 1980 became its new head office.

The next venture was a textile and handicrafts shop. For Amin, who was heading the Manikganj program at the time, the idea for this began when a group of people from the home office, including Marty Chen, visited the district for a survey and misplaced the keys to their car. Amin used the delay to raise an issue that had been on his mind. He had recruited *shebikas*, or female "helpers," on a voluntary basis to conduct the functional-education classes. After six months of classes, the landless groups would begin receiving loans to jump-start their livelihoods. The *shebikas* themselves were not poor enough to qualify as BRAC group members, so they received nothing. Many of them had handicraft skills such as weaving and embroidery and had asked if BRAC could help them find employment.[1]

At the time, only one shop in Dhaka specialized in rural handicrafts, an artisans' cooperative called Karika. Amin asked Marty and the others to find out whether Karika would sell embroidered goods made by the Manikganj *shebikas*. Karika agreed to do so, but only on consignment—meaning that the women would not be paid until the shop actually sold their goods. It was often several months before the women actually received any cash. "That made me angry," said Abed, who thought rural artisans deserved to be paid on delivery, just as any buyer would treat a commercial supplier. "I said I'm going to show them." He applied for and received grants from Bread for the World and Inter Pares for about $150,000 to set up a BRAC shop to sell fabrics, baskets, embroidered mats, and other traditional crafts handmade by Manikganj artisans.

However, neither Abed nor anyone else at BRAC knew a thing about retail sales. He approached a friend, Paul Myers, who headed the Bangladesh chapter of the Mennonite Central Committee (MCC), the relief arm of several Mennonite and other North American Anabaptist churches. An early proponent of the "fair trade" movement, MCC would produce handicrafts like handmade paper Christmas cards in Bangladesh, export them to its headquarters in Akron, Pennsylvania, and sell them in its shops, called Selfhelp Crafts of the World (later renamed Ten Thousand Villages). Abed proposed that with BRAC donor funding, MCC be commissioned to run the BRAC shop, including hiring and supervising the employees, for two years. The shop was called Aarong, for "village market."

"For the first two years there was a little bit of tension as to where the loyalties of the employees should lie," Abed said. As far as he was concerned, the first Aarong staff "were all BRAC employees, but managed by MCC." He and others from BRAC visited the shop often and quickly learned how to manage retail operations. In January 1981, MCC officially handed over management to BRAC. Bahar Abed became the first director of Aarong, which started turning a profit in 1983. Still owned by BRAC and employing tens of thousands of rural artisans, it is now one of the largest Bangladeshi retail fashion chains.

By then, Abed was acting like a canny serial entrepreneur, on the lookout for moneymaking opportunities everywhere, as long as they would serve the poor while reducing BRAC's donor dependence. It came to his attention, for instance, that productivity per acre for Bangladeshi potato farmers was among the highest in Asia. The greatest obstacle to profitability was not productivity but the country's shortage of cold-storage facilities: Unlike rice, potatoes in tropical Bangladesh start to shrivel and rot soon after harvest. Farmers therefore had to sell their entire yield at harvest time, when prices were at their lowest, and smallholders, with no access to refrigeration and under pressure to repay loans, barely made a profit.

Backed by a \$1.4 million commitment from the United Nations Capital Development Fund, BRAC built a refrigeration facility, called BRAC Cold Storage, to store up to four thousand tons of potatoes from the area surrounding the city of Comilla. It was launched as a commercial venture, with the twin objectives of generating revenue for BRAC itself through the rental of refrigerated storage space and improving income for small potato farmers. In its proposal, BRAC estimated it would raise earnings for no less than ten thousand farmers. Most private cold-storage firms preferred large growers, due to the ease of handling fewer clients with greater volumes, but BRAC Cold Storage would reserve space to be rented to small growers.

⋆ ⋆ ⋆

In 1978, with backing from the Dutch government, Novib made the largest donor commitment to BRAC to date, about \$5 million for a five-year experiment called the Rural Credit and Training Project (RCTP), which offered loans to people (repayable with a small fee) and trained borrowers in technical skills like farm management. It was a deliberate effort to undercut predatory lending. It also heralded a major shift for Abed in two respects. First, for perhaps the first time, he acted on a prediction of where donors were likely to shift their attention. Through his conversations with Cole and others, including the higher-ups at Oxfam who pushed through internal resistance to support his out-of-the-box proposals, he gained a better sense of global trends in donor priorities. Family planning was still near the top of the agenda, since fertility rates in South Asia remained enormously high—nearly five in India and closer to seven in Bangladesh. Abed reckoned that, soon enough, donors would realize family planning would never catch on without boosting people's incomes. "Family planning was not going to take off just like that," he said. With the RCTP pilot, he wanted to be ready when donors began shifting their attention to poverty reduction.

It also would be a departure for BRAC to focus on a few things in a large number of locations rather than a large number of things in a few locations. In Manikganj and Sulla, BRAC had pursued "integrated development" with a wide swath of anti-poverty programming, including group organization, solidarity building, adult education, health, family planning, and myriad forms of economic support. The philosophy was that because poverty did not have a single cause, it could never have a single solution, so it was necessary to work in all these areas. By now, however, Abed understood that integrated programming, while ideal for an experimentation zone like Manikganj, had practical limitations: it was harder to scale up complex programs than simpler ones. "If you want to do a national program, an integrated program becomes more difficult," he said.

Abed asked Kaiser Zaman, his old colleague at Shell, to join BRAC for a two-year stint. Following the 1970 cyclone relief project, Kaiser had worked for the International Rescue Committee (IRC) in Dhaka, before relocating to Washington, DC, to study for an MBA, his second, at American University. There he fell in love with and later married an undergraduate American woman, Wendy Sacks. Abed tasked Kaiser with laying the groundwork for the launch of a standalone lending program, which would open in new districts outside the existing BRAC program areas of Sulla, Manikganj, and Jamalpur. This was effectively the birth of microfinance at BRAC.

Kaiser recalled the conversation that led to this development: "Abed said to me one day, 'Look, we know some programs are working well, and some are not.'" Functional education was going strong at that point, but

Abed recognized that, even if these classes made people feel empowered and hopeful, that in itself did not put food on the table. "He said, 'We have to give people money. They don't come for functional education; they come for loans. So what about starting a bank?' I told him that under law, we cannot start a bank. He said, 'I know, but we'll call it something else. Can you work out something and see if it's a feasible idea?'"

Kaiser also told Abed, "We need some point of reference." As far as he knew, nobody in Bangladesh was offering credit to the poor since "microfinance as a concept did not exist." Grameen Bank, another Bangladeshi organization, would later make microfinance famous and, along with its founder, Muhammad Yunus, win the Nobel Peace Prize for it in 2006. Yunus, an economics professor in Chittagong, is sometimes credited with "inventing" microfinance, but Grameen was not even a blip on the radar at this point, according to Kaiser. Yunus made his first loans in 1976 but would only start expanding beyond the Chittagong area in 1979, and Kaiser said he was unaware of Grameen or Yunus when he wrote the RCTP proposal in 1978.

Abed had previously met an extraordinary Indian woman named Ela Bhatt, who, in 1972, founded the Self-Employed Women's Association (SEWA), a sort of trade union representing women working in low-wage jobs in the informal sector. Based in Ahmedabad, the site of Gandhi's ashram, SEWA organized women in a variety of professions, including home-based weavers, laundry workers, and vegetable sellers, and offered them small loans through SEWA Bank starting in 1974. Abed suggested that Kaiser go speak to her, and Kaiser was soon en route to Ahmedabad for a study tour of Bhatt's organization. He had dinner with Bhatt and her husband, studied their operations, and met several SEWA Bank clients.

He then undertook a similar tour of villages and towns in Bangladesh to find out whether anyone besides informal moneylenders was offering such services—and if not, why? "For the first time, I realized that banks have branches in every small town, but nobody gives loans," he said. "They only did deposits." When it came to borrowing, the bank managers told him that "everything has to go to Dhaka." In the capital city, loans would go to well-connected people who often did not even have to repay them, and "if you are not connected, you'd better sell your wife's jewelry." Kaiser said the banking sector's modus operandi was "Suck the money from the rural areas and feed it to the cities, to the businessmen building factories, who are connected to the military."

In August 1978, Kaiser placed the finished proposal on Abed's desk. (Abed was visiting Jon Rohde in Indonesia at the time, hatching a scheme to treat fatal diarrhea in children—a plan that would fully unfold in the 1980s.) The project, Kaiser wrote, "will be essentially a five-year experiment" to see whether a combination of credit and farmer training would succeed in creating a basis for self-reliance for landless people, who are otherwise "forced to place themselves in the clutches of exploitative moneylenders and traders." The project would open fourteen new BRAC branches in scattered subdistricts, away from its existing locations. Loans and training for groups and individuals alike would be channeled through village organizations, of which every borrower would have to be a member. True to BRAC's Freirean roots, they would all begin the journey with functional-education classes. Loans would only be invested in ventures with the potential to make money, and since the borrowers had no assets to speak of, the vast majority of these loans would be collateral free, with security based on the front-line field staff's thorough investigation of the borrower's ability and the potential profitability of the proposed venture.

With RCTP, BRAC would learn to expand to new areas where it would do just a few things but do them well, as opposed to a host of activities concentrated in one geographic area. It would eventually seek to replicate these activities across the entire country. It was the start of a more siloed approach to development, in which activities were compartmentalized into separate programs largely on the grounds of operational efficiency.

To be clear, Abed never believed that credit alone would emancipate people. He thought it would always have to be linked to some form of borrower assistance, such as training. "Some people, in trying to admire the village folks, proclaim glibly that the farmer knows best," the RCTP proposal said. "BRAC does not go along with that. More often than not, it is precisely because of lack of knowledge of what is best that the farmer is exploited. If knowledge is power, then ignorance is lack of power and powerlessness is the attraction for exploitation. The biggest exploiter of the poor is their own ignorance, and though sometimes a poor farmer is aware of his ignorance, he has no means of removing it."

On its credit operations alone—that is, exclusive of training costs—BRAC projected it would break even on RCTP within five years. It would not end up doing so, but the project was nevertheless considered a success. As Abed had predicted, donors began pushing money toward programs that sought to boost people's incomes, and BRAC would soon receive additional funding to expand the program. Moreover, the loans would benefit BRAC's other businesses and vice versa. A rise in income for smallholder borrowers using the cold storage facility for potatoes would lead to higher loan-repayment rates for BRAC, for instance.

* * *

"I told Abed *Bhai*, 'Sorry, I'm not doing microcredit,'" said Khushi. "I was very much into Freire, and very much into mobilization and getting people their rights," but directly providing services, especially credit, was a different thing altogether for her. Abed transferred Khushi to the training section, but she also pushed back against aspects of that work, since BRAC was providing training to other NGO staff as well as its own. "I said I will not train anyone except BRAC staff in BRAC methods," she said, arguing they would have little control over how other organizations would use the training. "I don't know if they are utilizing it or not. I don't even know if they believe in it or not."

Khushi was not alone. There were at least two others among the senior staff who shared her views. Moreover, a group of eleven junior staff within the organization, which had more than four hundred employees at this point, were dissatisfied enough with their jobs to ally themselves with her—a number that would later grow. "There was a group of us, and we said we are not getting into this kind of thing," she recalled, adding, "There was still a lot of ideology and idealism in people then." By the time BRAC moved into its new five-story headquarters in Mohakhali in 1980, she said she "felt that this was not the BRAC I wanted to be in."

The schism caused an unprecedented level of acrimony within BRAC—and between Abed and Khushi, whom he and Bahar had considered a personal friend. Khushi wrote a letter to the board chair, Begum Sufia Kamal, whom she knew personally, asking the board to intervene. This letter no longer exists, so exactly what it said is disputed, though it is safe to say that it was explosive. According to Abed, Khushi accused BRAC of cronyism, citing the example of hiring Kaiser Zaman, a friend from his business days at Shell. "They engineered a kind of a coup," he said, adding, "The accusation was that he was getting all his friends into BRAC."

The allegations felt deeply personal to him, largely because Khushi had been so close to him and Bahar. "She was a close friend, and that she could do this shocked us," he said, adding that Bahar in particular had considered Khushi "one of her best friends," and the episode left her deeply hurt.

Khushi denied that the letter accused Abed or BRAC of cronyism, pointing out that such an accusation would have been nonsensical given that "this is how I got into BRAC, too." It is worth noting that her father, Akbar Kabir, was still on the board. The letter, she said, was "was about the way BRAC was being run and the way we were being treated." She felt that BRAC was being taken in a direction contrary to its original mission.

Abed said he was also "very angry" with the board chair for the way she handled it. Begum Sufia Kamal was a renowned poet and activist, and Abed had asked her to lead the BRAC board on account of the universal esteem in which she was held in Bangladesh. According to Abed, without first discussing it with him or asking him to respond, she called an immediate meeting of the full board. She had never called an extraordinary board meeting before. Decades later, Abed still expressed irritation, calling it "thoroughly unacceptable" to call a board meeting to grill the founder "just because you've got a letter with lots of innuendo" from one person. He said rumors began to spread within the organization that he was being removed from the executive directorship and replaced by Khushi's father. Abed brought this point up at the board meeting, with Akbar Kabir present. "That board meeting was very acrimonious," Abed said.

The meeting ended inconclusively, with the board chair suggesting to Abed that he find out what it would take to bring Khushi back into the fold. According to Abed's recollection, he spoke to her, and among her conditions was that she be placed in charge of the training division. Abed refused. The demands had nothing to do with microfinance at that point, he insisted. "The demand was who should be posted where and what job they should get."

Khushi's recollection of the affair is markedly different. She emphatically denied ever asking for a promotion, either for her or for anyone else. Nor was there ever any question of her father taking over BRAC, which he never would have agreed to even if asked. The demands were driven completely by ideology, she said: "We were a group of youngsters with a lot of ideology and nothing else." In the early days, BRAC had more space for internal dialogue, she added. "When BRAC began, it was very participatory. Abed would often convince us of his way, and he was very good at that." But that space for dialogue began to contract as the organization grew. In Khushi's view, BRAC had begun to lose sight of the Freirean ethos.

One of the junior staff who allied himself with Khushi was Abdur Razak, the journalist-activist who ran one of the feeding centers in Rowmari and then spent years keeping his eye on the property BRAC still owned there. Abdur Razak, who was then working for BRAC in Jamalpur, said the complaints of the junior group actually had nothing to do with an aversion to microfinance. They were feeling neglected and mistreated by upper management. One particular person charged with approving their requests for time off "treated us as if we weren't even human." They finally decided to quit en masse, drafting a single resignation letter for eleven people and hand-delivering it to Abed, who replied that if they wanted to quit, they each had to write individual resignation letters. "We were so frustrated at this point that we said, 'We're not accepting any more of your rules,' so we just left it there and walked out," he said.

Nevertheless, Abdur Razak credited Abed with handling the situation with such a calm temperament. "He always kept his cool, and when you're talking to someone with that much cool, you can't start screaming and shouting." This perception of Abed—unflappable, almost preternaturally even-keeled—is common among BRAC staff, even while those close to him knew he had a darker side that erupted periodically.

Abed's reputation took a hit as a result of the Khushi affair. "In the NGO circles, there was this feeling that there must be something wrong with BRAC," he said, adding, "The rumor mill had it that the Young Turks have left—and now we'll see how BRAC runs." Akbar Kabir was left off the next slate of candidates Abed put forward for board membership renewal, and Begum Sufia Kamal, feeling sidelined, asked to step down. The new board chair would be Humayun Kabir, Abed's old friend from Glasgow.

Abed and Khushi remained on bad terms for about ten years, but they eventually reestablished a civil relationship. Immediately after she left BRAC, Khushi joined—and soon became head of—an organization called Nijera Kori ("We Do It Ourselves"), which fought for the rights and voices of women in rural communities. She went on to become a prominent feminist and social activist, crediting Abed with teaching her much of what she knew of people's empowerment. She professed to harbor no ill feeling over her rupture with Abed and BRAC, as it was a vital part of her personal journey. It would have been difficult for Abed to pursue his vision for growth if she had stayed, and the split was therefore inevitable, in her view. Khushi was sacked along with the two other senior staff allied with her in August 1980. "If I were Abed *Bhai*, I would have behaved exactly as he behaved," she said. About forty others left shortly thereafter. Khushi later added, "It was good I left when I did. I would definitely not have become what I am today."

On that, Abed and Khushi ultimately agreed. "The clean break was a good thing," said Abed. "It was better to get rid of these people." Far from being hobbled by the schism, BRAC was about to enter its period of most rapid expansion.

* * *

In August 1980, Abed won the Ramon Magsaysay Award, often called Asia's version of the Nobel Prize. Named after a former president of the Philippines, the prize is awarded annually to individuals for outstanding contributions to various fields, including community leadership, Abed's category. Previous winners in the same category included the fourteenth Dalai Lama and, two years before Abed, Ela Bhatt.

As BRAC's first major international recognition, the award helped offset whatever reputational loss the Khushi Kabir fiasco might have caused in Bangladesh and cemented its position as the most prominent Bangladeshi NGO. In the citation's telling of the BRAC story, the first participants were suspicious of "outsiders with strange ideas," but Abed's solution "was to select and train, through non-formal education, alert villagers whose leadership was more readily accepted." BRAC staff "guide, assist, and expedite, rather than direct." Even then, though BRAC was a sliver of what it would grow to be, the award citation described its scale as impressive, with a staff of several hundred "creating local organizations to solve the problems of over 1.34 million people comprising 200,000 rural families in 700 villages."

Bahar, in particular, "loved the fanfare" of the award ceremony in Manila, Abed said. In his brief acceptance speech, he described his mission in language loftier than any he used before—or would ever use again. "Civilization is not the product of a few great men," he said. "It is the cumulative actions of all men, great and small. And yet, today, the majority of mankind are not able to act on their own behalf. They cannot seek food when they are hungry, nor can they seek shelter from sun and rain. Man is no longer a free agent. He is held in bondage by a poverty created by some who want to have more. This poverty is not the absence of resources. It is the unequal sharing of them. Yet when mankind started out it was the need to share which brought men together into communities. But where are the communities of today? They are, today, divided between those who have and control, and those who do not have and are powerless. A community of greed has replaced the community of need."

Years later, Abed admitted this is not something he would have said or written later in life. An older Abed would not posit the existence of a mythical past when people lived in harmony. However, he did write the speech himself. It ended with a call for governments and individuals alike "to ensure that the future struggle to which all give highest priority is the struggle of the powerless to regain their lost humanity." Whether one takes it literally or not, the concept of recovering a humanity that has been "lost"—or, more pointedly, stolen—comes directly from the first paragraphs of *Pedagogy of the Oppressed*, and it captures, as well as anything Abed ever said or wrote, the driving ethos behind BRAC.

16

A LONELY BURDEN

Tamara by now was seven. The family was still living in the house in Eskaton below her grandparents. "I was very friendly with a whole bunch of the slum kids, who would come and play football in our garden and play with our dollhouse," she recalled. She was especially close to two sisters named Subi and Nubi, whose mother worked as a maid in the house.

Mohammad Ali was nearly part of the family. He recalled one incident involving Tamara and Subi. He had driven the girls to the market during a rainstorm and left them in the car while shopping. When he came back, the car was empty. "They had gotten scared, left the car, and went God knows where," he said. "I was ready to lose my mind. I went back home without them, scared for my life."

Apparently, after the girls left the car, Tamara had found a nearby police station. The police had called Abed at home. The fact that Abed has a temper is likely surprising to those who only knew him from a distance, but family and close friends knew he was more than capable of manifesting rage. Marty Chen described his "dark moods," as she called them. "It doesn't come very often, but when he's got a temper, it's like a shadow takes over." When Mohammed Ali arrived home without the children, Abed grabbed him by the collar and struck him. Then he said, "We're driving to the police station." Mohammad Ali began crying on the way. Not until they reached the police station did Abed divulge the fact that the girls had already been found and were safe.

There would soon be one more child to look after. In November 1980, three months after their return from the Magsaysay Awards ceremony in Manila, Bahar found out she was pregnant again. Her first pregnancy had been difficult, and the memory had not faded. "She was not very happy about the pregnancy," said Abed. "She thought, 'Oh my God, I'm going to go through another one.'"

Tamara was old enough to understand that a brother or a sister was on the way. "I remember Dad touching Mum's tummy often, and I remember her being pretty big," Tamara said. "I remember me touching her tummy. All three of us would chat about it." Between themselves, Abed and Bahar hoped for another girl.

The pregnancy had no complications, and on July 10, 1981, at a nearby private clinic run by a well-known obstetrician, Bahar gave birth to a boy. At 10:30 p.m., Abed received the call at home and rushed over, arriving just as Bahar was coming back from the labor room. "Well, it's a boy," Abed said. "I thought we were going to get a girl."

Bahar smiled and replied, "Well, I suppose it's okay—a boy and a girl." They named him Shameran, Old Persian for "candle bearer."

Tamara recalled celebrating her brother's arrival at the house. "Before I went to sleep, we got news from the hospital that Shameran was born. I was at home with all the house help—which was Mohammad Ali, the maid, and Rustum, our cook—and we had our celebration, dancing around, banging pots and pans in the kitchen," she said. "Then I went off to sleep on the living room divan. I didn't go to the bedroom. I was waiting for my dad to come home."

Abed came back to the house briefly to eat supper and returned immediately to the hospital without waking up Tamara. Shortly after his return, the mood in the recovery room changed. "I saw the doctor suddenly becoming worried," he said. "She was taking her blood pressure, and it was going down. She didn't know what was happening." Bahar was still awake. "Obviously there was something going on within her. I don't know if she herself was worried or not, but I saw the doctor getting very worried."

With Bahar's blood pressure dropping rapidly, the obstetrician told him, "I don't know how to deal with this. I don't know what has happened." She asked Abed to go wake up another doctor who lived several houses down the street, about two hundred yards away.

Abed ran to the doctor's house and banged on the door. It was past midnight by now, and Abed waited what seemed an interminable twenty minutes for the doctor to rouse himself and get dressed. By the time they got back to the clinic, Bahar had lost consciousness. They tried giving her oxygen, but there was no oxygen in the clinic's tank. Abed grabbed her shoulders and tried breathing air into her lungs.

Bahar's sister Minu had stayed with her while Abed was fetching the doctor. As Bahar's lungs filled with fluid, she told him, her last words had been "I'm sinking."

Bahar died of a pulmonary embolism, a blood clot that blocks one of the lungs' pulmonary arteries. If there had been oxygen in the tank, it might only have given her a few more minutes of life. Abed reeled in disbelief. Bahar had just been with them, joking about having a boy and a girl. Now she was gone.

In Bangladesh, when a loved one dies, the custom is to immediately go to the home to grieve with the family. Tamara, asleep on the divan, was woken by the arrival of friends and relatives in the middle of the night. "I can't remember who told me my mom had passed away," she said. "But then people started streaming into the house. I was a bit delirious because I had just woken up from a deep sleep."

Bahar's body arrived in the morning and was laid out on the veranda. Mohammad Ali recalled the scene—the body on the veranda, the newborn child in his crib, and guests coming and going. "Abed *Bhai* didn't really speak that much with the guests," he said. "I felt like my heart was shattering, so I could only imagine what he was going through."

In the first days after her mother's death, Tamara did not completely fathom what had happened, in part because of the attention she received from relatives. She recalled her father's aunt, Farida Hasan—Baiju *chachi*, the widow of Sayeedul Hasan—spending an especially large amount of time with her. Having a new baby brother also kept her mind occupied, and there was full-time household staff to help take care of her and the baby. She could not remember her father ever explaining, or needing to explain, what had happened or what would happen. "I remember bonding and connecting silently," she said. "I don't remember any conversations. I remember feelings."

"That kind of shock I'd never had before," said Abed. "Everything sort of changed for me. I'd lost a comrade." Bahar had not just been his wife; BRAC itself had been a joint effort. "So it was very lonely from two angles—one from a personal angle, and another from losing a great partner in running BRAC."

Abed and Bahar had planned to spend the autumn of 1981 in Boston, where the Harvard Institute for International Development had invited him for a semester-long fellowship. Tamara and the newborn were supposed to come as well, with the whole family staying with the Chens, who had just moved there. Marty Chen was herself a visiting scholar at the same institute.

When Bahar died, Abed decided to go to Boston alone, leaving the children with their aunt, Minu. He did not do much in Boston. "I was so depressed that I did not enjoy Harvard," he said. He attended a few seminars and helped Marty edit her book on BRAC's early years, *A Quiet Revolution*, but mainly he remembered feeling depressed. Marty would drive him to the campus, where the university had given him an office, and pick him up in the evening.

Those few months are a blur for Marty, who was herself in shock over the loss of her best friend. Lincoln had just taken a job as the Ford Foundation representative in Delhi, so she was parenting their two children alone while hosting Abed. "I just remember it as an intense, wrenching time," she said.

During his time there, Marty said Abed was actively considering whether to continue BRAC. According to Abed, there was never any question in his mind of giving up. He reflected, however, on the fact that running BRAC would be a lonely business. "At least when Bahar was there, it didn't feel that lonely, the burden of running an organization. But without her it became doubly burdensome."

He also knew Bahar's death would have been unlikely in a richer country. In Bangladesh, even those with access to the country's best doctors were vulnerable. For the majority who gave birth at home with no trained medical personnel present, often on a dirt floor, fear and dread were constant companions. The loss of Bahar strengthened Abed's resolve to eventually tackle the problem of maternal health.

He returned to Dhaka in November, before the Harvard semester was finished. There was concern on Bahar's side of the family that Abed would not be able to raise two children on his own, even with the help of household staff. Another of her sisters, Anu, who had no children of her own, offered to take the children and raise them. "I said no, I want to keep them with me," Abed said.

Years later, he would reflect on this period. The defining aspect of death is that it is certain and final, he said. One cannot fight with it, argue with it, or seek any compromise. "You have to accept and go on, so that's what I did."

Abed's mother, Syeda Sufya Khatun, was a woman of quiet intensity, whom he credited with being his greatest teacher. One of her nephews said, "I used to feel shy just by looking at her." Like many of the women in Abed's life, she died at an unexpectedly early age. (Photo courtesy of BRAC)

The sons of Rafiqul Hasan, Abed's grandfather, were raised in the Calcutta palace of Nawab Syed Shamsul Huda, an eminent Muslim scholar and political leader, pictured here (center), with Abed's father, Siddique Hasan, seated on the left. (Photo courtesy of BRAC)

London, circa 1959. Abed (left) and his East Pakistani friends would meet, drink, and argue about politics and philosophy. Next to Abed is his best friend Viquar Choudhury, with whom he later cofounded BRAC, as well as Faruq Choudhury (center, with glasses) and Zakaria Khan (in profile). (Photo courtesy of Runi Khan)

Abed met Marietta Procopé, the daughter of a former Finnish foreign minister, at a party in London in 1962. The pair quickly fell in love and were soulmates during some of Abed's most formative years. (Photo courtesy of Ann Procopé)

"If you want to live a comfortable life, you shouldn't marry me," Abed told Bahar, pictured here on their wedding day in April 1973. Bahar became deeply committed to the cause of BRAC. She was the mother of Abed's children and a partner at the helm of the organization in its early years. (Photo courtesy of BRAC)

Abed and Bahar with their daughter, Tamara, born in 1974. (Photo courtesy of BRAC)

The BRAC founder, shown here on a dock in northern Bangladesh in the mid-1970s, was known for wearing a suit and tie even when visiting the most remote rural areas. (Photo courtesy of BRAC)

Khushi Kabir (right) with the wife of a Sulla project staffer, circa 1976. One of his first hires, Khushi was a personal friend of Abed's and part of the inner circle of BRAC until she and a group of fellow ideologues split acrimoniously in 1980. (Photo courtesy of Martha Chen)

Aminul Alam (right) was known as Abed's "field marshal" and rose through the ranks within BRAC. He was aggressive and hotheaded, often shouting at subordinates, but his tenacity and work ethic also earned people's loyalty. (Photo courtesy of BRAC)

Sukhendra (Sukhen) Sarkar, a former schoolteacher who joined BRAC in 1973, conducting a refresher training for oral rehydration workers in the early 1980s. Sukhen ran the oral rehydration campaign, a program still cited by scholars as a case study in mass behavior change. (Photo courtesy of BRAC)

Kaniz Fatema (pictured in Manikganj in 1982) had no previous workplace experience when Abed hired her. She often argued with the founder—always unsuccessfully—regarding the rapid expansion of BRAC's children's education program, which she led from its launch in 1985. Abed credited Kaniz with vigilantly guarding the program, which she continued to lead until more than a million students were enrolled in schools under her supervision. (Photo courtesy of Martha Chen)

Abed and Shilu, his second wife, share a laugh on their wedding day in September 1983. A rare Bangladeshi businesswoman, Shilu Abed often challenged her husband. She was the dominant force in his personal life for much of the 1990s, a period of staggering growth for BRAC. (Photo courtesy of Maheen Khan)

Mushtaque Chowdhury (standing left) leads a discussion with Abed as BRAC's head of research in 1986. A young statistician who joined in 1977, Mushtaque built a research unit that acted as an independent shop within BRAC. Though unfailingly courteous in his demeanor, his unvarnished reports did not always make him the favorite of program staff. (Photo courtesy of BRAC)

Sir Fazle Hasan Abed in his later years, visiting a BRAC school. (Photo courtesy of BRAC)

Sir Fazle Hasan Abed and his wife, Lady Syeda Sarwat Abed, at the World Food Prize ceremony in Iowa in 2015. Abed's marriage to Sarwat, a maternal cousin, was his longest, lasting from 2000 until his death in 2019. (Photo courtesy of World Food Prize)

The author with Shahida Begun, whose story starts this book, pumping water for her goats in 2019. (Photo courtesy of Nawrin Nujhat)

17

A SIMPLE SOLUTION

Abed was no stranger to loss, especially when it came to the women in his life. Both his mother, whom he credited with being his greatest teacher, and his beloved sister Nurani had died young, when he was living five thousand miles away in London. Marietta's suicide had shaken him deeply, even though their relationship was already over. Bahar's death, however, affected him on a different level. They had an intellectual bond, plus the bond of running BRAC together, but greater than any of these was the bond of parenthood. Discussing his many relationships, Abed pointed out that the closeness of having children with someone is unrivaled by anything else in life.

Bahar's death brought Abed closer to Tamara, but this closeness was not manifested in fatherly talks. Though she had her own room, when Bahar was alive Tamara would often sleep between her mother and father. After her mother died, Tamara continued to sleep in the same bed as her father until the age of nine, when Abed remarried. According to Tamara, they developed an unspoken emotional bond. It helped that her father did not treat Bahar as a taboo topic, but rather spoke of her freely, at the dinner table and elsewhere, as he would any other topic. "There was always an ease of talking about my mom with him," she said. "It's not like he didn't touch the subject or didn't go there."

This was the child's perspective, in any case. For Abed, the loss of Bahar was a void that could not be filled. He found himself in a deep depression, and the only way to dig himself out was to completely absorb himself in work. To be sure, he had two children at home, but the grandparents were still upstairs. Other relatives and household staff were also on hand to help. "It's a kind of solace to work for others, so BRAC became my sole preoccupation," he said. "That was the only way to sublimate the loss of Bahar."

And there was no shortage of work. Bahar's death came at a time when BRAC was about to enter its first steep growth curve, and Abed would soon have to deal with a new set of problems that arose from scaling up. To give one example, shortly after Bahar's death, Abed got wind of an alarming report about fake data coming from the field, emblematic of the types of large-scale management problems he would have to grapple with from then on. BRAC had recently embarked on an unprecedented campaign to teach mothers how to make their own oral rehydration solution at home. The idea was novel in its simplicity: recent scientific advances had shown that young children suffering from life-threatening diarrhea responded well to a precisely calibrated mixture of water, sugar, and salt administered orally, but success depended on mothers learning the proportions of each. Most women were illiterate and had to be taught in person.

To help ensure the training was effective, Abed developed an incentive scheme whereby the trainers were paid according to whether the mothers remembered how to make the solution. Teams of monitors would go back to the villages, thirty days after the training, to visit a 10 percent sample of those trained. They would quiz the mothers and ask them to demonstrate how to make the solution. They collected samples and sent them back to the Cholera Research Laboratory—now called the International Centre for Diarrhoeal Disease Research, Bangladesh (ICDDR,B)—to measure sodium and glucose content.

The report that had alarmed Abed concerned an unannounced visit of the program's managers to the temporary lodging of one of the monitoring teams. It was a day off, and yet the monitors seemed to be hard at work—mixing the solution themselves and putting it into vials to send to the lab. It was much easier to do this than to walk around in the heat and rain, collecting samples from distant villages. Abed had heard other reports of monitors hanging out at tea stalls, where they would fudge the survey forms instead of putting in the footwork to actually visit people's homes. He realized nobody was monitoring the monitors, even as the program was scaling up to eventually reach millions of households. This gap in the system was potentially fatal, since if the training was off by a big enough margin—say, if mothers were consistently putting too much salt in the solution—the program could end up harming more children than it saved.

It is unclear whether Abed or someone else came up with the solution to this problem; in any case, it was a clever one. Henceforth, during the initial training, the trainer had to ask the first name of the mother's youngest child.

That name was recorded but withheld from the monitor, who had to ask the same question thirty days later, during the follow-up visit. If the names didn't match, it meant the monitor had not actually visited the household.

Abed was proud of this fix and noted years later, almost gleefully, that he'd had to sack many of the monitors.

* * *

When Abed and Bahar went to Manila to receive the Ramon Magsaysay Award in 1980, BRAC had only about three hundred employees. That year, it moved into a new building on land it had purchased for the printing press in Mohakhali, an emerging commercial area north of Dhaka's overcrowded center. Abed had every intention of filling up all five floors. He had parted ways, bitterly, with a handful of upstart radicals who opposed the rapid growth of the rural credit and training program. That program was indeed growing, but the initiative that exemplified BRAC's ambition during the 1980s was the oral rehydration program, a ten-year effort fueled by a $14 million donor commitment to teach mothers across Bangladesh how to save the lives of their own children suffering from diarrhea, the largest killer of children at that time. Abed credited this project with giving BRAC the confidence that it could do things on a massive, nationwide scale. Although the project was conceived and launched when Bahar was still alive, its greatest period of scale-up came after she died. It is fitting that its impetus was saving others from needlessly losing someone they loved.

Abed's interest in oral rehydration therapy—the practice of administering water, glucose, and salts by mouth as a treatment for dehydration—went back years and was driven by several underlying concerns. As a father himself, the first and most obvious concern was for the pain and suffering caused by losing one's child. The under-five mortality rate in Bangladesh was about two hundred per thousand live births in 1980—meaning one in five children did not live to see their fifth birthday. The biggest killer was diarrhea. In places without piped water or sanitation, death would stalk its youngest victims silently in the form of water-borne bacteria, which would cause them to lose fluids and electrolytes through diarrhea faster than their small bodies could replenish them.

Anything that reduced these deaths would be good in and of itself, and yet Abed was also concerned with an even bigger picture—namely, Bangladesh's frighteningly high population growth. In the 1970s, the world seemed to know two things about Bangladesh: poverty and overpopulation. This was the era of *The Population Bomb*, Paul Ehrlich's 1968 bestseller, which predicted—quite wrongly—that the world was on the brink of an inevitable famine caused by overpopulation and that hundreds of millions of people would soon die as a result. Abed was never that pessimistic, but it was hard to discount the fundamental problem of overpopulation. By 1978, Bangladesh had already grown by ten million people since independence—about the population of Greece, added to a land only slightly larger than Greece itself. Economic output could barely keep up. As Abed saw it, without reining in the fertility rate, raising economic output, or both, Bangladesh would remain poor forever.

The link between poverty and fertility is one of the oldest mysteries of development. For reasons still unclear, when people have more money, they tend to have fewer children. The explanations are varied. John Caldwell, an Australian demographer, developed the "wealth flow theory," which posits that fertility is higher in societies where the wealth flows from children to parents rather than vice versa. In Bangladesh society, the value of children was deemed high, in part because it meant more people to work the land. Another theory holds that greater wealth brings greater access to education and contraception, and as economies develop, large numbers of women usually enter the workforce, giving them less time to bear children. In any case, contraceptive prevalence remained stuck in the single digits in Bangladesh, despite the government offering free condoms, pills, and injectables.

As part of BRAC's group discussions, facilitators would introduce the idea of limiting the size of the family. They would ask participants whether having six children (the average number of offspring at the time) was really a good idea, given that household resources were already strained. BRAC offered other family planning education and services. These worked to a limited extent: in Sulla, about 20 percent of couples of childbearing ages began using contraception, far greater than the rest of the country.

That number would not move any higher, though. It wasn't simply that women didn't know about modern methods of contraception, couldn't find them, or weren't allowed by their husbands to use them. In fact, most women were actively choosing to have more children than they could afford, in part because they had so little confidence their children would live to adulthood. Abed reckoned that if they could reduce childhood deaths, the fertility rate would follow. This was neither a guess nor a groundbreaking insight: though counterintuitive, the correlation between under-five mortality and overpopulation was fairly well established by that point.

However, there was another, more personal link that led Abed to embrace oral rehydration therapy as the solution to the problem. He happened to be friends with the people who discovered it.

* * *

Scientists have yet to fully decode the mysteries of the human gut. In the middle of the twentieth century, they were relatively clueless. The mechanisms by which water and electrolytes are absorbed by the small intestine were almost completely unknown. By the late 1950s, building on earlier work on rat and guinea pig intestines, researchers discovered that the presence of sugar (in the form of glucose) greatly accelerates the absorption of water and salt by the membrane of the intestinal wall. However, several years passed before it had any significant practical application. It would prove to be a life-saving discovery in places where cholera and other diarrheal diseases were rampant—places like East Pakistan.

Fast forward to 1968. The scene is Viquar and Runi's house in Gulshan, where friends and neighbors would gather on weekend evenings to gossip among the jasmine vines. Two American doctors from the nearby Cholera Research Laboratory, Richard Cash and David Nalin, were among this crowd of friends, a mix of expats and locals. On weekends, Abed would fly up from Chittagong, where he had a finance job with Shell. They would talk about politics—the East Pakistan question was at the top of everyone's mind—and their research at the cholera lab.

Richard and David had arrived in Dhaka the year before, when they were just twenty-six. Like others at the lab, they were Yellow Berets, the tongue-in-cheek name for young doctors who opted for overseas postings with the US Public Health Service in lieu of being drafted to go to Vietnam. Neither had much expertise with cholera or other diarrheal diseases. Even so, they began testing ways to rehydrate patients orally, building on work conducted six years earlier by a US Navy doctor, Robert Phillips, during a cholera outbreak in the Philippines. The pair had to tread carefully, for Phillips's work—though it showed that absorption of salt was possible in cholera patients only if glucose was present—had ultimately failed. He now happened to be head of the Dhaka lab, and, likely due to his earlier failure, the boss was not overly supportive of the young doctors' work.[1]

One advantage of oral rehydration was its ready availability in rural field settings. The common method for rapid rehydration, a bottle of intravenous fluid, was not practical in places where clinics and hospitals were sparse. Even if one had a steady supply of IV fluid, which was unlikely—its cost was beyond the means of most people in endemic areas—it would be hard to find people who knew how to insert a sterilized needle into a vein. The problem with the oral method, however, was that nobody had found the right protocol in terms of dosage, frequency, mix of ingredients, and how long to administer the solution to the patient.

Working at the lab during a cholera outbreak in 1968, Cash and Nalin finally hit paydirt. Along with two local researchers, Rafiqul Islam and Abdul Majid Molla, they found a protocol that worked, using a precise solution and dosage of glucose and electrolytes—water, sugar, and salts, in lay terms—that eliminated 80 percent of the need for intravenous fluid in the treatment of acute cholera in adults, even for critically ill patients. They published the results in *The Lancet*, the British medical journal, that August, sharing a byline with Phillips to credit his earlier work. Shortly thereafter, they published another paper, showing how the same therapy could work in field settings, far from a hospital. Later, they did the same for non-cholera patients, and still later, for children.[2] *The Lancet* would call this "potentially the most important medical advance this century."[3]

The treatment was a game changer when it came to diarrheal diseases, but it did not catch on widely—in part because it was counterintuitive. If somebody is vomiting and having explosive diarrhea, why would you give them more water? The conventional wisdom, taught worldwide in medical colleges at the time, was to give nothing by mouth during episodes of acute diarrhea and thus to "starve the gut." It seemed to make more sense; it just happened to be dead wrong. During the early 1970s, there were few successful large-scale efforts to promote oral rehydration therapy, and certainly no nationwide efforts undertaken by a government or nongovernmental organization, though the World Health Organization (WHO) and UNICEF were planning global campaigns to promote its usage.

When the Bangladesh Liberation War broke out, Abed's American friends in Dhaka were scattered to the corners of the world. Jon Rohde—the man who, with Viquar, had taken the first Shell dinghy to Manpura—went to Yogyakarta, Indonesia, in 1973 for the Rockefeller Foundation to work on rural health and research projects, including diarrheal disease prevention. Although he had not played a significant role in the groundbreaking research in Dhaka, Rohde was on his way to becoming a global proselytizer for the use of oral rehydration therapy.

According to Jon, he visited Dhaka from Indonesia, likely in 1978, and went to see Abed and BRAC's programs. He and Abed had a conversation, "probably talking over the fire in the evening when we were off in the village."

"What's the one thing that would really change health in Bangladesh?" Abed asked him.

Jon thought for a moment and replied that if every mother in Bangladesh were to spoon oral rehydration solution to her child during bouts of severe diarrhea, the under-five death rate would likely plummet. He soon returned to Indonesia and thought little more of the fireside chat.

Abed, however, dwelled on this conversation. The following year, 1979, had been designated International Year of the Child, and he wanted to do something big—or at least start something big—to mark the occasion. During one of his monthly visits to Sulla, Abed convened a staff meeting under the tin roof of the first BRAC building in Markuli. He asked his colleagues to brainstorm solutions: If they were to launch a large program focused on stopping children's diarrhea, how would they do it? Abed likely knew the answer already but wanted the field workers to come up with it on their own.

The head of the Sulla program at that point was Sukhendra Sarkar, the early hire who had struggled to comprehend *Pedagogy of the Oppressed* before becoming an advocate of Freire's method. Sukhen had soaked up Abed's approach to development—testing new approaches, listening, reflecting, and iterating. He and the other field staff were well acquainted with the myriad health problems that plagued Sulla and were frustrated by their apparent intractability. The first BRAC doctors posted to Sulla had found that about a dozen maladies accounted for 95 percent of all rural health problems, with diarrhea highest on the list for children. Few of these needed doctors to treat them, and yet the many solutions the team had tried—including training local paramedics to go village to village offering services like itinerant salesmen, as well as a micro-insurance scheme—had run into trouble of one kind or another.

The team came up with four solutions to children's diarrhea and discussed the pros and cons of each. The first was drilling tube wells so villagers had access to clean, uncontaminated water. They had already tried this approach and found they were too hard to maintain. The pumps would break and spare parts would be impossible to find; in any case, the villagers did not want to pay to fix them. Asking people to pay for water in Sulla was like selling sand in the desert.

The second idea was flooding the zone with doctors, but they had already tried that, too. There were few doctors local to Sulla, and outsiders did not want to be stationed so far from home. For every ten doctors BRAC recruited in the early years, perhaps one would prove willing to stay in the villages working as a general practitioner for the poor. Besides, Abed did not put much stock in doctors. They rarely thought outside the box; their only fix for diarrheal dehydration would likely be an IV drip, regardless of whether one was available.

The third solution was ORS (oral rehydration salts) packets—small sachets that people could mix with a liter of water to produce just the right proportions of glucose, sodium, potassium, and bicarbonate. This was the solution supported by the WHO, but there were few local manufacturers of these sachets, and back-of-the-envelope math showed that the country would need hundreds of millions of packets annually. Even if production capacity were to skyrocket, the logistics would be insurmountable. There would be no way to get the packets to the villages and distribute them efficiently.

The fourth solution was the clear choice: BRAC would have to teach mothers how to make oral rehydration solution from household ingredients. Due to widespread illiteracy and lack of access to mass media, they would have to do this the old-fashioned way, through face-to-face training.

In Indonesia, a few months after Jon's visit to Dhaka, Jon and Candy received a long-distance call from their old friend. "I want to come see you," Abed said.

According to Jon, "He didn't say anything else, and I thought, 'Well, that's interesting. Come along.' We were delighted to have him stay with us."

When he arrived, Abed asked Jon whether he really meant what he had said—that if he could do just one thing to help Bangladesh's health situation, it would be getting every mother to use oral rehydration. "Absolutely," Jon said. "But how are we ever going to do that?"

"That's *my* problem," Abed replied.

Jon showed him some of the projects he was working on, including one that involved a two-sided spoon—one side for sugar, the other for salt—with the instructions written on the spoon. Abed brought one of these spoons back to Dhaka and showed it to others, who agreed with his hunch that it would never work. Illiterate people wouldn't be able to read the instructions. Moreover, if they depended on an object, once the object was lost, they would no longer feel empowered. In Indonesia, Abed had seen one other reason that neither spoons nor packets could work in Bangladesh without additional training. In Sulla, few people knew how to precisely measure water, whereas in Indonesia, even villagers in the most remote areas knew exactly what half a liter was, if for one reason only: they all had access to Coke bottles.

* * *

Abed's friends and colleagues thought he had lost his mind when he declared, nonchalantly, that BRAC would conduct training on oral rehydration therapy throughout the entire country, in every village, to every mother. The WHO also opposed the plan, a fact that Abed could not help but be proud of. The WHO promoted sachet distribution and argued that it would be dangerous to try to teach illiterate mothers to make their own oral rehydration solution. If the mother got the proportions wrong, the excess sodium might cause more harm than the disease itself. A local WHO representative raised his objection with the government. Abed had more faith in the learning ability of those who lacked formal education, especially women. He found an influential backer in the Swiss Agency for Development and Cooperation, Switzerland's official foreign aid agency, which agreed to fund a carefully monitored project along with Swedish Free Church Aid and, later, UNICEF. The involvement of the Swiss got the WHO off Abed's back.

Abed had read an article in the journal *Tropical Doctor* that explained how one could make the solution properly using only one's fingers as a measuring tool. At his home in Eskaton, he went into the kitchen in the back of the house, normally the domain of his small household staff. According to Mohammad Ali, his bearer, he brought pots and containers out from the kitchen and set them on the dining room table, where Bahar would typically serve tea and samosas. There, he conducted a set of rudimentary experiments, searching for a recipe that anyone, even someone who had never gone to school and knew nothing of standard measurements, could learn by heart. Instead of white sugar, he would need to use *gur*, also known as *jaggery* in India—a sticky, semisolid brown sugar, halfway between molasses and refined sugar—since that was the only type of sugar available in villages. *Gur* contained ordinary sugar, sucrose, which converts into glucose and fructose upon digestion; it also had the advantage of having potassium to potentially offset the diarrheal potassium losses. Using his knuckles to measure the *gur* and salt, he sent several specimens to the lab for testing.

The first field trial started in 1979 in Sulla, the most remote area BRAC had access to. BRAC hired several dozen women, some of whom only had eight years of education, who formed the front-line corps of the program. They called them oral replacement workers (ORWs). Accompanied by a male supervisor who would act as a chaperone, teams of these women began going village to village on the country boats that plied the waters of Sulla. They would knock on doors—where the houses had doors—and convey the messages to every mother on a one-to-one basis.

The team refined the training to ten messages in the pre-pilot phase, including what diarrhea is, how to mix the solution, when to spoon it to a sick child, and when to stop. The ORWs showed the mothers exactly how to mix the solution, and at the end of every training, each was asked to make the solution herself. The days were long. Trainers would spend the day going from household to household and then come back to the camp and have dinner before another set of meetings, sometimes lasting long into the night, reflecting on the day's experience and planning changes for the next day. "Everybody was a researcher," said Sukhen, who was charged with leading the new program. "Every worker was testing, finding the correct messages and methodologies."

To convey the right proportions, they revised, several times, Abed's original recipe using knuckles, eventually landing on the simplest description that worked: "a pinch of salt and a fistful of *gur*" for every *seer* of water. The *seer* was a traditional unit equivalent to about half a liter, but many homes had no measuring containers, so the workers would carry beakers and etch an indelible mark into whatever vessel the household normally used to pour liquid.

⋆ ⋆ ⋆

Abed needed someone to help him crunch the numbers and make sure the project was really moving the needle on child mortality. That person, a young statistician named Mushtaque Chowdhury, turned into one of the stars of the project.

Mushtaque had joined BRAC in 1977, fresh from a bachelor's degree in statistics from Dhaka University. Among his first assignments was conducting a baseline survey of BRAC participants in Manikganj. He lived there for three months, sharing a room with another new recruit, Aminul Alam. The two men could not have been more different—Amin was gruff and often aggressive, Mushtaque was exceedingly polite—but they stayed up late listening to Bengali songs on the radio, the only form of entertainment there. It was the start of a lifelong friendship, one that would shape BRAC's future.

Abed was keen to develop the talent of his staff, especially when it came to population issues. Using a Ford Foundation grant, he paid for Mushtaque to attend a one-year master's program in demography at London School of Economics in 1978. On a visit to London, he and Bahar had met with Mushtaque and told him, according to Mushtaque, "You must come back as soon as you finish your studies, because we are starting a new project that you'll find very interesting, and we need you for that."

"He didn't go much into detail," said Mushtaque. That project was BRAC's oral rehydration program.

Mushtaque knew from the start that it would not be enough for women to simply remember how to make and administer the solution. "Retention was one thing," he said. "Use is different." During the pilot, he conducted a quick survey and discovered a massive gap between knowing and doing. Of the mothers who had received training, only 6 percent said they were using the new knowledge. According to Abed, the problem was evident within weeks of launching the pilot. The workers themselves—the ORWs who were training the mothers—thought the therapy was bogus. It made no sense, after all. Why would a mixture of such common ingredients mean the difference between life and death?

Abed brought all the women to Dhaka for a crash course on the basic physiology of rehydration at ICDDR,B, one of the world's most notable hubs of scientific research on diarrheal disease. They learned how diarrhea depletes the body of vital water and sodium and how sugar aids in the absorption of both of these through the intestinal wall. Despite their limited formal education, the women quickly grasped the science behind it. What's more, they saw profoundly dehydrated cholera patients coming to the ICDDR,B hospital and recovering thanks to the solution. From then on, all trainers would receive a similar backgrounder.

After the next iteration of training, the usage rate improved to 18 percent, which was still dismal. "Then we were very unhappy," said Abed. Mushtaque returned to Sulla to find out what was happening. Now the problem lay with the men in the household. The logic of focusing the training on women had been sound, on one level. The mothers were nearly always the ones who took care of sick children, and the men were usually at work in the fields when the training took place. But this failed to take account of the norms of rural households. When a crisis happened—and a child having life-threatening diarrhea constituted a family crisis—the men stepped in to make the important decisions. These roving bands of women who had come to the village during the day had no credibility with the men. In fact, they most closely resembled the government's unpopular family planning workers. Rumors would even spread through the villages that oral saline fluid would make people sterile.

After some discussion, the program management team decided that the male supervisor, who usually just sat in the boat all day while the women did all the work, could make himself useful. While the all-female ORWs were in the village doing the training, the supervisor would go to the next village, convene the men, develop a rapport, and brief them on the purpose of the next day's training. The men present at these meetings would include the village elders and even local purveyors of quack cures. Moreover, the ORWs themselves were instructed to actually drink the potion in front of the trainees to convince them it did not cause sterility.

This went on, one iteration after another. At one point, Mushtaque brought his wife, Neelofar, to the pilot site to observe the training. She was not impressed. "The way these women are teaching, they sound like parrots!" she told him. "There is no genuine conversation." Mushtaque relayed this note to Sukhen, who changed the training, adding visual aids and making it more interactive.

When the self-reported usage rate reached 50 percent, the team felt confident that the system was good enough to replicate and scale up throughout the country. "Once 50 percent use it and get effective results, then the others will be influenced," said Sukhen. "Then the demonstration effect will happen."

An incentive salary system formed a pillar of the program. The team decided, no doubt with Abed's guidance, that a flat salary would not get the most from ORWs. Instead, for each mother trained, they would receive the equivalent of zero to 27 US cents, according to the 1980 exchange rate. The exact rate would depend on how many of the ten points the mothers remembered thirty days later; however, for the ORW to receive anything, the mother had to at least remember how to make the solution correctly. Based on this calculation, an average ORW received the equivalent of about $40 per month, a decent wage at the time.

In 1980, with the system nearly perfected after nine months of piloting, the program began sweeping across the country. Each team consisted of about fifteen female ORWs, a male supervisor, and a cook who worked tirelessly to feed them all. They would travel the countryside together on public transport, often mistaken for roving performers of *jatra*, a Bengali folk theater, like a roving troupe in Elizabethan England. The local Union Council, the elected local government, would typically offer them a couple of rooms, which might be a schoolhouse or even a cowshed. When Sukhen visited one of the teams in Baniachong, Abed's home district, he was given a floor mat and a blanket to sleep on. He woke in the morning to find his blanket and clothes soaked in cow urine.

Mushtaque would continue to write monthly memos to Sukhen and his team, presenting the monitoring data on knowledge retention, the survey data on usage, and his subjective impressions from field visits. He and Abed also presented their findings to an advisory committee of experts—including Richard Cash, by then an instructor at Harvard School of Public Health—which would meet several times per year. Mushtaque worked full time on the program for two years. His unvarnished reports did not always make him the favorite of the program staff, though he minimized friction by being transparent and courteous. Abed's unqualified support helped more than anything, according to Mushtaque. Based on this feedback loop, modifications continued even as the program scaled up, with tweaks like cross-checking the name of the youngest child and reducing the ten points to just seven.

The project took ten years, ending in 1990, by which point BRAC had trained more than thirteen million mothers. Sadly, Bahar, who died just one year after the first phase of scale-up began, did not get to see the results.

* * *

For millions of middle- and upper-class Bangladeshis in the cities, the first they heard of BRAC was through radio and TV spots promoting oral rehydration, produced to reinforce the in-person training. Those who grew up in Dhaka in the 1980s can still recall, like a jingle stuck in one's head for life, the exact language of the Bengali-language ads, ending with "a message from BRAC." When the campaign ended, oral rehydration was part of the culture. Bangladesh still enjoys one of the highest oral rehydration usage rates in the world. In tandem with the fall in child mortality, the fertility rate plummeted, as Abed predicted it would, and is now roughly at replacement level.

How many lives were saved? From the beginning, Abed's intention was to measure the program's impact in terms of the reduction in childhood deaths. Mushtaque's work found that attributing causality was easier said than done, however. Registration of both births and deaths was spotty, and the reason for a child's death was often left unknown, with malnutrition, pneumonia, malaria, and measles joining diarrhea as leading factors. Despite this, he collaborated with other experts in the field to conduct five census-style surveys at six-month intervals in villages where BRAC conducted the training. Before and after the training, the data recorded a statistically significant decline in child mortality for children one to four, the exact age when deaths from diarrhea can be most expected. Nonetheless, with no control group—and to be sure, ethical concerns would likely have prevented the creation of a control group, given that the therapy was already known to save lives—it was difficult to attribute these changes to the program, at least according to rigorous scientific standards. BRAC therefore shied away from stating how many lives they must have saved. Mushtaque, who went on to write his PhD dissertation on the program at the London School of Hygiene and Tropical Medicine (along with a later book, *A Simple Solution*, cowritten with Richard Cash), concluded that mortality studies of this nature are costly and their value limited.[4]

Few experts in the field question the program's success, however, and scholars continue to consider it a case study in mass behavior change. A 2019 study in the peer-reviewed *Journal of Global Health* combed through the historical data to examine the drivers that made Bangladesh such a success in reducing childhood diarrheal deaths. The mortality rate for children under five attributable to diarrhea dropped steadily, year by year, in an almost straight line from 1980 until about 2005, by which time it was about 86 percent lower than when the program began. According to the authors, although BRAC's program was not the only cause for this decline, it was probably the most significant factor, especially in the early years before packets became widely available. Using 1980 as a baseline, oral rehydration accounted for forty-four thousand lives saved in the year 2000 alone.[5] If only a portion of these were attributable to BRAC's work, it would likely mean that hundreds of thousands of people are alive today thanks to Abed's decision to launch the program—a decision that many, at the time, thought was foolhardy.

Abed enjoyed telling a story about Donald Henderson, the American epidemiologist who headed the WHO's smallpox eradication program. Smallpox was one of the great scourges of human history; it is the only human disease, thus far, that we have eradicated completely. In 1978, at a meeting in Kenya to announce that smallpox had finally been removed from the face of the earth, Halfdan T. Mahler, the WHO director-general, turned to Henderson and said, "So, Dr. Henderson, what is the next disease to be eradicated?"

Henderson took the microphone and replied, "Bad management."

Like many successful public health programs before and since, ridding the world of smallpox was not merely—or even mainly—a medical issue. It was an incredibly complex management problem that involved thousands of human actors with competing interests and diverse cultures, operating under conditions that included abject poverty, widespread illiteracy, civil war, and famine.

Abed understood that delivering knowledge of oral rehydration was not a question of what medicine to deliver—the "medicine," in this case, was about as simple as you can get—but a question of how to deliver it. That "how" depended on excellent management. Though bottom-up community involvement was essential, tight top-down supervision, with carefully calibrated checks and incentives, was equally so.

For most people in Bangladesh, as elsewhere in the world today, it was long assumed that the death of one's child was a matter decided by fate and perhaps ordained by a higher power, like the monsoon rain or the phases of the moon. Giving women the knowledge that they needed to wrest this decision from the hands of fate and save their own children's lives was not just a triumph of good management. It was also the pinnacle of human empowerment.

18

CHANGING THE PATTERN

The drama and disruption that took place around the turn of the decade—including the schism with Khushi and her group, BRAC's growth and its move into the multi-story headquarters in Mohakhali in 1980, and the death of Bahar in 1981—signaled a turning point in Abed's life. He was no longer a local "oddity" on the Dhaka scene, as Ian Smillie described him in the early 1970s, but a national figure and, increasingly, someone whose opinion was sought internationally. His inner turmoil was not easily read by others. "My dad's way of coping with grief and loss is basically to put himself into his work," said Tamara. In the years to come, he retained his outward poise but became susceptible to darker moods, including infrequent but explosive outbursts.

On the home front, Abed found life as a widower too lonely. He admired the example set by Golam Kabir, the father of Humayun Kabir, whose mother died when Humayun was four. He was impressed that the man never remarried and therefore spent half his life as a widower, even with children to look after. "I am in awe of people who have done that," Abed said. He could not. The void left by Bahar's death was too great, especially when he came home from work. He craved the domestic normalcy of a marriage.

In 1983, two years after the death of Bahar, his aunt Baiju became his matchmaker again, introducing him to a businesswoman named Nazme Ara Ahmed, who went by the name Shilu. They married on September 27, 1983, less than six months later. A widow whose husband had died in 1974, Shilu was an extrovert, a socialite, and a driven entrepreneur, having launched two restaurants and two craft shops, including one at the Dhaka Sheraton. Though she had sold her companies, she remained active in business associations promoting the handicrafts industry. "She was not the social service type," Abed said. "She was more business-oriented, but she loved crafts and craftspeople."

It would have been difficult for anyone to step into Bahar's role, both as a mother and in commanding the respect that Abed's first wife had within BRAC, so any comparison is bound to be unfair. That said, Shilu Abed was the polar opposite of the quiet, bookish Bahar. Shilu cared about clothes and makeup in a way that Bahar never had, and she liked it when people mistook her for a foreigner, often dying her hair red. Although she had two older children—her daughter, Maheen, was seventeen, and her son, Marco, was in his early twenties when she married Abed—she was not especially motherly. That Abed remarried so soon, and to a person whose personality was so plainly different, caused friction with Bahar's family, especially the children's aunts. "There was no problem with the older generation," said Abed, referring to Bahar's parents. "It was the younger generation that thought maybe Shameran and Tamara would not have the right kind of mother." Bahar's sister Minu, who had been present at her death, stopped speaking to him entirely.

Tamara, age nine, did not take the news well, either. Abed recalled her being "very angry." He told Shilu, "Look, maybe Tamara should get a bit older before we get married."

Shilu, who had already gone nine years without a husband, would have none of it. She replied, "Either we get married or we don't."

"There was no point in waiting another seven years for Tamara to grow up," Abed said. He decided Shilu was right and reasoned with Tamara, who "was a little unhappy for a week or so, but after that, she was fine. She was a child, after all."

Tamara, reflecting on her initial reaction and how quickly she got over it, said that even at such a young age, deep inside she knew that getting remarried was the best thing for her father. "There's no way I was expecting that at the age of forty-five, he would get widowed and remain single for the rest of his life." She soon became protective of her father in the face of those who commented on his decision. "When other people would mention to me, 'Oh, your dad got remarried,' I would always fiercely defend him—like with my aunts, other family members, or the house help."

Tamara went on to have a strong relationship with "Shilu Auntie," as she called her stepmother. "I would actually hang out with her one-on-one quite a bit," she said. "I would decide with her what she was going to wear, matching her jewelry with her clothes. I would put nail polish on her hands. I would pin up her sari before she went out for dinner." She added,

"She is a big influence on my life. She made me strong. She'd always talk about being a strong woman."

Abed and Shilu complemented one another in many respects, for while Abed was by no means antisocial, he had a limited appetite for socializing, whereas Shilu was a "networking guru," according to her daughter, Maheen Khan. While Abed was living in London in the 1960s, Shilu had been one of East Pakistan's few female entrepreneurs. On the personal side, marrying Shilu forced Abed out of his shell. Maheen recalled that her mother once joked, "When I go to parties, I get lost, because I know Abed is going to say, 'Let's go home.' I get lost so we can stay a little longer." On the professional side, Shilu took over the management of Aarong, BRAC's handicraft shop, and within two years began expanding it to new retail locations.

The relationship was more equitable than Abed's first marriage, but it was also far less harmonious. Bahar had looked up to Abed, and they never argued. Shilu, however, possessed a special talent for getting under his skin, and although he "didn't try to crush her style or control her," according to Tamara, both husband and wife were prone to combativeness in their relationship. "When they would fight, it would erupt. They had the ability to get pretty angry with each other and scream at each other, and then it would be over," said Tamara. The topics were rarely anything of consequence. "She had the ability to really irritate my dad, but she would also have the ability to stand up to my dad and tell him like it is. Not many others did that." As Tamara grew older, she acquired her stepmother's strong will and sometimes even found herself taking Shilu's side in the arguments. She would have her own fights with her father as she entered adolescence, and then adulthood, and credits her stepmother's influence with giving her the confidence to hold her own: "I think I got the guts to scream at him from her." Abed could be rational to a fault, failing to understand others' feelings—why they might be upset, or how their feelings motivated their behavior, for instance. "My dad is sometimes emotionally very clueless," said Tamara. "He can irritate the hell out of me."

By the time Abed's son, Shameran, who was born in 1981, started forming his own memories, Abed and Shilu were already married. Shameran therefore grew up calling her *Amma*, or "Mom," even though he always knew his real mother had died giving birth to him. The fact that Shilu did not fit the mold of Bangladeshi women of the time—she drove her own car and went to work, which was not typical, for instance—was "probably what drew my father to her," said Shameran. It also led to many of their conflicts.

Shameran recalled his father having an air of impatience about him throughout his upbringing. True explosions were rare, but they happened. "Anything taking time would irritate him," he said. "But he almost never lost his cool. You wouldn't see him getting upset or angry a lot—but then sometimes he would, and when his temper went, it was a sight to behold. God help you if you were on the receiving end of one of those. Growing up, the one time a year my father lost his cool—oh my God, we just ran away." Once, when his sister was a teenager, Shameran recalled his father getting so angry at Tamara that Shameran thought he might hit her, and she had to leave the house and stay with relatives for several days. "I was too young to remember what it was, but I saw that a few times. It was scary."

Few people knew this side of him at work, especially in BRAC middle management. Notably, even some of his senior colleagues claim they never saw him get angry. It is unclear whether this is because they genuinely never experienced it or if they chose their memories to reflect a cultivated myth of imperturbability. "I worked as BRAC advisor for sixteen years," said Faruq Choudhury, an old friend from the London years who joined as a senior advisor in the early 1990s. "I can't think of a single occasion where I found him agitated or angry."

* * *

By the mid-1980s, Abed was traveling abroad enough that even his young son noticed. Starting with the launch of the school program in 1985—a story told in full in the next chapter—Abed was preparing BRAC for its biggest growth period, which would come in the 1990s. "I remember him being away a lot," Shameran said. "Even on birthdays, he would typically be somewhere else, and I'd get a call from some other part of the world." He recalled Abed phoning from Nairobi on his fourth birthday in July 1985, one of his first memories. It is impossible to think that this absence did not have an effect on his family; perhaps even more notable is the fact that they so readily approved of it. "From early on, we got a sense that he was doing something very important," Shameran said. "We knew we were going to have to share him with his work, and that was okay."

The shifts on the home front in the early 1980s coincided with a change in how Abed thought about his work. Though he remained focused on changing Bangladesh, his concerns started to be more global, for, at the very least, he would need to expose himself to trends in international development by attending conferences and visiting donors abroad. Being on the road boosted Abed's confidence, as there were few others doing what he was doing on the same scale—and even fewer organizations that were indigenous to what was then called the "Third World." He viewed his approach as entrepreneurial, in the sense of being willing to try new ideas and take calculated risks, even if the gains he was pursuing were non-financial.

In 1987, Abed received a visit from an American named Bill Drayton, a former consultant for McKinsey & Company who had served in the Carter administration. Drayton had started an organization, Ashoka, that sought to create a global network of what he called "social entrepreneurs," a term he popularized. He was seeking like-minded people from around the world and found a kindred spirit in Abed. "When I arrived in Bangladesh, our approach was to go to everyone who looked like they might belong to our community," Drayton said. "So of course, we went to see Abed as one of those people. And of all of those people, he is the one who understood it instantly—and I have a lot of practice watching people hear this for the first time."

Drayton had a theory to explain the phenomenon of social entrepreneurship, which he situated in sweeping historical terms. He thought Abed, by thinking innovatively to tackle issues that had previously been the exclusive domain of governments, was in the vanguard of a global shift in how social problems are solved. From Drayton's point of view, societies had long been divided into the commercial and social halves—the one concerned with business, the other with human welfare. From ancient Rome to about 1700, the West saw close to zero growth in per capita income. It then exploded because the business half became competitive and innovative. From 1700 to roughly 1980, the social half remained stagnant and lagged behind, for two related reasons: first, governments found it easy to pay for social sector programs like schools and welfare systems by taxing the burgeoning business sector, thus relieving the pressure on anyone else to solve those problems; and second, governments maintained a monopoly on such programs, which stifled competition. The gap between these sectors became too large to sustain around 1980, when rising democratization of societies led to an increasingly innovative and competitive "citizen sector."

Drayton thought social entrepreneurs like Abed and Yunus would drive the citizen sector in the future. "The defining quality of leading social entrepreneurs is that they cannot rest until they have changed the pattern in their field *all* across society," Drayton would later write.[1] A business owner out to make money for himself is just a business owner; one who strives to change the way business is done across the board is an entrepreneur. The same holds for the social sector, according to Drayton. There were social entrepreneurs in the past, including Florence Nightingale, who did not just care for wounded soldiers but also modernized the practice of nursing, and Maria Montessori, who did not just teach well but also redefined good teaching. They were exceptions, however. Increasingly, social workers would be replaced by social entrepreneurs like Abed who, in part because the government was so incapable of solving the country's problems, would compete in the marketplace of ideas with solutions that aimed to change entire societies. "Abed was at the cutting edge of the whole system changing," said Drayton.

Abed bought into Drayton's theory and became a member of Ashoka's World Council, selecting social entrepreneurs to receive Ashoka fellowships. "I want to do this because you have spotted a global pattern," he said, according to Drayton.

At the start of the decade, BRAC was already working in every major area of human development except one—children's education. When he met Drayton in 1987, even that had changed, for, by then, Abed was two years into a program that exemplified the shift Drayton described, as it attempted to change the ways of a moribund state monopoly. In the realm of schooling, Abed would indeed try to change the pattern of the whole field.

19

THE ONE-ROOM SCHOOLHOUSE

There is a tale that lives on in BRAC lore of a mother in an adult education class who asks, "What about our children? Must they grow up illiterate and wait until they are old enough to come to your program?" That question inspired BRAC to launch its own schools in 1985, setting off a decade of eye-popping growth for its education program—or so the story goes. The anecdote about the mother first appeared in a 1993 annual report and has been repeated countless times, but it is likely apocryphal. Many staff, and likely some participants, had asked a similar question, but, according to Abed and others involved in the school program, there was no one mother who set it all in motion.

The real story is better than the myth. By the mid-1980s, children's education was one of the few areas of human development that BRAC had yet to explore. Most participants' children did not attend school. No matter how much help they gave the parents, Abed knew they would never break the intergenerational cycle of poverty if this did not change. Children's education had long been part of his plan, according to Abed. When his daughter Tamara was born in 1974, he thought BRAC would have opened schools by the time she was old enough to attend one. Reality did not keep pace with this ambition due to the myriad problems with the Sulla program and the slow pace of development in general; nor were donors ready, at that point, to fund schools run by an NGO. As time went on, Abed also realized the educational needs of the children of landless laborers differed radically from Tamara's situation. To start, their parents would be illiterate, and they would likely enter primary school never having held a pencil. Tamara would never fit into such a school. It would call for an entirely different model attuned to the needs of children born into poverty.

By 1985, BRAC was finally ready. It launched a small pilot of alternative schooling, geared exclusively toward children from extremely poor households. These one-room village schoolhouses became BRAC's Model T Ford: they may not have invented the model, just as Ford did not invent the automobile, but they designed a system of mass replication that took it to the largest scale the world had ever seen. From the initial pilot of twenty-two schools in 1985, the number of schools and students multiplied annually, eventually creating what was almost certainly the world's largest nongovernmental, nonreligious school system.

Abed set bold and, some argued, unrealistic goals for this program. At one point, he declared an ambition to open one hundred thousand schools. He had to stop expanding at "only" sixty-four thousand. He would often clash with his chief deputy in charge of education, a woman named Kaniz Fatema, who had a psychology degree but no previous workplace experience. Kaniz would often tell him such rapid expansion was impossible—and then proceed to do it anyway, until she found herself in charge of tens of thousands of schools educating more than a million students.

The real hero of the story is neither Abed nor Kaniz, however. It is a teacher—or, rather, tens of thousands of them.

★ ★ ★

When they first began popping up around Bangladesh, these one-room schoolhouses were sometimes likened to American prairie schools, where a local woman in a frontier settlement taught all the neighbors' children in a single group. Mazeda Khatun was one such woman. She was born in the backwaters away from the main market area of Manikganj, where bamboo footbridges cross swamps and streams, and paths are built on steep embankments lined by straw heaps and pumpkin vines. In 1985, this was not a frontier in any physical sense, for it was only forty miles from Dhaka, with regular bus service to and from the capital. But it was a frontier of development in the sense that about half the children in the area were beyond the reach of the state-run education system. To be sure, there were government primary schools nearby, but they were ill equipped to serve children from poor families, and, as a result, only the better off attended.

In 2019, Mazeda sat on the same plot of land on which she had been born, one of nine siblings, six decades earlier. She recalled the events of her life with a thoughtful expression and, occasionally, a wicked sense of humor. "When I was young, we had one room," she said. "All nine of us would sleep on a single bed with our parents on the floor. There were so many holes in the roof that when it rained we would roll up the bedding and put plates and saucers everywhere." This by itself was nothing extraordinary, as most of her neighbors in Manikganj were similarly poor, but one aspect of Mazeda's upbringing stood out: unlike most girls, she was kept in school by her parents until the age of sixteen, when they finally married her off.

Mazeda's husband died in a bicycle accident while she was pregnant with her second child. Relations quickly soured with his family, so she returned to her parents' village. "My husband's younger brother behaved very badly with me, and I didn't want to put up with it," she said. "I came back here and never left." As a widow with landless parents, there was little she could do to support herself. She earned tiny sums tutoring school-going children, who knew her as "madam," but she barely survived on this pittance. On some days, her meals consisted of the starchy water that remains after boiling rice.

In 1985, a former neighbor visited to share news of an opportunity that turned out to be life changing. The neighbor had moved to a nearby village where a new type of primary school would soon open. It needed a local teacher. Getting a job as a government schoolteacher required a secondary school certificate and months of formal training, usually coupled with good connections with local officials and perhaps a payoff. However, this job was different. The school would be run by BRAC, an organization Mazeda knew slightly from its activities in the area. To teach in this school, all one needed was a tenth-grade education—Mazeda's one meaningful asset.

More details about BRAC's plans soon filtered out into the community. Mazeda learned that each classroom would have only thirty students, mostly between the ages of eight and ten, compared to a national average of fifty-one students per classroom in government schools. The "honorarium" for teaching would be just 250 taka per month, then the equivalent of about $10.

She recalled the day of her interview at the local BRAC office. "We were seated in a room, and most of us had never been in an interview before," she said. "In the back of my mind, I knew this was an opportunity I couldn't miss, for it would mean I could support my family. If I didn't get this job, I'd be back to where I started. I was the third one to be called into the interview. When the other two came out, before I had a chance to ask them what the questions were, I was called into the room. I walked in and sat down." Across from her were a group of BRAC people, including a woman about twenty years her elder. "Nobody introduced themselves."

The older BRAC woman asked her to state her name and livelihood. Mazeda explained that she walked around the village giving lessons to the neighbors' children. The woman then asked Mazeda how many children she had of her own. Thinking of her two children and the planned size of the BRAC classroom, Mazeda deadpanned, "I have thirty-two children." That was the end of the interview, she said. She got the job—one of the first batch of twenty-two BRAC schoolteachers.

★ ★ ★

Some may have argued that Mazeda, so obviously underqualified and untrained, had no business being a schoolteacher. Yet BRAC's teachers, of which she became one of the best and longest serving, were the lynchpin of a system that would go on to produce better results than government schools in terms of drop-out rates and standardized testing. This was despite the obvious disadvantages of the pupils, many of whom were the first in their families to learn to read and write. In fact, one of the most miraculous aspects of the growth and quality of the BRAC education program was that almost no one in the chain of command—from Abed on down—had a formal background in education.

The older woman interviewing was Kaniz Fatema, the head of the program, who had never worked in a paying job before she joined BRAC through family connections, four years earlier in 1981. Kaniz's brother, four years her elder, was Humayun Kabir—Abed's old friend from Glasgow, now the board chair of BRAC. She had been born in Calcutta in 1935, the last of five children. Their mother, Sara, died when Kaniz was two weeks old. Her father Golam—the loud snorer, who so impressed Abed by never remarrying—was a senior officer in the provincial government of Bengal under the British Raj. At Partition, he opted for Pakistan, so Kaniz continued her education in East Pakistan, where she eventually married and had four sons in Dhaka, surrounded by her extended family.

In 1979, Kaniz's fourth and youngest son, age six, attended a birthday party and, for reasons that never became clear, woke up vomiting that night. Kaniz gave him anti-nausea medication and reluctantly took him to the hospital after he continued throwing up. "I'm scared of hospitals, so I was hesitant," she recalled. "But I really didn't know what to do." He was admitted and was supposed to stay overnight. "They said he would be discharged in the morning."

But in the early morning, her son—"a totally healthy child, very joyful"—unexpectedly died. She was told the hospital staff had mistakenly over-administered intravenous saline. Barely able to eat or sleep, Kaniz sank into a state of depression for more than a year. She sought treatment from a psychiatrist, "but it didn't help me," she said. "I had to take so many tablets, seven or eight, that he said, 'This is the limit. After that, we can't give you more.'" Eventually, her brother Humayun suggested she travel to the United States, where one of her sons was studying in Chicago, for a change of scene. "The traveling really helped, because I had to cook, I had to clean, I had to do everything," Kaniz recalled. "My son was a student, so we didn't have much money." Her condition improved over several months.

She realized that to avoid the cloud of depression, she needed to stay busy, so when she returned to Dhaka, she asked her brother where she might find a job. Though she had a master's degree in psychology and had volunteered with social welfare groups like the All Pakistan Women's Association, Kaniz had no work experience. She had been a housewife her entire life. Her brother inquired with Abed about having her work at BRAC. According to Kaniz, her brother said to Abed, "My sister needs a job, but not only a job—she needs a lot of work. She must be given a kind of job where she has to work really hard."

Abed replied, "We'll see what she can do."

⋆ ⋆ ⋆

Kaniz entered the organization in the midst of a period of rapid growth and uncertainty. The conversation between her brother and Abed took place just prior to the unexpected death of Bahar Abed on July 10, 1981. When Kaniz appeared for her first day of work on August 11, the organization was reeling from the loss of one of its most beloved figures. The wounds of the rupture with Khushi Kabir and her faction were also still fresh. Meanwhile, the organization had just doubled in size. In the year after moving into its new five-story headquarters in Mohakhali in 1980, the full-time employee headcount grew from 471 to 1,067. Its annual operating budget jumped from $1.4 million to $2.4 million, driven by the growth of the oral rehydration campaign and the Rural Credit and Training Program (RCTP), which in 1981 had twelve thousand members in its village organizations.

Kaniz and Abed were the same age, and they maintained a formal and respectful relationship. It is unlikely they ever opened up to one another on a personal level. Had they done so, they would have found they had much in common, both immersing themselves in work to fill the void left by loss. Kaniz floundered during her first years at BRAC, however, struggling to find her place within it. The emptiness continued to tear at her every day when she returned from work.

The solution was long hours. The growing programs required continual training of BRAC participants, field staff, and the expanding ranks of middle management, so there was a pressing need for good trainers, and Abed initially thought the job might suit Kaniz, given her psychology degree. "When she came on the scene, I put her in the training department," he recalled. "I didn't think she was very happy there."

Kaniz confirmed this: "I'm not the trainer type." She shifted to the materials development unit, which was always producing new posters and training materials. "As a materials developer, I didn't have any kind of assigned job description, so it became quite boring," she said. "I was very excited about the whole thing, but there was no work at all." To keep her mind occupied, she would browse development journals and photocopy the articles she found interesting and then share them with senior management.

In late 1981, when Abed was in the United States for his Harvard fellowship, one of the administrative heads at BRAC asked Kaniz whether she would be interested in representing BRAC at a workshop on adult literacy organized by the Institute for Education Research at Dhaka University. At the workshop, Kaniz asked questions with a newcomer's lack of guile. "There were a lot of NGOs talking about adult literacy programs," she said. "I asked people, 'You are talking a lot about adult literacy programs. Don't the parents ask about their children's education?' They said, 'Yes, they do ask us about their children's education, but you know—the problem is funding.'"

When Abed returned from the United States, Kaniz confronted him with the same question, which he had likely heard many times by now. He informed her of an existing pilot school for children at the BRAC training center in Savar, on the outskirts of Dhaka. These classes, an experiment that remains undocumented in official reports, were an attempt to teach children at the primary level along Freirean lines. Children learned from a set of posters that contained just one word each. Kaniz was not impressed. "It looked very odd," she said.

Kaniz was an outlier in BRAC in several respects. She had never had her "Freire moment"—the epiphany that BRAC's early cadre experienced with *Pedagogy of the Oppressed*. Even after exploring BRAC's functional-education program, she remained skeptical that the adults who attended the classes were actually learning to read. "They did have an animated discussion, which I liked," she said. "But the literacy-numeracy part was very poor."

Impressed by Kaniz's natural curiosity, Abed encouraged her to explore the topic of children's education. She started digging. Outside of work, her depression did not abate for ten years, she said—which explains why, when she finally found a project she wanted to pursue, she threw herself at it with abandon.

* * *

Though the 1972 constitution demanded it, by the 1980s Bangladesh still did not have a law extending free and compulsory education to all children, and it would not pass one until 1990. In reality, such a law would have made little difference. Other low-income countries had them on the books and found them unenforceable. In India, for instance, where primary education was compulsory, nearly 55 percent of children from the primary age group (roughly six to eleven) were not going to school. The numbers were similar in Bangladesh.

The challenges were well known, even to a newcomer to the field like Kaniz. In rural areas, it was hard to find locals who qualified as government teachers and often harder to find trained government teachers willing to live in rural areas. Of those who were hired, many received their jobs in exchange for kickbacks to local bosses. The rate of teacher absenteeism was shocking and it remains so in many countries today. (In 2017, researchers conducted surprise visits to about twenty-one thousand classrooms in seven countries in Africa and found that, 44 percent of the time, the teacher was not present in the classroom during periods of purported instruction.[1])

Moreover, "free" state education was never truly free. In addition to having to pay for clothes, shoes, transportation, lunch, and various other fees—including the cost of supplemental tutors, such as Mazeda, without whom no learning would take place—parents had to consider the substantial opportunity cost of sending their children to school. Starting from a young age, children were needed to help earn money for the family. This could mean feeding the animals, gathering firewood, or caring for younger siblings. Even if they were not earning money directly, they would be doing essential work that would otherwise have to be done by an income earner.

A myth persisted that parental awareness was to blame. If only parents' attitudes would change, enrollment rates would rise, or so the thinking went. However, in many respects, parents were actually making a calculated, rational decision: given the poor quality of the education their children would receive in government classrooms, sending them to school was not worth the cost.

Kaniz began looking for a viable model of schooling that met the needs of children born into poverty. The hours of schooling would also have to be short, flexible, and convenient to account for the need for children's help at home. Nor could the teaching rely on parents supporting their children's learning at home—by helping them with homework, for instance. No model that she was aware of dealt with these issues, nor was there one that addressed the lack of qualified teachers in rural areas.

In the library of the local UNICEF office, one booklet caught Kaniz's eye: a UNICEF periodical called *Assignment Children*, which had dedicated an entire issue to emerging forms of "nonformal education," a term that had slowly gained traction in development circles since its emergence in the 1960s. As development jargon, the term was vague, encompassing any teaching that took place outside the walls of a traditional classroom, including Freirean functional education, farmer training, and even children's gymnastics classes. One article in particular, describing a specific nonformal approach directed at primary-age children in India, struck a chord with Kaniz.

Authored by Chitra Naik, a prominent Indian pedagogue and social worker, the article described an "action-research" project targeting out-of-school children. In areas near the city of Pune, about three hours inland from Bombay, the Indian Institute of Education, which Naik had cofounded with her late husband, ran about two hundred experimental "schools" that looked nothing like schools in the traditional sense. Classes took place anywhere available—sometimes in the teacher's house, sometimes even in cowsheds. Kaniz was struck by one photograph showing a goat tied to a bamboo pole inside a classroom. Classes were run under the supervision of a village committee, consisting of local residents who selected the teachers and decided on key matters like class timing.

Her interest piqued, Kaniz asked UNICEF staff if she could borrow the booklet. "They said, 'No, you can take that booklet,'" she recalled. She gave it to Abed, and "he read it within half an hour," she said. "He asked me to come discuss it with him, and said, 'Why don't you go to Pune?'" Kaniz, who had only worked at BRAC for five months at this point, was surprised the executive director would send such an inexperienced person on an exposure trip abroad. Before long she was on a plane to Bombay.

* * *

Chitra Naik wrote with clarity of the Indian school system's shortcomings, which were similar to those of Bangladesh. Gandhi himself had identified their common root in the policies of British India, where "the schools established after the European pattern were too expensive for the people," as he had told an audience at London's Chatham House in 1931.[2] Long after the colonial period, lip service to "education for all," which in practice meant costly attempts to emulate Western education systems, helped ensure that education remained the prerogative of the few. Poverty, Chitra Naik wrote, "has made a mockery of the elitist cry of full-time and 'quality' education for all."[3]

When she visited Pune in January 1982, Kaniz found herself across the dinner table from Chitra Naik herself. "They chalked out a beautiful program for me," she said. BRAC was well known by now, and Naik, having heard of its work, wanted to learn more about Kaniz's interest. "It was a very embarrassing situation. They thought I was a senior person at BRAC." Kaniz visited a handful of villages, even spending the night in one, observing classes held in the evenings by the light of kerosene lanterns after the children had finished their chores. She even recognized the goat from the photograph in the article she had given Abed.

Kaniz was inspired by Naik's alternative to formal, full-time state education. The classes had flexible hours, and the instructors were drawn from the communities themselves. These teachers were farmers, laborers, artisans, and housewives who were given short training courses on pedagogical methods. For about three hundred evenings a year, they would guide children through two-hour classes, aiming to raise previously unschooled pupils to the equivalent of an American third- or fourth-grader within two years. Curricula were tailored to the village environment, with material using scenes from rural life, and the classes were deliberately joyful, with songs, dances, and physical exercises instead of the alphabet recitation and multiplication tables common in government schools. Of the 1,400 children in the program, about 1,000 were girls—a remarkable portion, given the belief that the poor did not value girls' education. The project, later called Propel (for Promoting Primary and Elementary Education), would continue for several years after Kaniz's visit.

When she returned, Abed merely commented on her exposure to the sun. "You've become so dark," she recalled him saying. "It's good you have some experience now."

There was no immediate follow-up. For the next two years, Kaniz was given free rein to prepare child-oriented material, even though BRAC had few child-oriented programs. "A kind of rough shape was coming in my mind with the Pune experience," she said. She wrote a primer for early readers and a teacher-training manual that used games with sticks and stones to help preliterate and prenumerate children ready themselves for entering school.

In Manikganj, Amin opened a handful of primary schools. He asked Kaniz to help train the teachers, who were mostly male and, in Kaniz's view, entirely unsuited for the job. During one visit, she found the teachers had apparently taught the children to read aloud from the primer she had written. It was impressive, until she flipped the primers back several pages and asked them to repeat, starting from the middle of the book. "They couldn't do it," she said. "That came as a shock. I realized they had actually memorized the whole thing."

Amin closed these schools because he had trouble motivating the teachers and did not want to be seen to be competing with government schools. This early experiment in children's schooling barely warrants a mention in the archive of BRAC innovations, and Abed himself admitted he did not even remember it happening. The experience of seeing those ill-equipped teachers stuck with Kaniz, however.

* * *

Abed was biding his time. The BRAC education program was born from his hunch that donors would turn their attention to children's education in the 1990s, and when they did, BRAC would need to be ready. The vogue among donors in the 1970s had been functional education and family planning; by the 1980s, their attention had turned to livelihood programs and child survival, the latter driven largely by the passion of James P. Grant, UNICEF's executive director. Abed was already seeing one earlier prediction coming true—that interest in family planning would lead to more funding for economic development programs for the poor, like RCTP and Grameen Bank. He was now ready to bet on the idea that donors would realize that poverty could not be beaten without education.

"There were two predictions I made in development that came true," Abed said. "The first was that family planning would not happen without poverty alleviation. The second was that in order to reduce poverty, you have to have education. These would come one after another. Without education, rural development would not happen, and without education, family planning would not happen. I said that even if donors are not funding education right now, they will come to the conclusion that it's needed, and ultimately, money will flow. And it happened."

Others confirmed this guess. According to Sukhendra Sarkar, as early as 1977, he and his colleagues were pressing Abed to launch a general education program for children. Abed counseled patience, saying the time was not yet ripe. "If you go for health, the world will come forward to help you, but not general education," Abed had told him. "Maybe the 1990s will be the decade for general education." According to Sukhen, "He told us to think twenty years ahead."

Kaniz, who had shown impatience with BRAC's halting move into children's education, said Abed told her brother, Humayun, "I know she is becoming frustrated, but the decade of education will come in the 1990s."

In 1984, an opportunity for an education pilot emerged with Inter Pares in Canada, which had a strong relationship at the time with the Canadian government's foreign aid agency. Kaniz recalled when a male colleague mentioned, almost offhand, that Abed had asked him to work on a proposal for a pilot of BRAC primary schools. "My heart skipped a beat," she said. Trying to conceal her excitement, she approached Abed. Kaniz was bolder than other BRAC employees "because I was a little mature compared to the rest of them, age-wise, of course," so she asked outright whether she could help write the proposal, "and he said, 'Of course, why not?'" Since she had never written a proposal before, Abed gave her a yellowed typewritten copy of the first functional-education proposal he had written for Oxfam, ten years earlier, and told her to follow the same format. Kaniz said she oversaw the Inter Pares proposal using this as a guide, farming out different sections to various staff and consultants, and finally enlisting John Paul Kay, Abed's long-time friend, to edit the final document to ensure consistency.

That is Kaniz's version of the story. Just as it is impossible to say who invented the automobile, it is hard to say who really designed the BRAC school model. Abed, who said the ideas originated with him, recalled that he wrote the proposal himself. However, when told Kaniz's more detailed version of the story, he replied, "Could be."

Proposal in hand, Abed flew to Canada and made the pitch directly to Inter Pares, who agreed to a grant of $165,000, most of which originated with the Canadian aid agency, for a three-year pilot of twenty-two schools. Kaniz said it took days for news to reach her that BRAC had won the grant. "He comes back from Canada and doesn't tell me the news! I was the only one who was excited." One day, Kaniz showed up for work to find that Abed, despite her inexperience, had put her in charge of the pilot. "I went back home at lunchtime, and when I came back the next day, there was a circular saying I am the project leader," she said. "Maybe he thought I had the passion. I was the crazy one."

Before long, Kaniz was sitting at the Manikganj branch office interviewing the first set of BRAC teachers, hearing Mazeda Khatun tell her she had thirty-two children.

* * *

The model they created exists today. There are no corridors in a BRAC school, nor a principal's or headmaster's office. Imagine, instead, a one-room building akin to a large shed, with glassless windows cut into walls of corrugated metal. The room is filled with the raucous sound of singing and rhymes. There are no desks, and the children do not sit in a row but in a large U, facing the center of the room. Barefoot, they kneel or sit cross-legged on woven mats laid down over a dirt floor, their flipflops in a neat circle outside the door. Arranged neatly in front of each child are his or her learning materials—usually a slate and a primer, with chalk and pencils in a plastic cup or repurposed tin can.

They called it nonformal primary education (NFPE). The term "nonformal" would be useful because it provided cover, in the sense that the government would be less likely to view nonformal schools as competitive to its formal school system. In reality, there would be nothing especially nonformal about BRAC schools besides the fact that BRAC ran them. Like the instructors in the Chitra Naik's Propel project, the BRAC teachers would be drawn from the local community, with classes held in rented or borrowed spaces. In practice, almost all would be women with a modicum of education like Mazeda. Most were unemployed housewives, and some had as little as eight years of schooling. The timing would be adjusted to meet the needs of parents and children, who would have to help out at home for much of the day. Each class would have no more than thirty children, and, by design, the majority would always be girls, since without extra attention from BRAC, parents were more likely to make girls stay home and do household chores.

Shortly before launching the first pilot of twenty-two schools, Abed told Amin, who had spent eight years in Manikganj, that it was time to move back to Dhaka to help him oversee the next phase of BRAC's expansion. According to Amin's wife, Gulrana, Abed said to him, "What are you doing there? You need to come to Dhaka." She added, "He was very upset about that." He was in his element in Manikganj, going village to village on his motorcycle, close to the farmers, fishermen, and village artisans at the heart of BRAC's work.

BRAC's Mohakhali home office now had the air of a large professional organization, even though the founder's three chief deputies—Amin in charge of rural development, Sukhen directing the nationwide oral rehydration campaign, and Kaniz in charge of the new school program—had zero experience working anywhere other than BRAC. Kaniz quickly grew into her role. "She, in her field, was as effective as Amin was in rural development, even with no experience at all," Abed said. "She was energetic and committed to what we were doing. She brought in her own ideas about how to run things and do things, and she was a great leader. She argued with me from time to time—the only one who would argue with me, in fact. Amin never argued. She was my age, so she could be my equal. I was not a guru to her or anything like that."

Amin and Kaniz had completely different personalities and management styles, which allowed Abed to get what he wanted out of both—an aggressive pursuit of scale from Amin and a focus on program quality from Kaniz. Those who worked with them at the time said Amin treated Kaniz, older by fifteen years, with deference. She was perhaps the only one apart from Abed he treated this way. "I was the only one who was not scared of him," said Kaniz. "We had a good relationship." Among her memorable moments was riding the dirt roads of Manikganj on the back of Amin's battered Honda, going from village to village to choose the sites of the first BRAC schools. They would pull off the road and discuss their plans with residents "on a mat on the side of the highway."

That said, Amin wanted to try everything under the sun to improve people's health and livelihoods, even if it meant encroaching on Kaniz's turf. He also had the persuasive qualities of a bulldozer. He was excited by the idea of a front-line cadre of schoolteachers advancing the development agenda. "Amin would see tremendous possibilities of these teachers being used for other things," said Abed. "He would suggest the teachers be mobilized for immunizing children, for instance. Kaniz would say, 'No, no, no! I want my teachers completely focused on education.'" Abed credited Kaniz with guarding the program vigilantly. "Ultimately Kaniz won that argument. Too many things, you don't do so well. One or two things you do well. Kaniz wanted that. She was a good manager in that sense." He added, "She would not take nonsense from anyone. She was in complete control of her program."

Abed laughed when he recalled some of his own arguments with Kaniz. "Now you have twenty schools," he told her. "Next month, I want to set up two hundred schools."

Kaniz threw up her hands and said, "You can't do that!"

"Of course we can," Abed replied calmly. "We'll train people. We can do that now that we have all these training centers."

Kaniz admitted that she resisted Abed's push to expand as quickly as they did. She recalled the initial proposal to expand to 150 schools. "For me it was unrealistic," she said. "And in the next few years, we were going to have a few thousand schools. I banged on the doors of Amin and Abed, but no one would listen to me. I said, 'You just can't do it!'" One BRAC insider called her a "plodder," which may have been the case, but this was fine as far as Abed was concerned. Vision and ambition were his domain; execution was hers. Ultimately, she was not experienced enough to insist, as others might have, that what Abed was demanding simply could not be done. This may explain a great deal of BRAC's story in general—people accomplishing the impossible because they did not know any better.

Interviewed at her home near Philadelphia in 2015 and 2019, Kaniz provided one of the more refreshing views on Abed and BRAC, for, while she greatly respected Abed, she did not lionize him as others did. Nor did she idealize her seventeen years at BRAC, which she described as an organization where "proper dialogue" was often lacking—yet that somehow succeeded in spite of itself. Gone were the heady debates of the early years and the firebrands like Khushi Kabir. Abed neither wanted nor needed these anymore. He had enough arguments at home. At work, he wanted people with the passion to execute his plans, not challenge them. Kaniz, who put up resistance to rapid growth but yielded easily, was just the type of person he was looking for.

⋆ ⋆ ⋆

It might be tempting, hearing Kaniz's story, to conclude that BRAC's NFPE pilot was based on Naik's Propel program. That would be a mistake. The night classes in Pune were part of a highly supervised research project, with each class attended by one or two professionals from the Indian Institute of Education. Such a management system would never have allowed BRAC to scale the way that it did.

At BRAC, what happened in the classroom was only the tip of the iceberg. Beneath the surface, managerial discipline would keep costs in line. This included a system of curriculum development, distribution of teaching materials, teacher training, monitoring, and supervision, all designed to maintain the cost effectiveness of the model, which was sacrosanct. Kaniz points out that the idea of monthly refresher trainings for teachers, a pillar of the model's success, was not even mentioned in the proposal and only emerged after the program began to scale. Years later, a visiting scholar would liken BRAC's management of its schools to an industrial system of production where "the role of the supervisor was similar to that of a foreman in a factory situation."[4]

In any case, Abed did not attribute the ideas in the pilot to Kaniz's exposure trip to Pune. In his view, the one-room village school was an innovation born of cost constraints. He wanted the quality of learning to be higher than that of the abysmal government schools without exceeding their per-pupil cost, which was less than $20 per year in 1985. If he exceeded that amount, even if the schools achieved good results, he thought people would object that the model was unsustainable since the government would never adopt it, which was his ultimate goal. He felt strongly that education was the responsibility of the state.

Teachers' salaries took up most of the government's education budget. The only way to keep costs in line, therefore, was by developing local, low-cost teaching talent. By now, Abed knew there was untapped talent right there in the villages, and it was almost always unemployed women. There was therefore no need to pay the inflated salaries of graduates coming out of the teachers' colleges. BRAC created champion schoolteachers in just fifteen days of training and supervisory support, followed by monthly refresher training, where the women came together and often learned from their peers.

"BRAC is only piloting NFPE," Abed told Alan Rogers, a UK-based scholar on nonformal education who interviewed him in 1988. "This is the responsibility of the government. We are only covering a gap. It is not a parallel system but complementary, supplementary. Eventually the government of Bangladesh will have to be in charge."[5]

Kaniz said she was always skeptical that would happen—and on that, she turned out to be right.

⋆ ⋆ ⋆

The field staff maintained good relations with local administrators of government schools to ensure a good transition when BRAC students entered the government school system after grade four (later extended to grade five). Abed said he was surprised that the vast majority chose to continue their schooling. When they began entering the state system, teachers there said the BRAC school graduates were notably less shy than non-BRAC students. Vibekananda ("Bibek") Howlader, one of the three original program organizers, attributed this result to the small class size, which allowed for more direct teacher-student interaction, and the fact that BRAC schools did not have the traditional seats and benches of government schools. "The teacher is always moving inside the classroom," said Bibek. There were anecdotal reports that ex-BRAC students, despite coming from such disadvantaged backgrounds, were performing better than their non-BRAC peers in government schools.

The strength of the system was recognizing and capitalizing on the untapped talent of unemployed women in rural areas, like Mazeda. When recruiting the teachers, Abed thought back to his own mother and her talent for making people feel loved and important. "If she's a cold woman, I don't want her, even if she's the most educated and most eligible to become a teacher," he said. "I want an affectionate woman who touches the head of a child to say, 'Do it like this.'"

He insisted on a few essential things to Kaniz. Among them was that the schools needed to be fun. "Whatever you do, children must enjoy coming to school," he told her. "It's important that children enjoy the process of learning. It shouldn't become a great task. It's poor children, working children, and they've got other tasks at home—so they should be enjoying themselves when they come to school."

When she felt sick and took a day off, Mazeda said the students would show up at her house. "Sometimes the parents would come too," she said. "It wasn't so much to check on my health. They just wanted to take me to school."

Abed would often repeat the report he had heard after the first major flooding during the pilot phase. The paths through the Manikganj backwaters had become impassable, and most schools were shut down as a result. Instead of staying home, the BRAC students would put their notebooks and supplies into an aluminum pot, hold it above their heads, and swim to school. They did not want to miss a single day.

20

A TEN-YEAR PLAN

Shameran Abed was at a wedding with his family in the early 1990s, at age eleven or twelve, when a man approached the table and said, "You are the largest NGO in the world!" Years later, he remembered thinking: What the heck is an NGO?

It is unclear when people started referring to BRAC with that superlative. The first printed reference to BRAC as "the largest NGO [nongovernmental organization] in the world" is from a UNICEF publication in 1993. Whether or not it was true at that point, BRAC was getting undeniably huge in terms of its employee headcount and the number of people reached, the metrics people usually used to make such pronouncements. In 1990, BRAC had more than 7,600 staff, including the teachers, and Abed estimated it had reached sixteen million households—at least thirteen million through the oral rehydration campaign, which had just succeeded in covering the entire country, and three million more through its core programs. Total income for that year was about $23 million, of which $16 million came from donors. It was a sprawling organization, difficult to describe in a few words or keep track of as it evolved, with programs and subprograms in nearly every sector of human and economic development.

Abed's wife, Shilu Abed, had parlayed her experience in crafts and retail to drive the growth of Aarong, BRAC's textile and handicrafts retailer. In 1983, when Shilu took over as director, Aarong consisted of just one shop, mainly selling handmade goods from the women in Jamalpur and Manikganj. Its expansion started in 1985, financed by donors enticed by its dual mission of preserving Bengali folk crafts (including a traditional style of embroidery called *kantha* and the Mughal-era fine muslin fabric *jamdani*) and generating sustainable livelihoods for rural women. By the end of the decade, Aarong had six outlets in three cities.

However, the real driver of growth was the loans and training, now under the umbrella of the Rural Development Program, led by Aminul Alam, and the education program, under Kaniz Fatema. The numbers were eye-popping: At the end of 1990, more than four hundred thousand people were members of BRAC village organizations, rising to 1.4 million in 1995, at which point the number of BRAC schools reached thirty-five thousand, with more than one million students enrolled. In the area of health, after the child survival campaign ended, having reached thirteen million households, a separate women's health and development program emerged with a focus on maternal health, an issue that had become personal for Abed after the death of Bahar. BRAC began training thousands of traditional birth attendants (the women in the villages who usually functioned as untrained midwives) in safer birth practices, with the aim of having one trained attendant for every village. Major subprograms were also launched to fight tuberculosis and pneumonia.

Catherine Lovell, who had served as a consultant to BRAC, wrote a book, *Breaking the Cycle of Poverty: The BRAC Strategy*, covering the organization's development through 1990. In her book, Lovell paraphrases the note of caution often sounded by donor appraisals and evaluation: "BRAC is doing well now, but if it continues to scale up so rapidly we are not sure it can manage." She asked, rhetorically, whether there was a point at which BRAC would become too large, too complex, and too diverse to manage. "Perhaps there is a break point, but just where that point might be is impossible to anticipate."

Abed laughed about this idea years later. When that was written, he said he did not even consider BRAC that big. Abed was pursuing a long-term plan that would make BRAC unique among major nonprofit organizations, for both its scale and its sustainability.

* * *

To understand how BRAC reached this stage, and how it then erupted into its period of mega-scaling in the 1990s, we have to rewind to the late 1970s. Abed had planted the seeds in 1979, when he launched the Rural Credit and Training Program (RCTP). Though the emphasis on credit had led to the acrimonious split with Khushi Kabir and her followers, Abed had not forsaken the methods of Paulo Freire. At the time, BRAC also started a standalone functional-education program called Outreach, an experiment to see whether empowerment could be achieved through Freirean methods alone, without any economic support whatsoever. The program focused purely on "mobilization"—that is, organizing landless people into groups, or "participatory and powerful people's organizations," to demand their rights.

"We thought that we needed poor people to demand services from the government, so [if we] organize the poor, they will exert pressure on the government to provide them services," said Abed. "In Outreach, we would not give them any money. They would get as many services from the government as possible, such as health care—and if the government wouldn't give them, the people would demand them."

According to a 1982 report for the Outreach program, "the landless cannot imagine that the power they await lies within them, and therefore, they lapse into a state of passivity awaiting liberation from heaven or [a] messianic leader." The journey toward "breaking the shackles of present socio-economic enslavement" begins within people's minds. Only then can they turn their attention to the actual sources of their exploitation and seek redress from government offices, the courts, and, if need be, through national politics. The groups' economic activities had to be financed from people's savings.

Both RCTP and Outreach were attempts to streamline BRAC's programming such that the most effective activities could be replicated and scaled up across the country. "We saw the merits of taking one agenda throughout the nation to have an impact," Abed said. Neither of these two experiments were a total success, although RCTP could probably lay a better claim to it. Functional education was not mentioned in Kaiser Zaman's original RCTP proposal—the "training" in the project name referred to technical skills, such as how to be a more effective farmer—but from the start the program included Freirean consciousness-raising lessons. In theory, members of a village organization (VO) were supposed to attend these functional-education classes before taking loans. In practice, the groups often received their loans before everyone finished the course, and once a group received a loan, new members and those who had not finished the classes would skip them, in order to focus almost all their energy on the new livelihood scheme that the loan had financed. Of the VO membership of thirty thousand in 1983, only about 40 percent had received functional-education classes.

Outreach, meanwhile, suffered from a high rate of dropouts, especially from people living hand to mouth, who were so exhausted after working in the fields that they had no interest in attending night classes. The goal of "establishing a new social order through conscientization and institutional development, without providing direct financial aid," in the words of a 1984 expansion proposal, lay far off. Without access to outside resources, "the militancy of the target population, which was developed through conscientization, may not be sustained owing to continued dependence on the elite for wages and credit."

In 1986, RCTP and Outreach were merged into a single program, and Abed placed Amin, whom he had recently recalled from Manikganj after his eight-year stint there, at the helm. The Rural Development Program (RDP), as the merged program was called, would become the main vehicle for BRAC's expansion for the next decade and a half, and the three geographic programs—Sulla, Jamalpur, and Manikganj—were soon dissolved into it, though Manikganj would remain the development laboratory. RDP represented the essence of nearly everything BRAC had learned thus far, amalgamating the well-oiled practices of functional education and lending while adding other interventions that had emerged from the Manikganj proving ground. Essential health care, for instance, would be provided by *shasthya shebikas* recruited from the ranks of the VOs. This would remain part of RDP even when a separate health program launched in 1990. The schools run by Kaniz would remain entirely separate.

Training of village paralegals, piloted in Manikganj in 1986, taught people in the villages how to handle basic matters of law, including raising awareness of people's fundamental rights. The paralegals would offer their services to landless people who needed help asserting their rights when it came to a host of legal matters including land law, wage and sharecropping disputes, and inheritance. Within a decade, this approach would supplant the last vestige of the functional-education requirement for microfinance. Women eventually began to see the Freirean classes as a mere obstacle to getting a loan, rather than an empowering initiative unto itself.

Offering credit to the poor was a core activity of RDP, but it also included a handful of "sectoral programs," which invested in promising subsectors of the rural economy in an attempt to raise borrowers' meager incomes. The sectoral programs were among the ways BRAC stood apart from Grameen Bank, which by now had emerged as the other major provider of credit to the landless poor. Grameen's founder, Muhammad Yunus, had won the Ramon Magsaysay Award in 1984, four years after Abed. Yunus promoted a minimalist version of microcredit, offering affordable loans and nothing more. As his earliest proposals made clear, Abed never thought this would be enough to boost incomes significantly. The poor might lack access to capital, but they also suffered from deficiencies of power, skills, and knowledge; moreover, if they did have money, many of the traditional activities they might invest in were barely profitable.

The RDP sectoral programs thus sought to reduce bottlenecks in the rural value chains that kept incomes low for landless people. Many of the group members produced vegetables on their homesteads, for instance, both to sell and to consume. BRAC promoted this activity since it offered a chance to make more money while adding nutrients to the household diet. But farmers lacked access to good seeds, so, in 1986, BRAC launched a small seed-production farm that sold low-cost, high-quality vegetable seeds to those who wanted them, including its own borrowers.

Livestock and poultry were among the most promising sectoral programs. In one Manikganj village, BRAC had persuaded the women to castrate all their roosters and introduce, in their place, some twenty white leghorn cocks, which produced hens that yielded more eggs than local chickens. These were enormously successful, except for the fact that the new chickens were more susceptible to disease and often died. BRAC therefore began selling chicken vaccinations and training women to be local poultry workers, inoculating all the chickens in their village against common diseases. An entire system of poultry farmers, vaccinators, egg sellers, and chick-raising units emerged from this program. By 1990, BRAC had distributed half a million high-yield variety cocks and chicks to the sixty thousand women involved in the program.

Silk production, or sericulture, was another page in BRAC's portfolio. Apart from the region surrounding the northern city of Rajshahi, which was famous for its silk, sericulture had never been considered a viable livelihood in Bangladesh. BRAC changed that by encouraging women across the country to raise silkworms, an activity that, while labor intensive, could take place in or near their homes without disrupting other household tasks. It also did not require a huge investment of capital. Silkworms can grow in shoeboxes; in fact, all they really require is a steady supply of mulberry leaves, the only food they will eat before spinning the cocoons that constitute raw silk. By 1990, BRAC had planted several million mulberry trees on the verges of roadways and other spare patches of land. The end products of these trees were the silk saris sold at Aarong.

* * *

In early 1987, Novib, now one of BRAC's largest and most consistent donors, paid for a team of management consultants to begin the process of hammering out BRAC's strategy for the 1990s. The consultants thought BRAC could at least double its current rate of expansion and cover 5 percent of the villages in Bangladesh by 1992. It would have been difficult for

Novib and BRAC's other major donor, West Germany's Protestant Association for Cooperation in Development (EZE), to finance this growth. "Both of them said, 'You are becoming too big for us,'" said Abed. "Four to five million dollars every three years we can do, but we can't do anything bigger." They suggested asking the foreign aid agencies of major European states to fund BRAC directly. With the exception of the Swiss aid agency, which had funded the oral rehydration campaign, BRAC had never received funding directly from foreign governments. With the help of the Ford Foundation, Novib cobbled together a consortium of the Swedish, Danish, Norwegian, British, and Dutch foreign aid agencies, and in January 1989, at the Sheraton in Dhaka, Abed met with representatives of these governments and made his largest pitch to date, by far. He asked for $56 million over ten years. "We had never heard of this kind of money before," he said.

The basics of the proposal were relatively straightforward. Over the next ten years, Abed wanted BRAC to become largely self-reliant, generating enough of its own revenue that if donors were to jump ship, the organization would still survive. Revenue would consist largely of interest charges on small loans delivered through RDP. Abed knew the break-even formula for lending in RDP branches: a branch usually took about three years to become self-sufficient, which happened when the level of outstanding loans reached 7 million taka ($212,000 at the time) at a 16 percent interest rate. According to his expansion plan, RDP would begin launching new branches, and when these branches became self-sufficient after three years, they would be transferred to a separate unit called the Rural Credit Project. Designed to make a profit, the Rural Credit Project would require $30 million of the requested $56 million to set up.

The initial idea was to call the Rural Credit Project the "BRAC Bank," since that's what it essentially was. "When we went with the BRAC Bank project to the government, they said that without a license, you can't call anything a bank," said Abed. "So you'd better call it Rural Credit Project." With the donors, they straight out called it "the BRAC Bank project," because if they had called it Rural Credit Project, "they wouldn't think about $30 million, they would think about $5 million." The Rural Credit Project formed the basis for what became the BRAC microfinance program. The donor consortium bought the pitch, and RDP Phase II, along with the Rural Credit Project, commenced in 1990. In addition to the aforementioned Dutch, British, and Scandinavian governments, the Swiss aid agency joined the consortium, as did the Aga Khan Foundation, which also brought in the Canadian aid agency.

According to the plan, it would take about ten years for microfinance to start generating enough money on its own that it could open new branches without any additional donor support. If the plan was successful, it would mean that even if donor funding were to dry up completely, BRAC could still survive. Since every new branch needed to be subsidized for the first three years, the overall break-even point depended on the rate of expansion. Abed said he wanted to grow faster and thus reach sustainability sooner, but the donors insisted he be more cautious.

* * *

There was some skepticism in the room at the Sheraton. Abed encountered resistance to at least one aspect of his proposal—and as it happens, it was one of the last sparks of Abed's desire to create truly revolutionary change by upending the rural power structure. It was a major investment in irrigation, which he thought was one of BRAC's most promising sector programs. "Abed, for perfectly laudable but ideological reasons, wanted to make a risky investment in order to, as he put it, change the balance of political power in rural areas," said Geoffrey Salkeld, who then served as Novib's desk officer for Bangladesh and helped create the donor consortium.

The overarching "ideological" issue was control of water resources. Agriculture was still primarily rainfed, but even water-soaked Bangladesh needed irrigation to take advantage of the Green Revolution's huge jump in crop yields. Abed saw three main sources of power in rural areas. The rural elites had already captured the land, the first source of power, and though there was much talk of more equitable redistribution of it, land-reform efforts had always foundered, mainly due to endemic corruption. Even in cases where landless people got land, they often could not keep it, thanks to the elites' stranglehold on credit, the second source of power, which landless people required to purchase seeds, plows, and other necessary items. Water was the third source, and it was still up for grabs, since it was the one thing farmers needed that the elites did not already control.

Abed thought he had come up with a way to give landless people access to water rights. He was aiming high: his goal was nothing less than "an agrarian revolution." BRAC would loan money to landless groups for the purchase and installation of deep tube wells, which would tap into underground aquifers, thus ensuring a volume of discharge that could irrigate large areas of land during the dry season. BRAC would train these landless groups in proper management and well maintenance. As the tube wells' shareholders, the groups would strike deals with landowners, whereby the landless groups would collect a portion (usually a quarter) of the crop production from irrigated land. With this they would pay off the loan.

Abed admitted that "it was kind of an ideological thing, in the sense that whenever people talk about social revolution, they think of land reform—distributing land to the poor. I said that even without distributing land to the poor, you can give the poor other assets which are just as vital, like water rights. So give them deep tube wells, and they will have access to the productivity of the land."

Salkeld said he lobbied several of the skeptical donors in the consortium to allow Abed to take the risk, which they eventually did. The scheme turned into one of BRAC's biggest failures. In previous cases where BRAC fell short of expectations, Abed was often the first to own up to it. In this case, BRAC had grown so large that it lacked visibility into project performance. It was the donors themselves who discovered something was awry. In 1991, David Wright, an advisor to the British aid agency, visited twenty-four of the tube wells—there were several hundred at this point—and found only three were generating enough money to make the annual BRAC loan repayments. The donors commissioned the consultancy Mott MacDonald to do a deeper inspection, which found that 68 percent of the tube wells were unable to generate enough income to cover normal operating costs, loan repayments, and depreciation—figures that, "depressing as they are, understate the extent of the problem." Record keeping and monitoring for the project "is clearly some way short of its potential," the report stated. In 1995, BRAC wound down the program, wrote off the loans, took back ownership of the non-performing tube wells, sold them on the market, and refunded 100 percent of the shareholders' loan payments.

"Own up to your mistakes and learn from them," Abed said. "That has been my philosophy." The tube wells venture was known to be risky from the start, with revenue from the sale of water dependent on many factors, including the vagaries of weather, which affected crop yields; the cost of fuel, since the pumps ran on diesel and prices doubled during the Gulf War; and the ability of people with little to no formal schooling to manage a complex operation. According to Abed, the story was simpler than that, for it all came down to one thing—power. He failed to account for the fact that in the rural setting, contracts are meaningless. The landlords would make crop-sharing agreements with the landless groups to take their water and then renege on them. The rural power structure was such that the landless groups had no legal recourse. "Poor people could not get the landed people to pay their fair share of what was agreed," Abed said. "The landed people just took their harvest and didn't give them much. It was a power problem."

Abed was a risk taker, within limits. He could be critical of microfinance staff when the portion of past-due microfinance loans was too low, for instance. The percentage of loans in which borrowers have missed installments is known as "portfolio at risk," or PAR, and it is a widely used metric to measure the quality of microfinance operations. A microfinance chief executive complaining that PAR is too low is counterintuitive, since lower PAR means a healthier portfolio, but according to Abed, "If it's too low, it means you are not taking any risks, and you are probably leaving out the poorest people."

He emphasized, however, that he had never taken a risk that jeopardized the existence of BRAC itself. Despite the brouhaha over the tube wells, the loans that financed them constituted less than 10 percent of BRAC's total loan portfolio—not enough to derail Abed's ten-year plan for self-sufficiency. Nonetheless, the lesson was significant, for the failed project likely represented the last gasp of Abed's hope that rural landless people might become a proletarian political force. He said the failure of the tube wells scheme "may be what convinced me that in Bangladesh, you won't have an agrarian revolution led by the poor."

⋆ ⋆ ⋆

It helped that microfinance had become popular among donors, thanks in large part to Yunus, who by now had captured the attention of the international development community with his singular focus on micro-lending. Grameen Bank was the only other Bangladeshi organization attracting this kind of money at the time. Though the two organizations' stated goals were similar, their methods were not—even though, as time went on, the loan products they offered would become increasingly similar. Abed and Yunus had no mutual animus, but they kept a polite distance from one another.

Abed did not believe that credit alone would provide a ladder out of poverty—or when it did, it was the exception rather than the rule. A detailed examination of the financial lives of the poor in places like Sulla and Manikganj had taught him that rural economies were rife with inefficiencies, and it was nearly always the poorest who paid for them. No amount of small loans would make these inefficiencies disappear.

In 1991, Abed and Amin visited a northern village far from the main road. It was November, during the dry season, when the paths are walkable and the morning air is cool and misty. The village itself was about a mile from where they parked the car. They walked down the dirt path, alongside ponds choked with water hyacinth, an invasive weed that covers the surface of the water. The air during this time of year would have smelled of cow dung mixed with the sweet scent of night-blooming jasmine.

When they finally reached the village, they met a woman who had recently borrowed the equivalent of $100 to buy a cow. Most of BRAC's microfinance clients could previously never have dreamed of owning a cow. "You must be doing very well now," Abed said to her.

Her blunt reply, had it been heard in policy circles in Western capitals, would have diffused the hype surrounding microfinance that was building at the time. "My cow produces only two liters of milk per day," she told him. "I sell this for about 7 taka per liter. I'm using that to pay back the loan you gave me. After that, I've got nothing left."

Abed, ever the cost accountant, began crunching numbers in his head. The price of milk in Dhaka was 25 taka per liter, the equivalent of about 52 US cents at the time, but the woman had no way of accessing that market. Milk goes bad quickly, and there were no refrigeration facilities nearby, which meant she would be lucky just to sell it to her neighbors. Abed thought that if he could devise a system to collect milk from women like her, refrigerate it, and transport it to the cities, perhaps he could pay her 15 taka per liter—more than double her current income—while covering the costs of collection and distribution, and even, just maybe, make a profit.

After several years, the Danish government backed Abed's plan to create BRAC Dairy and Food Project, launched in 1998. The enterprise employed milk collectors, usually men with bicycle carts, who went around to nearby villages collecting milk and depositing it at chilling stations, where BRAC then picked it up and hauled it by tankers to its plant in Dhaka. Tens of thousands of rural farmers sold their milk this way, and BRAC packaged and marketed it nationwide, eventually becoming one of the country's largest private dairies. Compared to earlier plans to upend the rural power structure, women getting more for their milk was more evolution than revolution, but unlike previous failed schemes, this one succeeded—and it often made the difference between sending their daughters to school and keeping them home.

* * *

In the 1970s, when Abed was a younger man and BRAC was just a few hundred employees, he had decided it needed to become "large and powerful enough to be reckoned with." His view on what constituted "large enough" likely changed as the organization's size broke through one ceiling after another. BRAC schools were something they were "only piloting" until the government could take over, he had said in 1987. In reality, donors proved to be more attracted to the program's success than the government was.

BRAC's village schoolhouses attracted international attention and high-profile visits. In 1990, UNESCO (the UN's education agency) organized the World Conference on Education for All in Jomtien, Thailand. The event established education as a priority for major donors, just as Abed had predicted would happen, and BRAC was singled out as an exemplary model. Shortly after that, Audrey Hepburn visited Bangladesh as a UNICEF celebrity ambassador. Abed took her to one of the primary schools, where a student asked whether she herself had gone to a BRAC school. "I was not lucky enough to go to a school like this," she replied.

By late 1989, fueled by about $1 million in funding from the Norwegian and Swedish aid agencies, the program had expanded to 2,500 schools reaching about 75,000 students. Another donor consortium of government aid agencies, separate from the RDP consortium, came together to back the mega-scaling of the education program in the 1990s, when BRAC opened tens of thousands of schools. For something initially designed as a pilot, Abed had tossed away any constraint on ambition, for even at such a massive scale, the program was only meeting a fraction of the country's need. At one point, he put forward a proposal to open a hundred thousand schools and began shopping it around. For one of the first times in his life, he found he was unable to raise the money for a major proposal.

Unsurprisingly, Kaniz said she cannot fathom how one hundred thousand schools would have been possible, anyway. "I was trying to stretch myself," she said. "How many managers do I need? How many program organizers do I need? I was trying desperately to calculate it. But I couldn't do it." The number of BRAC primary schools maxed out at "only" thirty-five thousand in 1995, with more than one million students enrolled—still less than 10 percent of the children in Bangladesh. There were also multiple subprograms, including preprimary schools (which eventually brought the total number of schools above sixty thousand), clubs for adolescent girls, and community libraries.

Becoming this large had its drawbacks, mainly in the form of pushback—and even violence—from those who felt their interests threatened. Government schoolteachers were understandably opposed to being replaced by local women who were, in their view, underqualified. The teaching establishment had initially dismissed the BRAC schools, thinking them unserious places where children only sang, danced, and recited nursery rhymes. This misconception allowed the program to scale up without much opposition. When the program became too massive to ignore, their attitude changed, especially when BRAC began pursuing closer collaboration with the government to share what it had learned. There was even talk of involving BRAC in the management of public schools. These discussions were scuttled by opposition from the association of government teachers, who argued that BRAC was engineering a backdoor takeover of the formal school system.

Ultraconservative Islamists had their own reasons to oppose schools where the majority of the students were girls. For years, rumors had spread that BRAC was some kind of Christian plot—the logic being that most NGOs were foreign, most foreigners were Christian, and BRAC was an NGO—but the rumors were easy to quash. Bibek Howlader, one of BRAC's first front-line organizers for the education program, in charge of a portion of the initial twenty-two schools in 1985, recalled a day in the first year of operation when every student in one school failed to turn up for class. He called a meeting of all the parents to learn why. "There was a rumor spreading that the children would be shipped to America and converted to Christianity," he said. Over the course of a several-hour discussion, he explained that neither of these things would happen. The children returned to school the next day, and that was the end of the matter.

Religious resistance surged in late 1993 and early 1994, when fundamentalist preachers of the Wahhabi sect, which was active in rural areas, began more actively circulating bogus stories about BRAC. Women taking loans, they said, were required to place the Koran beneath their feet when they received their money, desecrating the holy book. They claimed BRAC buried the dead children of its village organization members in an unholy black cloth. The branch offices, moreover, were actually sex dens. This time, the rumors inspired arsonists to burn down fifty-nine BRAC primary schools, with sixty-six more forced to close temporarily in a fifteen-day period. Such numbers would have been catastrophic for most organizations; for BRAC, it represented less than half a percent of its schools at the time. More than 100,000 of the 6.7 million mulberry trees BRAC had planted were also destroyed.[1]

BRAC weathered the storm via two strategies. On a national level, it kept a low profile lest it stoke the flames by taking an actively anti-Islamist stance. This was important, because the largest Islamist party, Jamaat-e-Islami, was part of the ruling coalition government at the time. At least one of the BRAC research division's reports on the disturbances was pulled from circulation. On a local level, BRAC stepped up its engagement with village elders and religious leaders to explain its true purpose. It helped that the rumors, so imaginatively contrived, were plainly false.

★ ★ ★

The quality of education in BRAC classrooms remained a huge concern for Abed. The fact that BRAC children would not otherwise be receiving any education did not make Abed amenable to compromises on quality; as a matter of principle, he thought BRAC children deserved a world-class education. From the earliest years of the program, anecdotal evidence, including comments from the teachers who taught BRAC graduates after they transitioned to government schools, suggested BRAC students performed better than those who had attended government primary schools during their first years. It was not until much later that hard data emerged to support this belief. In fact, an early World Bank study on the initial three-year pilot, comparing BRAC students with their counterparts in government schools, actually found that BRAC students performed slightly worse in terms of testing, although vastly better in terms of drop-out rates: less than 3 percent of BRAC students dropped out over three years compared to more than 40 percent of their peers in government schools. Considering their disadvantages—BRAC students came from largely illiterate households, after all—these were not bad results.

It was not good enough for Abed. Because he and his top managers lacked formal education training, expertise would have to come from abroad. Erum Mariam, the wife of Humayun Kabir's son and therefore Kaniz's niece by marriage, joined the education program in 1992 and took over as program head in 2001. "Abed *Bhai* would visit schools and say, 'I'm very concerned. Are they memorizing or are they reading?'" she said. Abed recalled reading an article in the *Times Education Supplement* about the countries with the best teaching: New Zealand was the best for mother language teaching, the Dutch excelled at math, and so on. He immediately launched a drive to find the world's top pedagogues to improve the BRAC curriculum and methods. "It all started with this article he read about the New Zealanders being good in languages," said Erum. "After that article, he was very excited, saying we needed to get different people from around the world."

Thus began a parade of global experts on short-term consultancies. An educator from New Zealand brought more storytelling into the BRAC classroom. A British specialist in mathematics education from the University of Leeds revamped the way BRAC taught math, using art to teach pattern recognition. Susan and Dennis Malone, two literacy and education specialists from SIL International, a Christian nonprofit, brought in a method for teaching indigenous children who did not speak Bengali at home, which proved so successful it was eventually adopted throughout the BRAC system, even for Bengali speakers.

The latter method, which Abed called the "Habirbari system" after the cluster of villages where it was first piloted, built children's confidence by encouraging free-flowing creativity and writing. According to Susan Malone, the key is to refrain from correcting children's mistakes, to encourage the flow of ideas around specific themes they already know about, such as their mothers. "Everything begins with what the children already know and builds on that," she said. According to Abed, building children's confidence made them receptive to new knowledge.

Abed was fond of telling the story of a visit to Japan, where he asked a rice farmer about his harvest. The farmer replied, "Not very good, because I went away for eleven days to my sister's wedding, and those days are crucial for water and fertilizer." Abed found it hard to imagine getting a similar answer from a Bangladeshi farmer. "He could monitor and evaluate exactly what is happening to his plants and why," he said of the Japanese farmer. "If you ask a Bangladeshi farmer how his rice is growing, he would say, 'It will be very good if Allah wills it.' One puts everything to fate, the other to what he has done, to human activity. That's the change that we need to make among Bangladeshi farmers." Abed would tell this story often to stress the importance of improving the quality of learning in the classroom.

In the 2000s, BRAC's own research unit finally published an analysis of data that showed BRAC students were indeed performing better on basic competencies than their government school counterparts. Yet despite the scale, the attention, and the apparent success, the government never adopted BRAC's methods or took over the system. "I thought that we would teach something to the government," Abed said in his acceptance address for the World Food Prize in 2015. Laughter broke out in the audience, even though he had not intended it as a joke. "I was disappointed. The government didn't want to learn anything from us."

* * *

His ambition was not just size. Credit and education were the biggest drivers of growth, with the lines on the chart showing the volume of loans and the number of schools climbing higher each year. The organization also continued to sprawl outward, adding new enterprises and activities designed to break the bottlenecks in rural value chains that kept people trapped in low-income micro-enterprises.

In order to ensure the health of the dairy stock for BRAC Dairy, BRAC trained four hundred para-veterinarians and set up a bull station to provide artificial insemination services, with bull semen from Friesian and other high-milk-producing cattle. On the backs of motorcycles, thousands of trained agents brought bull semen directly to cattle farmers' homes.

Meanwhile, the rising number of chickens running around people's homesteads led to a scarcity of quality poultry feed. In 1994, BRAC began sourcing hybrid field-corn seeds from Australia, but it struggled to get farmers to accept the idea of growing corn, a new crop at the time. BRAC, confident in rising demand, offered a buyback guarantee. If the farmers failed to sell the corn on the open market, BRAC would buy it at a guaranteed price. The farmers would have no obligation to sell to BRAC, and, indeed, most of them eventually found buyers willing to pay more. Field corn is now an established crop in Bangladesh. In 1998, following the government's opening of the sector to private competition, BRAC entered the market for seeds of the country's dominant crop, rice, importing hybrid seeds from China and field testing them in different ecological zones. Aarong, BRAC Seed, and BRAC Dairy would become the most profitable of the organization's social enterprises.

Abed's wife Shilu was the dominant force in his personal life during this period of phenomenal growth, often challenging him. The marriage was an evident source of stress, but despite their arguments, they had a solid and respectful marriage, and she continued to helm Aarong. She never achieved Bahar's level of popularity within BRAC, however.

In early 1997, Shilu survived a heart attack, and shortly thereafter she flew to Singapore to undergo balloon angioplasty to unclog a blocked artery. She was otherwise in good health and returned to work at Aarong quickly. For several weeks after she returned to Dhaka, it seemed she was on the road to recovery. However, at around 4 p.m. on April 23, about a month after the surgery, Abed received an alarming call at his office. Marco, her son, had visited her at home for tea and, finding her looking pale and unwell, had taken her to the clinic. She stopped breathing about halfway through the fifteen-minute drive, according to Marco. He had to carry her into the clinic.

When Abed arrived, the staff were in the midst of trying to resuscitate his wife of thirteen years. They pronounced her dead after about twenty minutes. She had likely died in her son's arms before reaching the clinic. Shilu Abed was fifty-five. Despite the previous heart attack, her death was sudden and unexpected. "She had gone to work and made promotions the day she died," said Maheen Khan, her daughter.

Shameran, age fifteen, was home at the time, unaware that anything had happened until Abed came back from the hospital and entered his bedroom. Shilu was never especially motherly, but she was likely the closest thing Shameran ever had to a maternal figure. According to Shameran, Abed broke the news and then turned around, left the room, and walked to his own bedroom, where he sat down. Shameran followed, and he and his father sat together in silence for some moments, until Shameran asked what he should do. "Start calling people," Abed replied.

It had not been a perfect marriage, but they had loved and supported one another for nearly fourteen years, far longer than Abed had been married to his children's mother. Abed grieved but did not stay depressed for months this time, as he had following Bahar's death—at least not outwardly. "Tragedy was getting a little repetitive in his life," Tamara said. BRAC was in the midst of its biggest growth period, and, as always, there was work to be done. "My dad always functions," his daughter added. "And that's something we learned as well: If something is difficult, or if there's change, you don't just throw your hands up in the air and sit there. You function. Day comes to night, night comes to day, you eat, you shower, and so on." Abed was seven years into the ten-year drive toward self-sufficiency. He had a plan in place; all he had to do was follow it. According to those close to him, inwardly he entered another period of deep loneliness.

21

THE MYSTERY OF THE POISONED COW

With the precision of a police report, Amina Begum shared an hour-by-hour account of a fateful day fourteen years earlier. Her one-room dwelling in the northern district of Nilphamari sits amid a warren of jute-stick fences and corrugated iron, where the air smells of cows and damp straw. Her face was leathery and lined, graying hair visible beneath the wrap of a rose-colored sari.

On that day in 2002, she took her new cow, which she had received from BRAC, to a nearby field, tied it to a post, and went to the riverbank to gather grass for fodder. By the time she returned, the cow, Amina's most valuable asset by far, had come untethered and wandered onto the land of two local farmers, Farhad and Syed.[1] Farhad was not a particularly wealthy man, living in a tin house across the nearby river, but he owned some land and wielded clout in the area. Syed, his sharecropper, leased a plot from Farhad to grow chili peppers.

When she came up from the riverbank, Amina spotted Syed chasing her cow onto Farhad's land, whereupon Farhad began beating the cow. What happened next was the basis for a dispute that briefly captured the attention of all the surrounding villages.

According to Amina, the men initially said the cow had drunk from Farhad's bucket of pesticide, but then they retracted that story. "I asked several times if the cow drank the poison," Amina said. "They both kept insisting no." When Amina got back to her tiny homestead, the cow sat down in front of her doorway and refused to get up. She was finally able to drag it to the local vet, which led to a brief recovery. However, at about one o'clock that night, the cow began vomiting and flailing, and it soon died. Amina lay next to the body all night, wailing.

It would take an extraordinary intervention on her behalf by local BRAC officials and the village council for Amina to get the justice she deserved. As always, there is a story behind the story, and a story behind that one. In this case, the story went all the way back to the 1975 famine.

★ ★ ★

By the late 1990s, Abed spent most of his days in the air-conditioned office near the top of the new twenty-story building that had become BRAC's headquarters in 1996. He was likely there, sitting behind the same desk he had used when BRAC was founded, surrounded by stacks of reading material, when he first saw the research telling him that, after decades of work, he was still failing at one of his main goals.

A quarter century had passed since he'd decided to devote his life to helping Bangladesh's poorest lift themselves up. Much had changed. BRAC had grown from a bare-bones group of activists with a shoestring budget to a sprawling nonprofit employing thirty thousand people. It had built the twenty-story high-rise, and the swamp across the street from the building was now a teeming slum where rural migrants lived in tin shacks on stilts.

Most of BRAC's staff worked in microfinance, making loans as small as $100 so that women could buy moneymaking assets like dairy cows. BRAC's microfinance groups were, on the surface, picture-perfect renderings of rural empowerment and solidarity. In thousands of villages, on a dirt patch in a common area, groups of thirty to forty landless women would meet weekly. They would roll out woven mats, gather up their saris in a kaleidoscope of bright shades, and sit down to discuss investments, pay their installments to a loan officer, collect disbursements, and offer support to their neighbors. Their stories inspired legions around the globe. They had put solid roofs on their homes and sent their daughters to school, the first in countless generations to learn to read and write. With its promise of women pulling themselves up with nothing but small loans and grit, microfinance captured the hearts of Western donors.

However, there was a problem that could no longer be ignored. The idea behind microfinance was that the poor did not need handouts; what they needed was access to credit. When it came to the poorest, the data failed to support this. During the 1990s, a handful of scholars began exploring the limits of microfinance. Abed credits a report from the Power and Participation Research Center (PPRC), a research institute and think tank run by Hossain Zillur Rahman, a Bangladeshi economist, for showing that microfinance was not reaching the poorest of the poor—the bottom 10 percent of income earners, those living on the edge of survival, the chronically hungry, the shunned.

Syed Hashemi, a researcher with Grameen, Bangladesh's other major microcredit provider, also began seeing data telling a story at odds with the one told by his boss, Muhammad Yunus. "Microcredit was being oversold," he said. "I had problems with Professor Yunus's narrative." Hashemi oversaw a survey in four villages where BRAC and Grameen were active, in which only 57 percent of those deemed poor enough to use their services—that is, those who were landless, or close to it—actually joined the microfinance groups. Of those who didn't join the groups, the largest portion, about half, had self-selected out, saying they feared being stuck with debt they couldn't repay and having to sell their few possessions. The programs had failed to target the poorest people effectively, "resulting in most of them remaining outside the microcredit net," Hashemi wrote. About 13 percent said they had wanted to join but were barred from doing so by the rest of the group for various reasons, including the fear that their husbands would gamble the money away—or because they just didn't get along with others in the village.[2]

Another survey, conducted by a member of BRAC's research unit with scholars from the Rockefeller Foundation and Columbia University, found that, in an area where an estimated 76 percent of households fell below the poverty line, only 27 percent belonged to one of the BRAC groups. The report suggested "a complex calculus of exclusion" that blocked the poorest from joining.[3]

Abed had conceived of the rural credit program with the poorest in mind—those who were landless or near landless, with close to zero assets, less than half an acre of land, and only their labor to sell. But in village after village, researchers found these microfinance groups were systematically excluding an entire category of people—women so destitute, unskilled, and lacking in confidence that they would never be able to pay back a loan. The ultra-poor, as BRAC called them, were almost always women, often widowed or abandoned. They lived barefoot and in rags at the margins of the villages, in dwellings of sticks and thatch. They would beg or do menial labor for a pittance when able, and if no work was available, they might not eat for days. Some were reduced to foraging for bits of corn that rats had hoarded in their holes. For others, a meal might consist of the water left over from the neighbor's boiled rice—which Mazeda, the early BRAC schoolteacher, had once drunk for its trace of nutrients.

Abed may have been helping the moderately poor with microfinance, but he was not helping the ultra-poor. This realization was humbling, for it meant BRAC was still not living up to its founding mission—to give power and agency to those who struggled the most.

⋆ ⋆ ⋆

They would have to rethink their approach. The discussions were led by two of Abed's chief deputies: Aminul Alam, who ran microfinance, and Mushtaque Chowdhury, the head of research. Both had been with BRAC since the 1970s and had forged a lifelong friendship in Manikganj, where they had shared a room for three months.

The two men could not be any more different. Amin was as aggressive and hotheaded as ever, often shouting at subordinates. Many loved him; others were jealous of the attention Abed gave him. However, none disputed that he was brilliantly entrepreneurial, honest, and fiercely loyal. Even his detractors said he had an extraordinary capacity to work. He had little patience for academic research, for he was in his element in the field—working with sharecroppers to find ways to improve their meager harvests, for example.

Mushtaque was a gentleman who never spoke a harsh word to anyone. His research unit acted as an independent shop within BRAC, often collaborating with outside scholars on lengthy studies to determine which interventions were working, which were not, and how they could improve. He was the avuncular professor, usually more comfortable surrounded by academic journals than sitting for hours with a farmer in a patch of dirt—although Mushtaque and his researchers also spent their fair share of time collecting data in tough field conditions.

For all their differences, Amin and Mushtaque were good friends. They would argue at the office during the day; at night, they would dine together with their wives and entertain guests at one another's homes. They lived in the same apartment building, and their children would play cricket together in the building's parking garage.

Having led the scale-up of microfinance since the mid-1980s, Amin initially bristled when the findings were shared, but he quickly accepted the need for a new solution. He knew that microfinance group meetings could create intense peer pressure to make payments, and although the women had pledged to help one another, defaulters could be subjected to public humiliation, which was no fun for anyone. BRAC staff were complicit, too, since they felt pressure to screen out potential credit risks. For outsiders from the city—and especially for foreign visitors—all the women seemed poor. But the ultra-poor were in a different category and virtually invisible.

BRAC already had one program that showed promise in reaching the poorest—although, even there, they weren't getting the results they wanted. It provided a starting point, however.

★ ★ ★

In the wake of the 1975 famine, the government of Bangladesh began running a food-rationing program called Vulnerable Group Feeding, paid for by the World Food Program, wherein women received about thirty kilograms of unprocessed wheat every month. For a family of seven, that would give everyone about two small pieces of flatbread per meal for three meals a day. Notably, they received it as raw, unmilled wheat, which was easier to sell in the market for cash. The program gave out this ration for two years, during which the women were supposed to learn a trade or find a viable livelihood. At the end of the two years, the women would leave the program, and a new cohort of women would start receiving rations for another two-year period. This continued, one two-year cycle after another, long after the famine was a distant memory. To stress the idea that the program was supposed to help people develop long-term livelihoods, the government eventually changed the name to Vulnerable Group Development (VGD), but, according to Abed, the program did little in the way of "development." After two years, participants were left high and dry, and most slid back into destitution.

Abed recalled a discussion, likely in 1984, with Salahuddin Ahmed, a Bangladeshi who served as deputy executive director of the World Food Program. As it happens, they were related by marriage: Salahuddin had married the oldest sister of Bahar, Abed's late wife. "We are finding it very difficult to get this project funded knowing that nothing is happening," Salahuddin said, according to Abed. "The government is not doing anything to make these women self-sustaining. All they are doing is giving them this food ration for two years, and then giving the food ration to somebody else."

Abed suggested an alternative approach. Starting with a pilot of just seven hundred women already chosen for VGD, BRAC would augment their rations with livelihood training so they would have something to fall back on when they stopped receiving the wheat. The new BRAC program had an unwieldy name: Income Generation for Vulnerable Group Development (IGVGD).

For the idea to work, women would need viable work options, which were hard to come by in rural areas. Religious and patriarchal conservatism barred most women from working off the homestead. BRAC had pushed back on these norms through consciousness raising, but this hardly revolutionized the culture. In Manikganj, which would serve as the IGVGD pilot site, Amin had focused much of the women's training on things they could do at home—weaving saris, embroidery, block printing, and basket weaving—with BRAC selling their products at the Aarong shop in Dhaka.

At first, Amin and Abed thought handicrafts might be an option for the IGVGD women. Then they considered the sheer number of people they would have to train. The government was giving wheat rations to two hundred thousand women at a time. If it planned to cover even a portion of these, crafts wouldn't do, for they could only sell so many saris and baskets. "Two hundred thousand women every two years meant Aarong would have to contend with so many producers that we wouldn't be able to handle it," Abed said. "How many shops are you going to have? It wasn't possible to get them into artisanal skills. We would have to do something they can sell in the locality."

The answer was chickens. Using money they had saved from selling some of the unmilled wheat, the women would buy chickens from BRAC and receive three days of training, free of charge, on how to care for them. They could eat the eggs they laid or sell them locally for extra cash, all without leaving the homestead. Ten hens and one cock for each woman turned out to yield about six eggs per day, roughly the same value as the thirty kilograms of wheat they were getting from the government—but only if the chickens were a hybrid between the domestic variety and imported white leghorns. "Some of them would do very well, and would not have nine hens, but thirty or forty," said Abed. "But nine hens and one cock was the minimum they needed to replace the amount of wheat they were getting from the government." When the two years were up, they would have something of lasting value and might even avail themselves of BRAC microfinance to grow their brood.

Provided the chickens didn't die of disease, that is. Without vaccinations, the mortality rate of the white leghorn hybrids exceeded 40 percent. Amin approached this the way he did every problem, like a garage mechanic constantly putting the car on a hydraulic lift and tinkering with its engine. They decided to train a corps of "poultry workers," one woman for each village, who would serve as the local vaccinator. After a five-day training course, she would go door to door, vaccinating the neighbors' chickens for a small fee. The government livestock department provided the vaccines—although, in another snag, the vaccines needed to be refrigerated, and the fridges in the local livestock department offices would often break down. BRAC trained a corps of fridge repairmen to make sure they kept working.

This complicated scheme, funded under a government contract with World Food Program funding, spread to most of the country. By the early 1990s, BRAC was training thousands of village poultry workers each year. By 1996, it had more than thirty thousand active poultry workers in as many villages. The mortality rate for the vaccinated chickens fell to about 15 percent. By the mid-1990s, BRAC had 150,000 women in each two-year cycle of the program.

A World Food Program survey found that approximately two-thirds of the participants "graduated" from absolute poverty to become microfinance clients. Even four years after they stopped receiving the wheat rations and training, they were still borrowing and saving. That was not a terrible result. Yet, according to the same survey, fully a quarter of the women sold their chickens and slipped back into poverty as soon as the wheat rations ended.

One of the problems was that BRAC was still riding on the back of a government program. Local politicians had the final say in who was included, so corruption inevitably crept into the process. Women sometimes had to buy their way into the program by bribing a government official to receive a ration card. They would borrow money for the bribe from the rations distributor, who would collect on the loan by overcharging for the wheat.[4]

The program attracted positive attention from people like Hashemi, the Grameen researcher. However, for Abed, it wasn't good enough.

* * *

Martin Greeley, a veteran researcher with the Institute of Development Studies at the University of Sussex, UK, recalled the peculiar dynamic between Mushtaque and Amin. Wry and observant, with the detached air of a British academic, Greeley had been studying BRAC on and off since 1979. As research head, Mushtaque had hired him to do a scholarly deep dive into the performance of BRAC's rural credit program in the 1990s. Microfinance "was Amin's baby," according to Greeley.

To present the findings, the three men sat together in the home office in Dhaka. As Mushtaque summarized the results of the research, Amin swatted away each point with variations on the same rebuttal: we know that, and we're already doing something about it. "It was robust," Greeley said. "Outside the office they were friends. I had been at dinner parties at both their houses." During work discussions, "they felt they were doing their jobs and defending their patches." When BRAC resolved to create a new program dedicated to the ultra-poor, Amin's resistance dissolved. It helped that the order came from Abed, the one man whose directives he never questioned.

In a long process involving staff and outside consultants, BRAC began designing a program that sought to build on the modest gains of IGVGD. The full name of the new program was even more unwieldy: Challenging the Frontiers of Poverty Reduction—Targeting the Ultra-Poor" (CFPR-TUP). Greeley, who came up with that mouthful, confessed he had no idea the BRAC program would be saddled with the name for years to come. Hashemi, from the beginning, said he called it the "graduation program," which caught on as shorthand.

Like its predecessor, the new program would support women for a period of twenty-four months. After that, they would be on their own. This time around, BRAC, not the government or local elites, would have complete control over who entered the program, albeit with participation from communities. They would begin by convening groups of forty to fifty villagers and asking them to draw a map in the dirt, showing where the poorest people lived. Program staff would follow up with door-to-door visits, using questionnaires to determine who were the poorest. Were there multiple sources of income, just one, or none? Did the woman have shoes on her feet? How many meals per day were they eating? Were there school-age children in the household? Senior managers would spot-check and vet the final selection of participants to ensure that village politics did not corrupt the process. This rigorous process was designed to reduce the inclusion of people who did not really need the help.

Once they were in the program, women would get a package of intensive support: a big push that included a grant of cows, goats, chickens, or seeds; training in how to generate income; a cash stipend to give them breathing room while they learned their new livelihood; a savings account; and basic health care. BRAC also made sure their children went to school, encouraged them to adopt savings habits and good hygiene, and coached them in the basics of financial management. It was an intensive immersion course on getting out of poverty.

There was also a component of one-on-one coaching, which the old IGVGD program had lacked. A BRAC caseworker would pay each participant a personal visit once a week to make sure she was able to manage her new asset. If the cow proved too big for her to handle, they might switch it for chickens or goats. They would discuss whatever other problems she might be facing—in effect, holding her hand as she made the inevitably rough transition to self-reliance.

BRAC selected the first seventy thousand participants in 2002. Among them was Amina Begum.

* * *

The morning after her cow died, still weeping uncontrollably, Amina appeared at the local BRAC office to tell her story. Her cow was everything to her, and she was convinced that Farhad and Syed, who had long complained about it destroying their crops, had deliberately untied and poisoned the cow.

A BRAC branch office was a hub of many activities. Community health workers, who made the rounds on foot to local homes, refilled their satchels of basic medicines. People came to discuss their loans. Staff administered a slew of other programs like education and legal aid. All this business came to a standstill in the presence of the wailing Amina and her tale of the poisoned cow.

The BRAC officials, or the *bhais*, as she called them, gathered the facts and went to Farhad's house, across the river, to plead the case that he should remunerate Amina for her loss. Farhad denied having done anything wrong, dismissed them, and accused Amina of letting her cow run rampant over his crops.

The workers at the BRAC office continued to press the case. It came to a head two days later at the home of the local Union Council chairman, who served as the local boss, often adjudicating disputes in front of his own home. The entire Union Council—the unit of government in charge of a conglomeration of villages—was present. Farhad and Syed appeared at the hearing with their supporting entourage. Amina was backed by a party of BRAC officials. Since it was market day in the town, this assemblage drew an even larger crowd. All told, about five hundred people gathered inside and around the chairman's house to get a glimpse of the drama, according to Amina. She was the only woman. The facts were laid out, though (much to her displeasure) she was not allowed to speak.

It did not look good for Syed. The rope Amina had used to tie the cow to the post was not around its neck when Amina came up from the riverbank, nor was it next to the post. An eyewitness had told Amina he had seen Syed toss the rope away, and Amina had found the rope exactly where the witness said Syed had tossed it.

After hearing both sides, the chairman pronounced his verdict. Farhad, as the owner of the land, was partially responsible, so he and Amina should split the cost of the cow.

"Mr. Chairman," the BRAC *bhai* in charge of the case responded, "that's impossible. Amina has nothing. The cow was her only asset. If that's your decision, it's as good as making her destitute again."

The chairman conceded the point. In that case, Farhad and Syed should split the cost. Farhad then pointed out that Syed himself was only a sharecropper and hardly had the means to compensate Amina. At this point, perhaps seeing he was unlikely to win the day and eager for the affair to end, Farhad offered to pay the full value of the cow, or 3,900 taka (about $80 at the time). Recognizing his largesse, the other members of the Union Council joined together to chip in 1,900 taka.

Amina buried the cow behind her house. She got a new cow, and eventually more livestock, and grew bean plants over the cow's grave. Before long, the case of the poisoned cow faded into memory.

* * *

Across the pilot area, similar disputes arose. One woman, jealous of her neighbor's new goat, tried to steal it. Fighting broke out as neighbors complained about noisy chickens. An angry landowner refused to allow someone's new cow to cross his land to graze.

Time and again, the women were unable to stand up for themselves. "My neighbor stole my goat," a participant would tell her caseworker, even naming the culprit. Everyone in the village knew what had happened.

"Did you ask for it back? Did you protest?" the caseworker would ask. The women rarely put up an argument or even tried to negotiate.

The ultra-poor may have lacked physical assets such as goats and cows, but they also faced a more profound privation—a severe shortage of social standing and self-esteem. Any change, even the responsibility of caring for a brood of hens, tended to worsen their existing fear. Imran Matin was a Bangladeshi researcher who had completed his PhD in development economics at the University of Sussex, where Martin Greeley had served as his internal examiner. He joined BRAC's research division in 2001 and shortly thereafter began conducting studies on the early iterations of the graduation program. "All these dynamics started revealing themselves," Imran said. "The social status of the ultra-poor really started to become clear. They were treated as subhuman beings. For every little thing, it became obvious they needed us. They had no social voice, no social capital."

These seemingly petty disputes—though they were anything but petty for the women involved—had the potential to derail the entire program, since they consumed most of the staff's time. Unable to turn to anyone else in the community, the participants had to appeal directly to BRAC for assistance, often traveling long distances to do so. The women developed a relationship of dependence, akin to patronage, with BRAC, which was the exact opposite of what BRAC was trying to do.

★ ★ ★

To lead the graduation program, Amin had appointed Rabeya Yasmine, a young protégé of his who had helped design it, having led IGVGD since 1996. One of the most awkward things about BRAC was the fact that it was led almost entirely by men; even within an organization devoted to women's empowerment, the patriarchal culture was strong. Amin went out of his way to mentor women and promote them to leadership positions. Rabeya was one of them, and, according to Martin Greeley, "as far as she was concerned, the light shone out from Amin."

Rabeya took note of the various disputes, came back to Dhaka, and had a brief but formative chat with Amin. "Why don't you go and form a village assistance committee?" her boss asked her, according to Rabeya. That was all. There was no elaborate discussion, for that was not Amin's style. He would rather let his subordinates figure out the details.

"He was like a supersonic bullet," Rabeya said. "He would just hit you, and you'd have to absorb it." She went back to her desk and pondered his words. She had faith in Amin. He had paid his dues; he had slept on enough dirt floors to have gained wisdom and insight into village life. Therefore, there must be some merit in what he had just said.

Nearly everyone at BRAC knew that Abed's early experience had refuted the idea of relying on the "community" to solve its own problems. The village elites had always been the villains in the BRAC story. Bringing them onto a "committee," which seemed to be what Amin was implying, usually ended with the strong dominating and exploiting the weak.

Rabeya spent days strategizing over the village assistance committees, which later became known, at Abed's suggestion, as the Village Poverty Reduction Committees. She developed a detailed plan. Before adding the next round of participants to the program, they would approach the landowners, village bosses, business owners, and other respected members of each community. They would ask them to join a seven-member committee that would meet every month to offer advice and oversee local aspects of the graduation program's implementation.

Most important, Rabeya instructed her staff to speak to the village elites using a simple script, which went something like this: "This is your village. BRAC has started running a program to help the poorest here, but we are not a permanent solution. Who helped the poorest before we arrived? You did. When they were hungry, you gave them rice and leftover food. You gave them your old clothes. Now we want to help you do the same thing but in a more organized manner, to bring about long-lasting change in their lives."

It worked. In other circumstances, some of the same landlords and bosses might have tried to commandeer the program for their own gain. When framed in positive terms, appealing to their sense of good citizenship—when BRAC spoke of permanently ending the privation that everyone, rich and poor and all those in between, had long accepted as a fact of life—they began doing the opposite. In the next round of asset transfers, these committees began stepping in to adjudicate local disputes, protecting the participants and thus relieving the burden on the staff. Many even began offering free tutoring to children of the ultra-poor women. These Village Poverty Reduction Committees became a pillar of the program.

The astonishing changes that took place in the women's lives was evident long before independent research confirmed it. It was not just the extra income from cows, chickens, and goats. For the first time, the women found themselves accepted into the mainstream life of the village. They were invited to people's homes, to weddings and religious festivals. The women carried themselves taller, looked people in the eye when they talked, and smiled more often. According to Abed, a key element was the regular coaching and hand-holding by BRAC caseworkers, which gave people courage and hope, catapulting the program beyond the middling success of the IGVGD program.

The research and evaluation team produced dozens of working papers assessing all aspects of the program with a more objective eye. They found the health of women participants did indeed improve substantially. They took in more food and a greater variety of nutrients. The research culminated in a four-year randomized controlled trial (RCT) launched in 2007 in collaboration with a group of independent scholars. A new trend in development studies at the time, RCTs were usually used in measuring the efficacy of drugs, but they were fast becoming the gold standard in evaluating social programs as well. The RCT confirmed that the graduation program was having a significant and long-lasting impact on people's lives, leading to a 38 percent rise in earnings, which persisted long after they left the program.[5] People did not sell their goats and chickens at the end of the two years, in other words, but continued to climb the economic ladder. By almost every measure, the women who participated in this program were wealthier, happier, and more independent—and the change seemed to be permanent.

* * *

What creates a poverty trap? This is one of the oldest questions in economics, as the authors of the first randomized evaluation of BRAC's graduation program pointed out. According to one definition, a poverty trap exists when people, or even entire countries, cannot invest enough resources to improve their lot over a sustained period of time. Whatever paltry return they get on their investment is too small to make any long-term difference in their material needs. Even if they get a temporary boost, they eventually slip back.

In a classic nutrition-based poverty trap, a person's wages are so low they cannot earn enough to eat properly. They may not starve, but they remain weak and malnourished, which leads to low productivity and, therefore, low income and so on in a vicious cycle. Abhijit Banerjee and Esther Duflo, winners of the 2019 Nobel Prize in Economics, examine the evidence for this type of trap and find it wanting. They look at what tends to happen when extremely poor people gain more income. If the poverty trap were caused by undernutrition only, it stands to reason that hungry people would invest as much of their new income as possible in food, in order to get stronger and healthier, so they could work more, earn more money, and climb out of the trap. Often this is not what happens. Instead, food expenditure rises at roughly the same rate as overall consumption. This suggests that for the hungry, food is not the overwhelming priority we assume it to be. Sometimes people will even go hungry and save up to buy a TV to stave off boredom.[6] Despite this evidence—or lack thereof—the assumption that hunger causes people to remain poor still accounts for billions spent on food aid each year.

Duflo has explored an alternative theory, presenting evidence that hopelessness itself can be a source of poverty traps. The causal pathway runs through the stress of poverty itself. People experiencing stress tend to see the future, rightly or wrongly, in a more negative light. Evidence from psychology shows us that this, by itself, tends to lead to more negative outcomes, since people see the future as bleak no matter what they do and thus modify their behavior in a way that makes positive outcomes even less likely—for instance, by not working as hard. For those in poverty, such pessimism is often well grounded. Consider Abed's anecdote about the woman with the cow, whom he and Amin encountered at the end of a dirt path in the early 1990s. Due to the low price of milk, her cow barely produced enough to pay off her loan and would never boost her out of poverty. She had little incentive to work harder. Other times, however, even a small injection of hope yields gains. Duflo cites a study in West Bengal, India, in which mere exposure to local female politicians led to higher educational attainment for girls, despite no other changes in the education system. Aspiration led to hope, which led to better outcomes.[7]

For Abed, this explanation resonated with his experience more than any other. In the Bengali language, there is a word for planning—*porikolpona*, which literally means "arranging imagination." As Abed once pointed out, getting people to earn and save led to a transformation worth more than the money itself, for it arranged people's imagination toward a better future: "Regular savings, however meager, is a very powerful mechanism that gets the poor to arrange their imaginations for tomorrow and beyond."[8]

One can draw a direct line between the changes Abed saw in the early BRAC participants in Sulla, when the flames of self-worth began to flicker in the first classes based on the pedagogy of Paulo Freire, and the stories of transformation that occurred with the graduation program. As Abed saw it, poverty deprived people of the capacity to be fully human—to dream, to plan, to arrange their imagination to see a better future. They were trapped in poverty in large part because they felt their condition was immutable. Deep-seated skepticism of change—a conviction that one's condition was "ordained by a higher power, as immutable as the sun and the moon," as Abed put it—could become a self-perpetuating trap of hopelessness, sustaining itself based on a person's inability to imagine that a better world is possible. Only by nurturing their ability to imagine a better future, to cast aside fatalism and believe that one's destiny is, at least partially, in one's own hands, could the problem be solved. "People trapped in a cycle of destitution often don't realize their lives can be changed for the better through their own activities," he told the *New York Times* in 2015, in an article on the success of the graduation approach. "Once they understand that, it's like a light gets turned on."[9]

At the boundary between economics, psychology, and neurology, an emerging "science of hope," as Abed called it near the end of his life, suggests a well-placed injection of hope and self-esteem, provided it is combined with an adequate boost of material support, can make all the difference. Only by "nurturing their capacity to think independently, critically, and creatively" could empowerment programs live up to Paulo Freire's maxim that true education "makes it possible for students to become themselves."[10]

Shahida, whose story begins this book, was another member of the first graduation cohort. She had been carrying mud in a pail on her head at a brickfield, backbreaking work that paid pennies per day. The program made her a professional goat raiser, but it did far more than that. It turned her into a woman with swagger, not afraid to sass the police. When she put down her mud pail for the last time and began lavishing attention on her goats, it wasn't just a smart move that would give her a little more income. It was the triumph of hope over fate.

22

SELF-SUSTAINING MODE

Abed had always remained friendly with Sarwat, one of his cousins on his mother's side. She had been born in the home he lived in while attending Dhaka College, shortly before he left East Pakistan in 1954. When Abed was eighteen and she was a newborn, he'd been chosen to recite the *azan* into her ear; later, when Marietta visited Bangladesh, he'd taken a teenage Sarwat to meet her at the airport. Few people, even those closest to them, foresaw what would happen with Abed and Sarwat in the year 2000.

At this time, Sarwat was divorced with two grown children and living outside Dallas. She flew to Washington, DC, to visit Abed, who was passing through for a World Bank conference. It had been three years since Shilu's death, and Abed still felt the sting of loneliness.

During their meeting, Abed heard the following words come out of his mouth: "Life would be so much more pleasurable if I could marry you." He added, "If only I weren't so much older." He was sixty-four. She was forty-six.

Sarwat replied, "Is that *really* such a problem?" Cousins marrying one another in Bangladesh is legal and, though not common, not exceedingly rare, either.

They went immediately to a jewelry shop near Union Station, where Abed bought her an engagement ring before they returned to their respective homes in Dhaka and Dallas. Early one morning later that year, Abed picked her up at the Dhaka airport. She rested a few hours before an at-home wedding ceremony that afternoon.

"I really didn't see that coming," said Shameran Abed. Sarwat was never a particularly close member of the family, since she had lived in the United States for many years. His one adult memory of Sarwat, previous to the marriage, was when he and his father had visited her during a layover in Dallas in 1998, on their way to Tucson to visited Abed's old friend John Paul Kay, who by then was dying of a skin melanoma that had migrated to his brain.

When pressed on whether his DC proposal was really as spontaneous as it sounded, Abed conceded, "It was premeditated in the sense that I had thought about it. It came out at a particular moment. *That* was not premeditated. I didn't mean to propose to her at that point. It just came out of my mouth."

Abed said he fully expected to die around the same age as his grandfather, at seventy-two, or his father, at seventy-three. "I'll probably survive another five years," he told Sarwat.

She replied, "If we have a happy five years, that would be wonderful."

They ended up having far more than that. Indeed, his third marriage lasted longer than either of his first two. Starting at the age of seventy, every year on their anniversary, he would tell her, "Another bonus year for us."

According to Cole Dodge, the union brought an end to one of Abed's dark periods. "Sarwat was a godsend," he said.

⋆ ⋆ ⋆

The year 2000 was momentous for both Abed and BRAC. As per the plan of the previous decade, the microfinance program, having expanded nationwide, turned a corner and began making enough money to open new branches on its own, without donor funding. Abed had achieved one of his longest-standing goals: to make the majority of BRAC's operations self-financing. Only 25 percent of BRAC's $150 million annual budget now came from donors. Even if donor funding were to evaporate completely, he knew BRAC could survive with about thirty thousand staff "and maybe run a few thousand schools out of the surplus of microfinance."

This was the year, in his mind, that BRAC actually started becoming big. It now employed fifty-six thousand people, including the thirty-one thousand part-time teachers in its primary schools, with more than five million people counting themselves members of the village organizations. The numbers began growing more rapidly now that donors could no longer dictate the speed of expansion. With the repayment rate exceeding 99 percent, BRAC's credit portfolio more than doubled in the next six years. Much to his annoyance, people began asking whether BRAC was getting too large, to which he would reply, "Do you ask Shell why they employ so many people? No. So why do you ask us?"

And donor funding did not evaporate—far from it. A donor consortium continued to finance the education of more than one million primary school students, and, in 2001, another consortium backed the launch of the ultra-poor graduation program. "We decided to conserve our own resources as much as possible," said Abed. As long as donor money was available, Abed would use it, allowing him to use the internally generated revenue to grow BRAC's reserves, expand the existing enterprises, and invest in new businesses. The strategy was to "continue raising money from the outside and use as little as possible of the internal money generated," which remains the strategy to this day. "We were on to a self-sustaining mode, and I wanted to make it even more solid," he said.

⋆ ⋆ ⋆

For years, Abed had flirted with the idea of starting a proper bank. In the late 1990s, studies pointed to the existence of a "missing middle" in the credit sector—small entrepreneurs whose borrowing needs were too great for the small loans of microfinance, but who were still not served by existing commercial banks.

BRAC already had a small-enterprise lending program, which it had set up in 1996 to drive job creation by supporting entrepreneurs in the start-up or expansion phase. After three years of operation, an external review pointed to a still unmet need. Average loan size had grown from 26,000 taka (about $650) in 1996 to 46,800 (nearly $1,000) at the end of 1999, with no rise in delinquency. Based on interviews with field staff and district managers, the review estimated that the average loan size could easily be twice that. The main obstacle was the conservatism of a program whose decision-making process was still rudimentary. The assessment of borrowers' creditworthiness depended largely on the personal judgment of the front-line field worker, a far cry from the professional risk analysis befitting a proper commercial bank. The reviewers also said that without significant expansion, enterprise lending would not likely have much impact aside from "shuffling income and employment from one community business to another."

Opening a real bank, as people had reminded Abed several times over the years, would be impossible without government permission, and until now the erratic turns of national politics had failed to yield such an opening. Ziaur Rahman, the war hero turned president, had been assassinated in yet another coup attempt in 1981, and a ten-year military dictatorship followed, toppled by a student uprising in 1991. By then, two dominant figures in Bangladeshi politics had emerged, the daughter and wife, respectively, of the country's two late wartime leaders—Sheikh Hasina, one of the daughters of Sheikh Mujib who happened to be in West Germany when the rest of the family was massacred in 1975, and Khaleda Zia, Ziaur Rahman's wife.

Khaleda Zia won the elections in 1991, but her government proved unfriendly to the idea of a BRAC bank. (Notably, the earlier iteration of the "BRAC Bank" idea—described as the "BRAC Bank project" to donors in 1989 but as the "Rural Credit Program" in official documents—went on to become the microfinance program, which Abed now had every intention of continuing on its own track. The new BRAC bank would be something entirely different, focused on larger commercial loans.) After power shifted back to Sheikh Hasina's Awami League in 1996, Abed applied for a bank license again. "At the end of 1999, we were told that we would get the license, provided we go through the formalities of setting up a bank," Abed said. Donor money would not be needed, for BRAC was now sitting on tens of millions of US dollars, which it could invest anywhere it wanted. These reserves came from the profits from Aarong and other enterprises, as well as the gratuity fund for employees, which funded the lump-sum retirement payouts for BRAC staff.

There was one catch. In December 1999, the High Court Division issued an injunction blocking the first branch of BRAC Bank from opening. The court had responded to a petition from Muzaffar Ahmed, a professor of economics at the University of Dhaka, who claimed that BRAC, by pursuing banking activities, would be acting contrary to its objectives set out in its original 1972 memorandum of association as a charitable society, as governed by the Societies Registration Act of 1860. Abed put it more succinctly: "This guy didn't like BRAC or Grameen Bank." Ahmed was among those who felt BRAC was becoming too big and too powerful.

The case went all the way to the Supreme Court, which ruled in favor of BRAC in June 2001. The court conceded that the petitioner—that is, the professor—"is not a busybody or interloper," nor "a litigious person" with "a dubious goal for generating publicity for himself." Rather, he was a concerned citizen "whose heart bleeds for his less fortunate beings." Nonetheless, the professor had failed to show that he or "his less fortunate beings" would be harmed in any way by BRAC setting up a bank. The court ruled that a charitable society could invest its own funds as it saw fit as long as the returns were used solely for the charity's stated purpose, just as colleges and religious foundations frequently place their sizable endowments in dividend-yielding investments. Immediately following the Supreme Court's decision, BRAC Bank opened its first branch, focusing on lending to small- and medium-sized enterprises.

⋆ ⋆ ⋆

Abed had long preferred to empower the poor directly rather than through roundabout means like trying to change government policies. It is hard to say when he began to change his mind about this, but a shift was well underway by the mid-1990s, likely hastened by the failure of the deep tube wells project, which he had hoped would upend rural power structures. Abed then realized the landless poor would not become a political force unto themselves—not in his lifetime, anyway. If he wanted Bangladesh to be more equitable and less corrupt, change would have to come about through incremental means. The reins of power in society were held by a network of elites and would remain so for the foreseeable future. In order to change society, one had to influence the schooling of those elites.

According to Abed, the original idea for BRAC University grew from his recognition that the government, much to his dismay, would never adopt the methods of the BRAC school system without a mindset shift on the part of education officials. In fact, the government did not seem to be learning anything from BRAC at all, which led to what he named as the single most important lesson of his career: "More and more, I realize that improving governance is as important as development," he said in 2015. "In the old days, we used to think NGOs could solve all the problems."

There was an element of opportunism. Bangladesh had passed a law in 1992 allowing for the establishment of private universities, part of a global trend that saw the number of such institutions surge worldwide in the 1990s. According to his friend Cole Dodge, who by the mid-1990s was working full time on a revitalization plan for Uganda's Makerere University, this was "not only a window, but a large gate"—and Abed, he said, was actually slower to respond compared to others.

Many entrepreneurs saw for-profit universities as an opportunity to make money, catering to those who had the money to spend on a degree even if they were academically underqualified. Abed's vision was broader, unsurprisingly. He wanted to cultivate a new and more enlightened class of public administrators in education and other areas of service. He conceived of a university-educated "functional elite," which meant not just the country's rulers but also the emerging class of entrepreneurs, bankers, civil servants, and middle managers who had a hand in executing power. In Abed's conception, a truly functional elite would be responsive to the needs of society as a whole, not just themselves, in contrast to the dysfunctional, corrupt, rent-seeking elites that held power. He wanted university graduates to understand "the dynamics of deprivation" in low-income societies, so that higher education would cultivate ethical and empathetic leadership in all professions—not just "softhearted development workers."

Less than one half of 1 percent of Bangladeshis attended university. Abed thought higher education would help Bangladesh avoid the "middle-income trap," which sees countries rise from the poorest ranks and then get stuck. He theorized that the Asian societies that had broken free of the middle-income trap, like South Korea and Singapore, had done so by investing in higher education. Drawing on his connections, he brought together a committee of wise heads to help him. These included his old friend Lincoln Chen, now a professor and department chair at the Harvard School of Public Health; Derek Bok, the president of Harvard; and prominent Bangladeshi academics. The advisory group commissioned a feasibility study on starting a private university in Bangladesh and hired David Fraser, an epidemiologist who had served as president of Swarthmore College and later conducted strategic planning for the Aga Khan University in Karachi, to conduct it.

Abed favored the liberal arts model, which had its roots in Oxford and Cambridge but had proliferated most widely in the United States. A liberal arts education cultivated a well-rounded worldview and fine-tuned a capacity for critical thinking, as opposed to the technical and practical skills that would prepare students for immediate employment, like accounting and engineering. It is ironic that Abed himself never had anything close to such an education; inspired largely by his uncle, Sayeedul, he was an autodidact of the liberal arts.

In the hundred-page feasibility report he delivered in 1996, Fraser did his best to support Abed's case that a liberal arts university would help fix an educational system that was "underfunded, overstretched, and dysfunctional." The idea of liberal arts education was not especially popular in Bangladesh, which favored a more narrowly utilitarian model with its roots in the colonial system, born of British authorities' need to find suitable government employees. Even so, Fraser wrote, "With appropriate attention to tailoring the curricula to local needs and opportunities, such an innovation might be able to overcome resistance to 'liberal arts' education, as it is now understood in the country." In a 2020 interview, Fraser recalled that Abed was "in some ways standing the education development process on its head" by even considering a liberal arts institution in a place like Bangladesh.

There were two problems with the liberal arts idea, both of which proved to be insurmountable. The first was the price tag. To establish such a university, Fraser recommended Abed raise $56 million for capital outlays and endowment. This may have been easier with an ultra-wealthy benefactor like Fraser's former boss, the Aga Khan, the wealthy spiritual leader of millions of Nizari Ismaili Muslims worldwide. Without such a resource, it was an impossible sum for a country like Bangladesh, even with Abed's reputation among donors.

In any case, the law would not have allowed it. Following Fraser's feasibility study, Abed asked Cole to make the rounds of senior government officials to measure their receptiveness to a private liberal arts university—with Cole himself as the vice-chancellor, or chief executive. It was a hard no to both, said Cole. "It became clear there was no chance for a liberal arts curriculum according to strict government guidelines," he said. Nor would the establishment accept a foreigner as vice-chancellor.

So be it, said Abed. The university would have to start on a more strictly utilitarian basis and introduce liberal arts elements by stealth. Moreover, it would have to be funded almost entirely by tuition fees. In April 2001, BRAC University admitted its first class of undergraduate students, offering degrees in business administration, computer science, economics, English, and architecture. Jamilur Reza Choudhury, a prominent Bangladesh academic and civil engineer, served as the inaugural vice-chancellor. The start-up costs were just $900,000 from BRAC itself and $800,000 from Ford Foundation, most of the latter to fund a scholarship endowment. Tuition would pay for the rest. "The model adopted by Abed was clearly to treat BRAC University as an enterprise," said Cole. Graduate-level institutes were soon added, starting with the BRAC Institute of Educational Development, focusing on pedagogical methods, school administration, curriculum development, and teacher training. The James P. Grant School of Public Health, named for the former head of UNICEF and a champion of BRAC, would educate an elite cadre of public health professionals and midwives. Abed's wife, Sarwat, founded the university's Institute of Languages in 2005.

Abed considered BRAC University the capstone of his life's work. He often pointed out that, historically, universities have the greatest longevity among institutions, since they tend to educate a country's leaders, who go on to protect the universities' independence. Oxford, Cambridge, and the University of Bologna have existed for eight hundred years or more, outlasting parliaments and corporations. BRAC itself may or may not exist in a century. Abed was confident BRAC University would.

23

FROM TAGORE'S LAND

By 2000, the team at the top of BRAC consisted of five people, all men. Abed had appointed three deputy executive directors: Amin running the ground operations, Mushtaque leading the research division, and Salehuddin Ahmed in charge of training and other administrative functions like human resources, logistics, construction, and accounts. In the 1970s, Salehuddin had been one of the researchers behind "The Net," the BRAC research study that traced a sinister web of rural corruption. Articulate and well spoken, with a PhD in economics, he began representing BRAC in international forums and climbed the ranks to a senior management role.

The fifth man was one of Abed's oldest friends, Faruq Choudhury, part of the group of Bengali expatriates who had first come together at the East Pakistan student hostel in 1956. Faruq had gone on to a distinguished career in the Pakistani, and then Bangladeshi, foreign service. By the mid-1980s, he had risen to the rank of foreign minister, and he then served six years as the Bangladeshi high commissioner to India. After his retirement in 1992, Faruq became a consigliere-type figure to Abed, a chief advisor sitting outside the organizational hierarchy.

Of these five men, Abed's golden child was still Amin, who continued to do the work of several people. Amin suffered from one severe shortcoming, however. His communication skills were unpolished, and his English was fractured and heavily accented. "I once told Abed *Bhai* that if Amin spoke good English, none of us would even have our jobs at BRAC," said Salehuddin.

There was little non-BRAC experience on the team. With the exception of Faruq Choudhury, all had joined as young men in the 1970s, when the organization employed less than four hundred people. Abed would turn sixty-five in 2001, and he thought the organization was on solid enough footing that he no longer needed to serve as executive director, but there was nobody, even among his top deputies, whom he felt comfortable handing BRAC over to.

To replace himself, it is telling that Abed neither promoted someone from within nor hired a professional from the field of development, like a seasoned executive from a large NGO like Oxfam, Save the Children, or CARE. Instead, he chose a former government official who had himself just retired. Abdul-Muyeed Chowdhury, a career bureaucrat, had recently ended a long career in the Bangladesh civil service. He recalled being "accosted" on the golf course by Faruq at the end of 1999, with a message from Abed: "He wants you to be the new boss of BRAC."

BRAC had grown so large that executive-level engagement with the government was necessary, and Muyeed (as he was known) was highly respected in government circles, having worked in areas as diverse as land administration, narcotics control, and the finance ministry. He had even served as CEO of the national airline at one point, and he had overseen the completion of the Jamuna Bridge, a billion-dollar mega-project that finally linked the distant banks of the Brahmaputra, or Jamuna, which split Bangladesh in two. Muyeed had risen to the ranks of permanent secretary, the equivalent of a vice-minister or undersecretary, the highest non-political rank one could attain in the civil service. If an approval was stuck in ministerial limbo, Muyeed could unstick it. Two weeks after his retirement in July 2000, he took over as the new executive director of BRAC, only the second in the organization's history.

Abed would become chair of the governing body, a post long held by his friend Humayun Kabir, which would allow him to step back from managing the day-to-day affairs of the organization, at least nominally. In truth, though, Abed had no real wish to relinquish control. According to Mushtaque, this eventually became a classic case of "founder's syndrome," when a powerful founder of a company or organization has difficulty passing on the torch to anyone else.

* * *

Among Muyeed's first tasks was to explore and, if necessary, negotiate the terms of becoming part of Oxfam, the British charity that had been BRAC's first funder. The idea had emerged in conversations between Abed and Sylvia Borren, the executive director of Oxfam Novib, formerly known as just Novib. The Dutch organization had been one of BRAC's largest supporters through the 1980s, and it had joined Oxfam International, a newly established confederation of Oxfam-affiliated organizations, in 1995.

According to Borren, both she and Abed initially agreed on the mutual benefits of BRAC joining Oxfam. The combined entity would create a global advocacy network with the stature to convince governments to adopt policies that favored human rights and poverty reduction. BRAC would have a seat at the table of international dialogue, and Oxfam would benefit from having a credible voice from the "Global South," the emerging term for low-income countries. "I thought it would totally change the perception and the reality of Oxfam being a Western donor group," said Borren, who worked for two years to make the marriage happen.

After participating in several meetings with the Oxfam directors, BRAC's leadership, including Abed, said it would need to undertake a consultation with internal stakeholders, including middle and field-level management. A major sticking point was what BRAC would be allowed to call itself. According to the rules of the confederation, "Oxfam" would have to be a part of the new name, at least internationally. "The issue of changing or modifying the name stood out as the biggest challenge to BRAC's membership," according to an internal Oxfam report from April 2001.[1]

Borren recalled three successive instances in which she sensed this prospective partnership was falling apart. The first was observing Abed during several meetings of the Oxfam directors. He was "amazed at the endless deliberations," she said—and not in a good way. Bored and impatient, Abed was used to "running his own empire" at BRAC. A protracted style of decision-making was not for him. "He'd get sick of it and he'd disappear," she said. He would go back to his hotel room and work; later, "he'd come and ask me what happened, because he just couldn't spend his time like that." On another occasion, Oxfam leadership shifted the proposed site of a meeting in Bangladesh due to a fear of political unrest in the run-up to the 2001 general election. "This was very offensive to Abed," she said.

The final straw came at another meeting of Oxfam leaders, where one of the country directors raised a point on the supposed incompatibility of Islam and democracy by arguing, incorrectly, that no majority Muslim states were democracies. It was likely November 2001, though Borren cannot recall the location or whether it was before or after 9/11. A discussion ensued. "I sat there, and I watched the train crash happen," said Borren. Having worked closely with Abed for years, she understood from his muted reaction that the deal was off. "I watched Abed sit back," she said. "He didn't say much at first, and finally he said very quietly, 'Bangladesh is a mainly Islamic country and a secular democracy.'" There was no drama, and Abed said nothing about it afterward, but Borren knew him well enough to know that it was over.

The internal consultations went forward at BRAC, and the rank-and-file of BRAC decided the organization should keep its name and independence. Abed and others, including Muyeed, later cited the required name change as the reason, but Borren said this issue could have been solved and that Abed had already made up his mind. In hindsight, he was right, she added. "My opinion now is that BRAC was wise not to do it," Borren said in 2020. "It wasn't my opinion then, but it's my opinion now." Joining Oxfam would have significantly slowed down BRAC's international expansion, which would soon take off.

★ ★ ★

A number of significant changes took place in Abed's life in the three years following the turn of the millennium. Stepping down from the executive directorship was one of these shifts, but it probably had the least impact, for there was never any doubt that Abed remained in control. He was now the chair of several related entities—BRAC itself, the university, and the bank. The fact that micro-lending, which constituted a huge portion of BRAC's activities, had turned the corner into profitability gave Abed a level of freedom he had not known before. The direct results included the launch of the bank and the university.

His marriage to Sarwat proved to be a rock of stability. Aarong, BRAC's textile and fashion enterprise, was facing trouble and had to go through a period of restructuring, and Sarwat, like both of Abed's previous wives, stepped in briefly to manage the situation. Meanwhile, foreign aid contributions, especially from the British government, remained strong, allowing BRAC to break ground on new approaches like the graduation program for the ultra-poor.

There was already plenty happening in Bangladesh alone, but the circle of concern would soon grow much wider. The terrorist attacks of September 11, 2001, had profound consequences for Abed, both personally and professionally—although, to be sure, the realms of life and work were rarely distinct for him. The events of 9/11 and their aftermath seemed to have little effect on his worldview, for he retained his deep-seated hopefulness about the future of humanity, but they set in motion at least two developments with long-term implications. The first was the career trajectory of his daughter, Tamara, who was now twenty-six. Having been educated in India and the United Kingdom, she had finished her MBA at Columbia Business School and secured a coveted investment-banking job at Goldman

Sachs, located in New York's financial district. On just her second day of work, she was riding the subway to the office when the first plane hit the nearby World Trade Center. She emerged from underground in the seventeen-minute window between the two planes crashing. The streets were in chaos. Noxious black smoke and debris engulfed the entire district when the towers fell. Like thousands of others, Tamara fled lower Manhattan on foot, walking north, able to see only a few feet in front of her face.

Tamara had lived abroad for years, but this was the first time she felt far from her family. The events made her reassess her life priorities. Within half a year, she gave up her job at Goldman Sachs and moved back to Dhaka. Though her father never pressured her to do so, she took a job at Aarong, which her mother had founded shortly before her death twenty years earlier.

There were far greater changes in store for BRAC. As the US invasion of Afghanistan got underway, Abed received a letter from a United Nations Development Program (UNDP) official, telling him that after the expected fall of the Taliban, Afghanistan would need organizations like BRAC to help returning refugees resettle. He soon received a personal visit from the Pakistani head of UNDP's Asia bureau, telling him the same thing. Decades of civil war had forced five million people into refugee camps in Iran and Pakistan, and a million people a year were expected to begin repatriating once a new government was formed.

If there was one thing that made it clear that Abed continued to run the show, it was his seemingly abrupt decision to launch BRAC in Afghanistan. Up to this point there had rarely been any question that BRAC was a national organization working mainly for the betterment of Bangladesh. Aside from a few projects in which it provided assistance to organizations in other countries—sending education program staff on short-term assignments to help with Sudanese schools, for instance—BRAC had never worked abroad.

Faruq Choudhury recalled returning from a visit to the Pakistan border area during the US-led invasion. In addition to being Abed's chief advisor, he wrote for *Prothom Alo*, one of the country's top dailies. "They had sent me to cover Mr. Bush's bombardment of Afghanistan," he said. When he returned, Faruq went to Abed's office on the nineteenth floor of BRAC headquarters and debriefed Abed. He told him of the desperation he had seen in the squalid camps on the Pakistan side, where thousands had fled in a matter of weeks.

Abed hardly needed to hear stories of people's trauma or the acute needs in terms of health and hygiene, for he had already made a decision.

Abed informed Faruq, without so much as an opportunity to debate the matter, that BRAC would be going to Afghanistan. "I was surprised that I found he was already done thinking," Faruq said. "He informed me of the decision. He didn't ask for my views."

Faruq pressed his friend to articulate the logic behind it, which Abed proceeded to state plainly: BRAC had seen this before, having had a similar experience in its native Bangladesh, when millions returned to a nation reduced to rubble. From these ruins, it empowered people to rebuild their lives from the ground up. Now it had an opportunity to do the same elsewhere. As a Muslim country with a shared experience, Bangladesh had something to offer that Western aid agencies did not.

For its first foray outside Bangladesh, Abed set things in motion and stepped back, allowing his deputies to visit Afghanistan to lay the groundwork. The manner in which Abed handled this task—selecting people with certain skills and letting them figure it out as best they could—suggests he was keen, at this point in his life, not to micromanage such a momentous move.

Despite the sobering circumstances, these first visits of BRAC staff had all the elements of a caper in which they stumbled from one success to another. The team, consisting of Muyeed, Amin, and two others—Tajul Islam, the director of public affairs, and Jalaluddin Ahmed, a health specialist—had little to no international experience. "It came as a bolt from the blue," said Tajul, recalling the day Faruq Choudhury informed him, nonchalantly, that he was going to Afghanistan.

"Not really! When? Why?" Tajul replied, according to his own recollection. His main job thus far was in ensuring smooth dealings with government agencies and the press.

"Mr. Abed called me and said he wants you to go and do the lobbying, the permissions, licensing, and so on," Faruq said.

"Why me? I'm not a program person!"

"I don't know," Faruq said. "Maybe he thinks it's a PR job."

Any of them could have pushed back. None did. Even for senior staff, when the chairperson asked you to do something, it was taken as an instruction, not a request.

Had Abed not hired Muyeed, who was adept at pulling bureaucratic strings—and not just in Bangladesh, it turned out—things may have been considerably more difficult. To start, there was the matter of obtaining visas. There was a man in Dhaka whom Muyeed had met during prayers at Dhaka's central mosque, who nominally served as the Afghanistan consul, even though he had never pledged fealty to the Taliban. When the pre-Taliban regime fell in 1996, the consul stayed on, receiving no salary, a lonely presence representing a state that no longer existed. When Muyeed asked whether he could still issue a visa, the consul happily obliged, since the fee would be the first income he had received in years.

The team first flew to Islamabad, where Muyeed had kept in touch with classmates from his pre-independence training for Pakistan's civil service. Some now held powerful positions in the state bureaucracy of Pakistan, which he knew would likely be influential in the new Afghanistan. They were able to secure an orientation briefing from the agency handling Afghan affairs. From the capital they went to Peshawar to visit refugee camps. "We didn't know anything," said Muyeed. "We spent those days going around and meeting people and getting a feel for things."

Their connections with UNICEF proved invaluable. From Peshawar, they secured spots on two UNICEF flights into Afghanistan. Amin had decided that the group should split up, for he was eager to see parts of the country outside the capital. Amin and Jalal flew straight to the northern city of Mazar-i-Sharif—Muyeed called Amin a "daredevil" for insisting on this—while Muyeed and Tajul went to Kabul to meet with officials of the newly installed interim government.

In Mazar-i-Sharif, Amin and Jalal landed at an empty airport where every window had been blown out. "It was just a vacant room," recalled Jalal. "There wasn't even a counter. The wind was blowing from one side to the other." In the distance, they spotted several UN cars, one of whose drivers found and roused a sleeping immigration official, who led them to a plain table with a drawer, the only piece of furniture in the airport. From the drawer he removed a stamp for their passports and a registry book in which he wrote their names.

Accompanied by UNICEF staff, they went on to visit villages in the remote Jowzjan province, three hours outside the city, where they saw overcrowded health clinics and talked to students in local schools. A few questions revealed that the majority of children remained at home.

On the ten-hour road journey to Kabul, they passed hundreds of derelict tanks lining the Soviet-built road up to the twelve-thousand-foot Salang Pass. He realized the importance of Amin taking him so far afield before visiting the capital. The long drive gave him a far more visceral feel for what Afghans had endured.

Meanwhile, in Kabul, Muyeed and Tajul were trying to navigate the new Afghan bureaucracy. At the airport, the United Nations had opened an impromptu counter issuing visas on arrival. The officials were surprised to see the Bangladeshis already had visas.

UNICEF had brokered a meeting with Sima Samar, a human rights activist who had taken a post in Hamid Karzai's transitional government as the Minister of Women's Affairs. Like Abed, she was a recipient of the Ramon Magsaysay Award. Muyeed presented her with a letter of introduction that Abed had written. An admirer of Abed and BRAC, Samar guided them to the planning ministry, which would have to approve their application to provide relief and development services. She supported all their subsequent paperwork. Without the support of UNICEF and Samar, "it would not have been a cakewalk," said Muyeed.

Abed intended for BRAC itself to put up the seed funding for the launch of the Afghanistan program. This would allow him to move with the urgency the situation demanded. He was confident external donors would follow. Bangladesh's strict foreign-exchange controls regulated the amount of money that could flow out of the country, however. The problem proved to be "almost insurmountable," according to Muyeed. The central bank denied their initial request to transfer $250,000 to Afghanistan.

Muyeed met personally with the governor of the central bank to make the case: much of the money would come back to Bangladesh in the form of remittances from BRAC workers sent to Afghanistan, who would send their earnings home to support their families, he argued. Again, it paid to have a former government insider, Muyeed, leading the conversation. The governor agreed to make an exception.

The team returned to Afghanistan in April, minus Muyeed. By this point, it was clear how much goodwill they were generating simply by being from Bangladesh. At the foreign ministry, they entered a room crammed with applicants, including one representative of a Korean NGO who said he had been waiting for two months trying to get his application through. The foreign ministry officials saw the Bangladeshis as brothers and ushered them to the front of the line, according to Tajul.

Everywhere they went, they were welcomed with tea, nuts, and chocolate. Rasul Amin, a writer, professor, and the first education minister, embraced them when they appeared at his office, shouting, "Here come the people from Tagore's land! Bring them tea!"

While waiting to receive the promised approvals, Amin decided he wanted to visit a village outside Kabul, this time unescorted by UNICEF or any local intermediaries. With a hired car and driver, they drove for about an hour before reaching a military checkpoint. The soldiers strongly advised them not to go any farther due to security concerns, so they got out and began walking to the nearby village, asking the driver, a moonlighting Kabul pharmacist, to act as an interpreter.

A local man approached and greeted them: "Salam alaikum." His trepidation was apparent, and he asked whether they were looking for something. The village was a collection of mud brick dwellings seemingly from ancient times, smoke from cookstoves curling into the sky. Before they could answer, another man appeared. Both wore *shalwar kameez*, the traditional loose-fitting pants and tunic. Amin and Tajul tried to explain that they had come from Bangladesh and wanted to know how they would be received in this community if they offered services like credit, education, and health care.

The visitors soon found themselves seated on cushions on a clean dirt floor of a local home, the imam joining for a conversation about the needs of the village. There was only one well for two hundred people in the village, the men explained. There was no bank nearby, so when people were short of cash and needed money, they borrowed from a moneylender at an exorbitant interest rate. It was a familiar story.

Amin explained the concept of microfinance. Our organization, he said, offers loans with a minimum service charge. He did not use the word "interest," which is forbidden according to a strict interpretation of Islamic law. He explained that they would have to open an office and pay people's salaries to make the service available, so they added a service charge, typically 12 to 15 percent. This was not going to enrich anyone; it was simply to cover the costs of making the money available in the village. He asked whether this would be acceptable. A series of murmurs and exchanges in Pashto followed. The men replied, through the driver-translator, that they saw nothing wrong with this proposal.

Amin and Tajul asked about schools. One man had mentioned his son had walked miles to school previously but had stopped because of the war and now was on the verge of entering the workforce illiterate. Amin explained that they ran thirty-four thousand schools in Bangladesh for those who had been left out of government schools—all of them free of charge. "They said, 'How many?' They couldn't believe it," Tajul said.

"If we open a school here, would you send your children?" Amin asked. The men said they would.

Amin and Tajul were approaching an obviously delicate topic. According to Tajul, he turned to Amin and asked him in Bengali, "Should we ask about sending girls to schools, or do you think they'll beat us up?"

Amin considered this question for a moment and replied, "You ask, but first, let's get ready to run back to the car."

Tajul cleared his throat. "If you don't mind, we have one more question. If we open a school here, will you send your girls?"

They men looked at each other, and the house owner replied, "Why not?"

The imam then took over. "Let me explain," he said. "The Prophet said that learning is compulsory for every faithful boy and girl, male and female. And he said to seek knowledge: if you need to go to China, go to China." (The imam was quoting an apocryphal hadith, a saying attributed to the Prophet Mohammed.)

"Right, right, right," the house owner continued. "Our children cannot go to China. But if you open a school here, it means China has come to our village!" The men had one condition: separate schools for boys and girls.

BRAC soon received permission to start microfinance, health, and education programs. Tajul found a call center from which he phoned Abed to tell him their applications had been accepted. Abed simply repeated "thank you" several times. "He is reserved in the way he expresses his emotions, but he was very happy, and he said thank you, thank you, thank you, twice or thrice," Tajul recalled.

Amin decided they would start with branches in areas surrounding Mazar-i-Sharif, which he likened to the Rangpur district in Bangladesh's far north, and in a district forty miles outside Kabul called Jabal Saraj, which would be BRAC Afghanistan's version of Manikganj, the more accessible proving ground.

Before the year's end, the Swedish foreign aid agency, Oxfam Canada, and UNICEF were all donors to BRAC Afghanistan. By the end of 2003, they had enough donors to keep the operation afloat without any more money coming out of Bangladesh.

* * *

Abed returned to Kabul in October 2002, his first visit since 1971 when he himself had been a war refugee, arriving via bus after a day's journey over the Khyber Pass from Peshawar. The Kabul to which he returned thirty-one years later was unrecognizable, the hippies and miniskirts long forgotten. There was hardly a building without bullet pockmarks. He looked for the cheap guest house where he had stayed for a week, waiting for the telegrammed reply from Marietta. He could not find it. He met with several ministers before embarking on a road trip with one of his oldest friends.

Accompanied by Amin, Abed and Faruq Choudhury flew to Mazar-i-Sharif and hired a car and driver for the overland journey to Kabul, the same ten-hour journey that Amin had taken through the Soviet-built tunnel at the Salang Pass. Abed shivered as they ascended the Hindu Kush on the route said to have been taken by Alexander the Great. For both men, one of the most memorable aspects of the trip was the proud Afghan driver, who played and sang along with a Bollywood love song the entire journey—the same song over and over again, according to Faruq. The driver professed pride in the fact that years earlier, the great Indian actor Amitabh Bachchan had come to Mazar-i-Sharif to film one of his movies.

According to Abed, the greatest challenge of working in Afghanistan proved to be an obvious one: the persistence of Islamic fundamentalism, which was of a different variety than what Abed had encountered at home. In Bangladesh, local mullahs objected to girls singing and dancing, calling such behavior un-Islamic. In Afghanistan, the hardcore Islamists objected to girls going to school, period. Abed showed he was amenable to compromise on some accounts but had no patience with those who would willingly keep half the population living in ignorance. He was not religious, but he was rarely unsettled by the prohibitions of Islamic conservatism, even if he did not agree with them. He had no problem keeping Afghan girls and boys in separate schools, for instance; when Amin and Tajul told him about their first unfiltered conversations in the village outside Kabul, Abed remarked that one could not expect BRAC's programs to be lifted out of Bangladesh and dropped into Afghanistan unaltered.

Likewise, when communities objected that girls could not be permitted to walk to school without an escort, Abed thought an agreeable compromise would be to recruit an older, married woman—an aunt-like figure, called a *khala* (literally "auntie" in both Bengali and Dari)—to chaperone groups of girls to school. He often said, "The purpose of development is to change culture."

Abed had a linear view of social progress, even if that progress was slow. As he saw it, if the current generation of Afghan girls could not walk to school alone, at least they would go to school; it meant their daughters would likely walk to school on their own.

The practice of microfinance threw up its own set of obstacles, though they had little to do with the nature of credit itself. Though Islamic law prohibits interest charges, most imams had little argument with non-predatory lending, including the "service charges" that financed the branch operations, provided these charges covered the costs of lending rather than enriching the lender. The problem was that most women in rural areas were fully covered and would not show their faces to unrelated males. If women were the clients, the loan officers—who convened the group meetings, disbursed the funds and collected repayments—would also have to be women. And initially women said they would not go to the villages without being accompanied by a man.

According to Abed, it was Amin, not him, who drew the line here. If microfinance was to be self-sufficient, every additional cost would have to be borne by the clients themselves. Amin therefore decided there would be no male chaperones. If a woman wanted a job as a BRAC loan officer, she would have to go to the villages on her own. "So many Afghan women needed a job and a monthly income that they took on the challenge," Abed said. "We insisted on it, and it worked."

⋆ ⋆ ⋆

On December 26, 2004, the third-largest earthquake in recorded history shook the ocean floor off the coast of Sumatra, Indonesia, causing a series of tsunamis that reached fourteen countries and drowned 230,000 people. In modern times, only a handful of natural events (the 1971 Bhola cyclone among them) are known to have killed more people.

Just as Afghanistan tested BRAC's readiness to respond to human-made disasters, its launch of operations in Sri Lanka did the same for natural ones. The island nation saw thirty thousand die in the tsunami, second only to Indonesia in the death toll. BRAC opened its third country office here and began relief operations. Immediate needs came first, including stopping the spread of water-borne infections and restoring a sense of normalcy to people's lives. BRAC constructed latrines, repaired broken and contaminated wells, and replaced lost and damaged school materials. Within months, the shift to longer-term development priorities had begun, as BRAC began convening small groups of women to offer microloans.

Abed knew that BRAC could not remain in Asia, which no longer had the highest count of people living in extreme poverty. That distinction now belonged to sub-Saharan Africa, and they would have to go there if they were to prove that poverty solutions born in Bangladesh made sense for the rest of the world. BRAC had already dipped a toe in these waters, sending educational consultants to southern Sudan. In 2006, international operations began expanding at a faster pace, with BRAC launching programs in both Tanzania and Uganda. That same year, an affiliate office, BRAC UK, opened in London, followed by New York–based affiliate, BRAC USA, in 2007. The choice of countries that followed—Sierra Leone, Liberia, southern Sudan, Pakistan, and, following the 2010 earthquake, Haiti—reflected Abed's strategy to focus on post-conflict and post-disaster settings, where immediate humanitarian assistance would serve as an entry point, allowing BRAC to establish a foothold, get people back on their feet quickly, and transition to long-term development needs. The programs differed from country to country, but they typically included health care, agriculture programs, and microfinance; BRAC schools were opened in several of these countries. Adolescent girls' empowerment programs became especially important in sub-Saharan Africa.

When Abed asked friends and supporters, including Lincoln Chen and Richard Cash, to help launch independent BRAC affiliates in the United Kingdom and United States, it signaled his intent to create a more global organization, albeit one that retained its worldwide headquarters in Bangladesh. It reversed the typical practice in aid and development, whereby people in rich countries decided what was best for people in distant poor countries. These affiliates were charged with raising BRAC's international profile and fundraising for its international operations, but they were on the distant marches of the realm; the locus of decision-making remained BRAC's home office in Dhaka.

* * *

Abed alone made the decision to expand beyond Bangladesh. In the case of previous big moves, he had plotted quietly in advance, sometimes for years. In 1985, he timed the opening of the first BRAC schools with an anticipated surge in international donor interest in childhood education, which colleagues say he had predicted as early as the 1970s. When this surge happened in the 1990s, Abed was ready. Years of planning paid off, allowing BRAC to quickly scale up to tens of thousands of schools.

Yet there is no record, prior to 2001, of Abed telling anyone that he planned to expand BRAC internationally. He could hardly have predicted that a US-led coalition would overthrow the Taliban. In fact, had the contemplated merger with Oxfam happened, expansion anywhere other than Bangladesh would have been unlikely. BRAC would have become known as the Bangladeshi outpost of Oxfam, its global identity absorbed into an international nonprofit conglomerate. His confidence was likely given a boost by the declaration by BRAC's rank-and-file that the organization should retain both its name and independence.

The logic of going abroad was hard to refute. After all, poverty was a human problem, not a Bangladeshi problem. As long as Abed had the opportunity, it would seem shortsighted not to extend BRAC's solutions, almost universally lauded in the development community and yet little known anywhere else, to other countries. Years later, in an interview with development scholars, Abed would recall an exchange at an international forum between two unnamed former prime ministers of Canada and Sri

Lanka. The Canadian, according to Abed, got on his case about his international ventures. "So, has BRAC finished all the work in Bangladesh?" he asked. "Why is Abed going to Africa?"

Abed did not have to defend himself, because the Sri Lankan former prime minister jumped in to do so. "Do you think Southern NGOs can't go anywhere else?" he asked. "Is it only Northern NGOs that can go to other countries?"[2]

Going global may not have been part of Abed's original master plan, but it was a decision born from finally having a sizable flow of internal, unrestricted revenue, and that was indeed something Abed had been building toward for years. This position allowed him to respond quickly to global needs, unconstrained by what was fashionable with donors.

It was also the result of a more expansive, global mindset that began coming about during BRAC's major expansion phase in the 1990s. As it turned out, the first decade of the millennium saw a growing appetite for solutions originating from the so-called Global South, the twenty-first-century term for what used to be known as the Third World. The development sector had long been tainted by a white savior complex, a term for the obnoxious insistence, usually born of good intentions, that richer Western countries impose their solutions on people who didn't know better. Soon enough, it became unfashionable to ask why Abed was going to Africa.

24

THEY CRIED LIKE THEY'D LOST A SON

Abed mellowed as he grew older. His rare but explosive fits of rage became even rarer until they ceased entirely. Instead, his temper became quicker, the outbursts more frequent but less intense. He became irritated more easily—people being late especially bothered him—and shouted at people from time to time, but he stopped losing it completely like he used to, according to Shameran. "It became more regular, but milder," his son said. He likened the change to the general irritability and crankiness that often comes with aging.

In 2002, Abed's younger brother, Murshed, died of pneumonia following treatment for a rare disease called amyloidosis. Abed was by his bedside until the end. Their parents, Siddique Hasan and Syeda Sufya Khatun, had raised four sons together, in addition to Abed's late sister Nurani. The four brothers remained close their whole lives, and Murshed was the first to die. Abed would eventually be the last.

The loss brought him closer to his extended family, especially as his brothers' children grew older. According to Murshed's daughter, Tanya Murshed, he acted as mentor and advisor to his nieces and nephews and seemed to have special relationships with each of them. Tanya would often host Abed when he visited London, where she had grown up. She would eventually become a barrister, an immigration judge, and the founder of Evolve, a criminal justice development organization in Uganda. Despite their overlapping interest in human rights, her uncle's advice was often of a more practical nature. Abed reached back to his years as a London bachelor to coach her on basic life skills, like the right way to use an iron, pack a suitcase, fry an egg, or make the perfect toast. Though he always spoke highly of the men in the family, Abed was noticeably more affectionate with his brothers' daughters than with their sons, according to Tanya. "He was always much better with women," she said. No matter how short his visit, it became tradition to gather the relatives in London for a meal at a Chinese restaurant.

Abed seemed to fall easily into the role of older mentor even with people he did not previously know. Around 2006, Wendy Kopp, the founder of Teach For America, received an email from a professional acquaintance saying that Abed, whom she knew only by reputation, had requested an introduction to her. Abed, who was visiting New York at the time, had no motive other than wanting to learn more about her plans, according to Kopp. "This just never happens," Kopp said. "He's running an NGO, a huge one—the world's biggest—and decides to get together with this other social entrepreneur?" She was surprised that Abed even took the time to inquire about something "only tangentially related to his own pursuits."

Founded in 1990 based on Kopp's undergraduate senior thesis at Princeton, Teach For America recruited recent college graduates to work as teachers in low-income areas of the United States. Kopp fit Bill Drayton's definition of a social entrepreneur, for her goal was to change the pattern of how young people approached the profession of teaching. Kopp was considering whether to take her work abroad but had yet to make up her mind. Her board, not wanting her to lose focus on her US work, was unsupportive. She had just finished a board meeting that "went horribly," she said. "No one thought it was a good idea." The decision was complicated by the fact that she had three children and a fourth on the way, and many people—"and they were all men, by the way"—suggested it would be irresponsible to take on the task of international expansion in light of her family obligations.

During a three-hour dinner, Abed persuaded Kopp that she could—and should—help those in other countries launch organizations similar to Teach For America, as part of a global network that became Teach For All. She could do this from her home in New York without sacrificing the time spent with her family. "He was immovable on that point," she said. "And I left completely certain that he was right and that I should persist." Kopp launched Teach For All in 2007.

* * *

BRAC's growing international footprint positioned it for wider recognition than its status as a Bangladeshi NGO would ever have given it. As a tactic for global expansion, microcredit was the sharp end of BRAC's spear. If done well, it could generate revenue to maintain a network of small offices in any country, covering the overhead for other programs like health and education. The guiding philosophy was "credit-plus," which meant that access to affordable credit, while essential, was not a silver bullet for ending poverty. Health care, hygiene, clean water, family planning, skills training, and decent schools all needed to be part of the mix.

To BRAC's friends around the world, this was a compelling story. Many of them were therefore surprised in 2006 when the Norwegian Nobel Committee awarded the Nobel Peace Prize to Muhammad Yunus and Grameen Bank, but not BRAC. The Nobel committee had sought to highlight the global importance of microfinance. In this area, BRAC was as much a pioneer as Grameen. The difference was that BRAC did many things, whereas Grameen did one thing and promoted it exceedingly well.

There were grumblings among BRAC's supporters that the Nobel committee was misinformed or had fallen victim to hype. However, if Abed had any complaints about being passed over, he kept them private. Abed said Yunus deserved the Nobel not only for his work but also for his successful advocacy, which established microfinance (including micro-savings and other financial services) as a viable mechanism for reducing poverty in the eyes of Western donors. "I give him credit for what he has done, which is advocacy at a global level for financial services for the poor," he said. Unlike Abed, he was good at soundbites—"colorful language that sticks in your mind," as Abed called it—like saying that poverty will one day be in a museum.

"Grameen was essentially a global marketing effort," said Bill Drayton, the Ashoka founder who popularized the term "social entrepreneur." He did not seem to mean this in a pejorative sense, since Drayton has also named Yunus, along with Abed, as one of the world's pioneering social entrepreneurs. "Yunus has made an incredible global contribution to marketing a social change idea globally, and he developed all sorts of mechanisms for doing this," he said.

When it came to the international conversation on microfinance, "Yunus didn't just have a seat. He designed the table," said Syed Hashemi, the former Grameen researcher who became a proponent of the graduation approach to ultra-poverty. Microfinance may not have been the silver bullet that the hype implied it was, but its rising profile benefited BRAC, Grameen, and many other institutions—along with millions of borrowers.

* * *

As Abed's "field marshal," as Marty Chen called him, Amin kept up his workaholic pace, overseeing microfinance in Bangladesh along with the start-up of new international operations. When he traveled with his driver within Bangladesh, he would work from morning until night, taking his pillow in the car and sleeping between stops. His wife, Gulrana, had no way of knowing whether he ate regularly or took his medication while traveling, which was problematic, since he suffered from heart disease, high blood pressure, and diabetes. Mohammad Shafiqul ("Shafiq") Islam, his driver of fourteen years, who traversed nearly every road in Bangladesh with him, said he would often skip meals, which would have risked low blood sugar. As for taking his medication, "If he remembered, he did, and if he didn't, it didn't matter to him."

By 2006, the microfinance industry had become large enough that the Bangladesh government saw fit to set up a regulatory agency. Upon its establishment, the Microfinance Regulatory Authority requested the country's microfinance institutions—and by now there were many in addition to BRAC and Grameen—to provide a list of all branches. The BRAC program already had more than two thousand offices at this point, which was remarkable, given how small the country was in terms of area.

Amin thought the demand for credit was still unmet, and he suspected that as soon as the authority was up and running, it would require permission every time he wanted to open a new branch. He therefore generated a list of about six hundred previously unplanned branches, added these to the existing branch list, and submitted that to the authority. "He started setting up branches all over the place," Abed said. New staff were recruited for each location to rent office space and conduct surveys of the local population to determine who was eligible for credit. Combined with the existing rate of expansion, this meant doubling the number of outposts in a twelve-month period. In 2007, BRAC recruited close to eighteen thousand new staff for microfinance alone.

Amin drove his subordinates hard to meet targets during this period, according to Reaz Uddin, one of his deputies. More loans meant more income, which meant more branches and more loans. By this point, Reaz had worked under Amin for more than two decades, and he knew, from his earliest encounter with him, the importance he attached to microcredit. In 1984, Reaz had joined the Sulla program, which was organizing landless groups without offering any economic support. At the time, the program had run out of donor funding and was operating from the income of the printing press. When Amin was put in charge of that program, "we had already heard from other staff that he's very aggressive and quite angry most of the time, so we had an idea of what to expect," Reaz said. The staff was surprised by his gentle demeanor during the first meeting in the Markuli office, until Amin wrapped it up by saying, "I don't know what you guys are doing, sitting here in the middle of the *haor*, just talking and mobilizing people, which doesn't even count as real work." Amin thought that without giving people the means to build their livelihoods, other work would ultimately be fruitless.

By 2007, Amin's purview was huge. He was expanding and launching new operations in Afghanistan, Tanzania, and Uganda, while overseeing the breakneck expansion of mainstream credit operations in Bangladesh, including the small-enterprise lending component, which Reaz was in charge of. The program was also piloting new financial services, including, for instance, a collaboration with Western Union to receive remittances from Bangladeshi workers abroad.

One night, according to Reaz, while Reaz was visiting a BRAC office in the western district of Kushtia, Amin called him at 10 p.m., asking how much the enterprise lending program had disbursed that month. It was late in the month, and the program had already met its monthly target, so Reaz had stopped disbursing. (It was common practice, though not BRAC policy, to stop disbursements during the last several days of the month. As the timing of future repayments was based on the calendar month, this would give borrowers a few days' grace period before they were officially in default.)

Amin was furious. The lowest tier of microfinance, which gave loans of about $120 on average, had failed to meet its target. If Reaz had continued disbursing until the last day of the month, microfinance as a whole would have met its target. "I don't care where you are now!" he shouted. "I want to see you in my office at 8 a.m. tomorrow morning." The drive from Kushtia to Dhaka is six hours on a good day, but a thick winter fog covered the roads that night, and visibility was close to zero. Despite having worked for Amin for more than twenty years, Reaz thought he was about to be fired. He managed to convince a reluctant driver to take him as far as the Dhaka outskirts, which he reached in time for the 5 a.m. call to prayer. He took a bus the rest of the way, walking into Amin's office at 7:45 a.m. "Good," Amin said. "You're here. I'll call you later." Amin did not call him for the rest of the day.

Amin called him in at 9 a.m. the next day. "I made you suffer because I was angry," he told him calmly. Microfinance disbursed, on average, about $76 million per month at that point. Amin explained to Reaz that had his program disbursed 30 million taka (about $440,000) more, microfinance would have met its target for the month. "You have to consider the whole program, not just your part of it," he said.

It soon became clear that something was amiss beyond a single missed target, however. The staff that had been sent to run the new branches received, at most, a one-day orientation. The surveys were done hurriedly, leading to poor borrower assessments. "We ended up selecting clients who never should have been clients to begin with," said Reaz. When borrowers began falling behind on loan repayments, many of the staff feared losing their jobs and found ways to cover it up, including by creating fake loans to nonexistent borrowers. They used these "ghost loans" to repay previous loans—obviously a disaster waiting to happen.

Amin's management process depended largely on personal observations and a superhuman work ethic, but he had failed to develop a system to track basic processes like client selection and loan performance at scale. Perhaps this was the "break point" that the scholar Catherine Lovell had warned about in the early 1990s, where BRAC simply became too big. In fact, internal monitoring was good enough by then that the problem was visible before the bubble burst, and the ghost loans never accounted for more than 2 percent of the portfolio. It was clear to Abed that the program was expanding too fast, however. "Obviously, management was not ready for it," he said. It didn't help that Amin's employees were so fearful of his wrath that they would not come clean with him.

Abed had to intervene. The organization shut down hundreds of branches, wrote off several million dollars of bad debt, and declared a one-time amnesty on managers who had approved false loans. Amin had finally reached the limit of what he could handle. Abed removed the Bangladesh microfinance program from Amin's portfolio and told him to focus exclusively on expansion abroad. "It was too much for him," he said. "He was not able to manage it properly."

It was a blow for Amin. "Amin was a winner," said Reaz. "The fact that he could lose something, or not be able to meet a target—he was not ready to accept that."

* * *

One morning in 2007, while waiting for the elevator at BRAC headquarters, Amin collapsed and began vomiting. He soon lost consciousness. Shafiq, his driver, and three security guards picked him up and loaded him into the back of the car. According to Shafiq, he regained consciousness and began muttering en route to the hospital. "This has happened before," he said. "Take me home." The three others in the car could not persuade him otherwise. "We couldn't force him to go to the hospital, because he was our boss," said Shafiq.

Several senior colleagues, alerted that his car had been diverted to his home, followed them. At Amin's home, they joined Gulrana in insisting he go to the hospital. After much prodding, he relented. Three hours passed between his initial collapse and his arrival at the hospital. The doctors confirmed he had suffered a serious heart attack and admitted him. Within days, they operated and installed three stents.

Reaz recalled seeing him in the recovery area following the operation. Amin was still in a restricted area, so only BRAC senior managers were allowed in, but Amin spotted Reaz outside and requested that he come sit next to the bed. When the others left, Amin spoke to him quietly. Reaz leaned in, wondering what Amin had to share after his near-death experience.

"Reaz," he said. "How many remittances have we received in the Western Union pilot? This is a new program. Pay attention to it."

* * *

Despite the setback with microfinance and the heart attack, Amin did not slow down. He accepted Abed's decision to transfer him and shifted all his energy to international expansion. He began taking insulin to manage his diabetes. When he was in Dhaka, Gulrana would pack him fruit to eat in the office to keep his blood sugar up, but it would often return home untouched. She still had no idea whether he took care of himself while traveling.

On October 2, 2010, two days after returning from a work-related trip to Pakistan, Amin suffered a second heart attack at home. He died in a Dhaka hospital, leaving behind his wife, Gulrana, and two sons, Andalib and Shamma. Aminul Alam was sixty-one.

At its headquarters, BRAC held a *qulkhwani*, a Bengali ritual that takes place after burial in which relatives and friends pray for the departed soul's salvation. Women from the early BRAC groups in Manikganj traveled to the capital for the memorial. "They cried like they had lost their son," said Andalib. Unbeknownst to the family, he had kept in touch with the women all those years. "I had heard about it, but I had never seen that side of my father. And he was always in touch with them, like they were extended family." At BRAC, people still speak of Amin with reverence, not just for his work ethic and commitment but also for the way he empowered and inspired others around him, especially female colleagues.

It is often said that Amin only cared about BRAC. "Nothing mattered for him other than BRAC," Abed said. His driver, Shafiq, used similar language: "There was nothing in his universe other than BRAC."

However, this was not true. Miraculously, he somehow found the time to play the role of the elder in his extended family, which, with eleven siblings, was huge. He visited nieces and nephews on weekends, counseling them on jobs, schooling, and other life matters. At home, he was a carefree husband and father who enjoyed talking about football or cricket with his sons, Andalib and Shamma. He rarely discussed work. Gulrana, not Amin, was the disciplinarian. "We were always scared of our mother," said Andalib. "Our father was more like a friend."

Asked how she would like her husband to be remembered, Gulrana replied, "He was just another simple human being who loved his work. He was not a superhuman."

⋆ ⋆ ⋆

By the time of Amin's death, BRAC had become, by and large, the organization that exists today—a massive institution active in about a dozen countries, mostly self-financed, with a university, a bank, commercial enterprises, and large standalone anti-poverty programs in nearly every sector of development.

In February 2010, as part of the British New Year Honors, Abed knelt on a velvet investiture stool at Buckingham Palace while Prince Charles laid a sword on each of his shoulders and dubbed him Sir Fazle Hasan Abed, a Knight Commander of the Order of St. Michael and St. George, in recognition of his services to humanity. BRAC's star shone bright in the wake of Abed's knighthood, with *The Economist* hailing it as "by most measures the largest, fastest-growing nongovernmental organization (NGO) in the world—and one of the most businesslike." With annual disbursement of roughly $1 billion in microloans and a diverse portfolio of programs and enterprises, the organization "has probably done more than any single body to upend the traditions of misery and poverty in Bangladesh," the magazine said. Its scale-up abroad had been so rapid that it was already the largest NGO in Afghanistan, Uganda, and Tanzania, "overtaking British charities which have been in the latter countries for decades."[1]

That year, BRAC's global employee headcount, including part-time teachers, reached 120,000. In foreign aid and development circles, BRAC was known as an exemplar of effective and innovative anti-poverty programming, running at a scale that would rival most governments, reaching at least one hundred million people and likely many more, either directly or through a member of the household. To most people outside of Bangladesh, however, it remained unknown.

25

A VISIT FROM AN OLD FRIEND

In 2016, Abed received a visit from one of his oldest acquaintances, Zafrullah Chowdhury, the doctor who had set up Gonoshasthaya Kendra ("People's Health Center") shortly after Bangladesh's independence. In the wake of liberation, Zafrullah had been the only other Bangladeshi doing anything of note to help the fledgling nation's long-suffering poor.

Zafrullah's hair had turned white, but otherwise he had barely changed. He still had a walrus mustache and hair that reached his collar, and he appeared on the carpeted nineteenth-floor executive suite, as he did everywhere, with a rumpled, untucked shirt. He had the willfully unkempt look of a man who did not give a damn what you thought of him.

Zafrullah came to Abed with a modest request. He needed 350 million taka (about $4.5 million) to set up a center that offered low-cost dialysis services to low-income people with kidney disease. He had 100 million secured and reckoned he could come up with another 50 million, leaving a gap of 200 million ($2.6 million).

Abed officially turned eighty that year, and Zafrullah, five years younger, still treated him like an older brother. Markedly different in so many ways, the pair had a bond like old soldiers, forged during their wartime activism in London, when Zafrullah had befriended Abed's ex-girlfriend, Marietta; she had tried to leave him a sizable donation in her suicide note.

Zafrullah was known for being outspoken, more so than Abed. In the 1980s, he had successfully taken on multinational drug companies by pushing for reform of Bangladesh's drug laws to make essential medicine more widely available and affordable. He did not have Abed's reputation for effective management, and Gonoshasthaya Kendra had never reached anything close to BRAC's size, but Zafrullah knew how to get things done through sheer force of will. He had set up more than forty hospitals and health clinics for the poor, a low-cost insurance scheme, a medical college, and a drug manufacturer. Like Abed and Yunus, Zafrullah's work had secured a place for himself in the nation's history. All three men had won the Ramon Magsaysay Award, Asia's greatest prize for social work.

Zafrullah sat across from Abed's desk and made his case. A four-hour dialysis session cost the equivalent of $35 in Bangladesh, three times more than in India. Patients usually needed two to three sessions weekly. These expenses were compounded by the cost of blood tests and erythropoietin injections, putting treatment out of reach for nearly all low-income workers and their families. Zafrullah had firsthand experience of this issue: he himself suffered from kidney disease and needed regular dialysis, which he never could have afforded were it not for his relatives. He met patients who had bankrupted themselves for treatment. What must it be like, he asked Abed, for rickshaw pullers and laborers? Unable to afford a transplant or dialysis, about forty thousand Bangladeshis died of kidney disease each year. When the victim was the household's breadwinner, the consequences were devastating. Entire families fell into destitution.

BRAC had money, but this was no small request. Abed ran an organization that took donations—often from the same donors that supported Gonoshasthaya Kendra—not a grantmaking foundation. Abed had quietly supported causes he deemed worthy, like the Dhaka Lit Fest (an annual showcase of Bengali literature), and BRAC had recently made small grants to other nongovernmental organizations (NGOs) that were struggling. But this was on a different level.

Abed said yes on the spot, pledging 100 million Bangladeshi taka ($1.2 million) of BRAC's money to Zafrullah's project. BRAC had never made a grant that large to a nonaffiliated organization. Perhaps Abed, having turned eighty, was adopting a more expansive view on how to effect social change. BRAC did not need to do everything; it could now be a philanthropist itself. That still left the doctor needing $1.2 million, but Abed had a plan for that, too: ask Yunus for the rest.

This was assuming BRAC's new executive director approved the plan. Much had changed in the previous six years, and it was no longer a given that BRAC would approve the founder's decision.

★ ★ ★

The death of Aminul Alam in 2010 had shaken the organization. Years later, people still spoke of him with a mixture of fear and reverence. One might be forgiven for thinking he had been the second-in-command, though he never held that role in any official capacity. If there was a formal number-two person at BRAC, it would have been the executive director of BRAC itself—sometimes called BRAC Bangladesh, to distinguish it from BRAC's other country operations, which remained small by comparison. The role had thus far been filled by people who came from outside BRAC.

The second executive director after Abed, Abdul-Muyeed Chowdhury, had been a retired senior officer in the civil service. Slightly younger than Abed, he had joined in 2000 and left after six years. The third, Mahabub Hossain, was a development economist known mainly for his research in the field of agriculture. He joined in 2007 at the age of sixty-two and stepped down in late 2013, shortly after suffering a heart attack. He remained an advisor until he passed away in 2016.

Though both were respected and competent, neither of these two men made a tremendous mark on the organization. In the parlance of BRAC, neither Muyeed nor Mahabub had been considered "one of the *bhais*." The Bengali honorific for an older brother denoted, in this case, the surviving inner circle of Abed's management team, along with others who had been with BRAC for decades—people like Mushtaque Chowdhury, who had joined as a researcher in 1977, straight out of university, as well as the chief financial officer, S. N. Kairy, who had joined in 1982. (Salehuddin Ahmed, understanding he was not likely to be promoted to executive director, left for a career in academia, including a stint as pro-vice-chancellor of BRAC University, and later became a journalist.)

It is questionable whether Abed, and those close to him, ever really allowed the executive directors to lead. Though he had formally stepped back from the day-to-day running of the organization, Abed found it hard to remove himself from the picture. Many colleagues who had worked with him for years trusted him and no one else. As long as the founder continued to come to the office, they would go to him with their problems, rather than an outsider, even if the outsider was formally their boss. Abed seemed to do little to stop this.

Abed would speak of his retirement, even as he continued coming to the office every day. Age was taking its toll. Knee-replacement surgery in late 2011, the year he turned seventy-five, had slowed him down physically, and he began walking with a cane. A health scare several months later, which turned out to be nothing more than a persistent fever, coincided with BRAC's fortieth anniversary celebration, landing him in a hospital in Bangkok, where Abed and Sarwat watched the ceremonies from a hospital room. Asif Saleh, the communications director, delivered Abed's speech.

"In these twilight years of my life, I feel a sense of comfort and satisfaction in knowing that we have an able and competent leadership team at BRAC," Abed had written for his speech. It had the tone of someone passing the baton to a younger generation. He expressed confidence that the team would carry on "when I call time on providing leadership to this organization that I have built." He called gender equality "the greatest unfinished agenda not only of my life's work but of our time."

Yet it was hard to imagine BRAC without Abed. He recovered quickly from that illness, and before long he was back behind his familiar desk, the same one he had used for four decades, with its neat stacks of correspondence and reports. Even so, in the years that followed, he began showing his age. He became harder of hearing, and, in private conversations, he lamented that his memory no longer functioned like it used to. For a man who prided himself on being able to recall numbers and dates, and who could recite long passages of Shakespeare and T. S. Eliot, this was hard.

* * *

With power residing with Abed and his cadre of lieutenants, insiders began quietly voicing concerns that a younger generation of leaders-in-waiting had yet to emerge. In many Asian corporations and NGOs, founders appoint their children or other younger relatives to leadership positions, effectively making them heirs. Well over half of South Asia's listed companies are effectively family businesses. Where Westerners might see nepotism, Asians tend to see trust, stability, and longevity, and studies indicate that Asian family businesses tend to outperform others.

In hindsight, it may seem like it was inevitable that Abed's children would eventually come into the fold. However, Abed genuinely believed that everyone, his children included, had to follow their own path. He never asked Tamara or Shameran to join BRAC. On her own accord, Tamara had joined Aarong, the textile enterprise, in 2002. Ten years later, she was promoted to senior director of BRAC, making her part of the senior management team, and soon thereafter put in charge of all social enterprises.

By then, her brother Shameran had also joined. After graduating from Hamilton College, a liberal arts college in upstate New York, Abed's son had studied law in London before returning to Bangladesh in 2006. For a time, he wondered what he should be doing. He loved writing and worked as a journalist covering Bangladesh's messy politics for a daily newspaper. He contemplated practicing law or even entering national politics, which were, as ever, enmeshed in corruption scandals. He assisted his father on the side with secretarial work. Those around him, including his newspaper colleagues, questioned why he hadn't already joined BRAC. It seemed the natural thing to do. In 2009, Shameran was on a break between jobs and still "trying to figure out what the hell I wanted to do," in his words. He received a call from S. N. Kairy, BRAC's head of finance, who asked him to come to his office. "Until this day, I don't know if my father put him up to it," said Shameran.

Kairy informed him that microfinance was going through some trouble and had a new director, Ishtiaq Mohiuddin, Kaniz Fatema's son, who wanted to turn things around. "Why don't you come and work with him for a while?" Kairy asked him. Shameran joined as the number two for BRAC microfinance in late 2009. He had a quiet but commanding presence, much like a younger version of his father. It helped his stature within the organization that microfinance began performing well again. The crisis of 2007 proved to be a mere hiccup in the end. The program was profitable again within two years and began growing quickly. Shameran moved up to program director in 2014.

Another member of the senior leadership team soon became family. Tamara married Asif Saleh, the former communications director, who, like her, had recently been promoted to senior director. Whereas five years earlier, few would have called BRAC a family-run organization, by 2015 few would doubt it.

This was more comfort than concern for Abed. The advantage of relying on family was precisely that they were reliable. None of them, he said, were likely to leave anytime soon.

* * *

Midway through the decade, the organization was in good shape financially—at least in Bangladesh, which remained the site of the vast majority of its work. In the 2010s, the microfinance surplus began reaching staggering proportions, averaging about $75 million annually between 2011 and 2015—greater than the entire ten-year philanthropic commitment of the donor consortium in 1990—and growth showed no sign of slowing. Other flows of self-generated revenue also continued to rise. The annual surpluses from BRAC's enterprises averaged $17 million over the first five years of the decade, most of it coming from Aarong, BRAC Dairy, and the seed enterprise. Other investment income, consisting mainly of dividends from BRAC Bank, contributed an additional $6 million in an average year.

Among the increasingly valuable businesses in which BRAC had a stake was bKash, a mobile money platform. Described as a subsidiary of BRAC Bank, it was actually a joint venture between the bank and two Bangladeshi-American brothers, Kamal and Iqbal Quadir. Launched in 2009, it allowed people to transfer money through their mobile phones—sending money from the cities back home to their village, for instance, where a local bKash agent would dispense cash to family members. On the strength of an initial handshake agreement with Abed, bKash scaled up throughout Bangladesh using the BRAC branch network. By around mid-decade, it had eclipsed Kenya's M-Pesa as the world's largest mobile money platform, measured by the number of regular users (more than twenty million) and monthly transactions (more than one hundred million).

Donor funding, meanwhile, continued to flow. Abed had always spoken of donor money as fickle—"here today, gone tomorrow," as he once said. Tomorrow, in this case, was a long time coming, for the donors did not seem to be going anywhere. Combined donor financing for BRAC and BRAC International reached about $260 million in 2014. The British and Australian taxpayers were by far the largest contributors, their foreign aid agencies having inked a five-year commitment of £358 million ($567 million) in 2011 to BRAC Bangladesh. The agreement was unusual in that the donors offered unrestricted support that was not linked to any specific program. Within bounds, BRAC could do what it wanted with the money. Excitement over BRAC moving into Africa had fueled initial interest from donors like the Mastercard Foundation, which gave more than $90 million to BRAC Uganda between 2008 and 2012.

* * *

After the departure of BRAC's third executive director, Mahabub Hossain, the position remained vacant for about a year and a half, from the end of 2013 until mid-2015. Abed was effectively at the helm during this period, back to the job he had for BRAC's first twenty-eight years. Sarwat said the only thing that got him to relax during this time was Words with Friends, the online Scrabble knockoff, which he played obsessively on his iPhone. According to Tanya Murshed, his niece in London, he would often pester his opponents, including relatives and strangers around the world, to make their next move.

Abed understood, at least in theory, that he could not stay in charge forever. The fourth executive director would need to have a different profile than the previous two. It would make sense to put a development professional in charge. The prolonged search for an executive director came to an end in 2015 with the appointment of Muhammad Musa, a thirty-year veteran of CARE International, another of the world's largest charities. A medical doctor by training, Musa, unlike BRAC's previous two executive directors, had decades of experience running large operations in the development sector. Though he was Bangladeshi, most of his time with CARE had been spent abroad, in Ethiopia, Uganda, Sudan, Tanzania, and, finally, India, where he served as chief executive of CARE India. Two decades Abed's junior, he was also much younger than both of his predecessors. And, as it happened, at the beginning of his career, Musa had worked for Zafrullah Chowdhury.

Musa was of a different breed. The BRAC work culture was staid, especially in the executive suite of BRAC headquarters. Musa came from a middle-class background and brought a breezy informality to the setting, interspersing his conversations with jokes and stories, often told in a singsong tone. Thin and balding, with wisps of long hair, he wore a suit without a tie, often with a baseball cap, and would sometimes take phone calls perched on the back of his desk chair in his office, his feet on the seat.

* * *

Musa joined during a period of retrenchment. BRAC had enjoyed years of expansion; however, in 2016, Musa's first full year on the job, BRAC laid off thousands of people in Bangladesh. Many were long-serving employees. Abed spoke of a letter he had received from a person who had worked at BRAC for much of his life, only to be let go. He was clearly moved, though he showed no sign of second-guessing the decision to downsize.

The growth of donor funding had begun to slow, and there was a sense that perhaps it had even peaked. In Bangladesh, where the UK aid agency was the most generous BRAC supporter, a temporary weakening of the British pound led to a reduction of support in terms of local taka. The second-largest supporter, the Australian government, reduced its funding commitment as it made dramatic cuts to foreign-aid spending across the board. Donor-financed programs across the organization were strapped for cash. Employees used the words "funding crisis" to describe the situation, a characterization Abed did not dispute.

In fact, this overstated the severity of the situation, since the revenue-generating arms of BRAC remained extremely healthy. For microfinance, annual loan disbursement rose to an eye-popping $3 billion in 2016, up 26 percent from the year before and triple that of 2010, with a surplus exceeding $170 million in Bangladesh alone.

Things were largely proceeding according to the long-term plan created by Abed years earlier. Years of investment in the credit and enterprise arms of BRAC had all but guaranteed a steady flow of internal funding. Even a complete evaporation of donor funding, an unlikely scenario, would not pose an existential threat to BRAC, though it would force severe restructuring.

Donors still financed roughly a quarter of BRAC's overall expenditure in Bangladesh. This oft-cited figure, though accurate, was potentially misleading, since it included the expenditure for microfinance, which was entirely self-reliant and constituted more than half the expenditure pie. Another quarter of the pie consisted of BRAC's social enterprises, which were also self-reliant. Education, health care, the ultra-poor program, and other social programs—the remaining quarter of the pie—were still largely reliant on donors.

"To some extent we are dependent on foreign donors," Abed said. "Gradually we would like to become less and less dependent on them." He clarified that he never wanted BRAC to become 100 percent self-reliant, for the organization, in that case, would be accountable to no one except its own board. Donor funding kept BRAC on its toes. "To become completely self-financed means that you will not seek anybody's money," he said. "Therefore, you don't seek anybody's advice or anybody's scrutiny into your organization. That means there is a chance that things may go wrong and you wouldn't even know about it. So it's better to be in the market, going for money that other people are also trying to get." The ideal portion of donor financing is about 10 to 15 percent, he suggested.

There was a more systemic reason that BRAC Bangladesh could no longer rely on huge inflows of donor cash, and this was good news cloaked as bad: the country's needs were not as dire as they once were. By now, the indicators of Bangladesh's success were widely reported. Maternal mortality was 75 percent lower than it was in 1981, when Abed's wife died in childbirth, and infant mortality was half of what it was in 1990, when BRAC finished the nationwide child survival campaign. As a country climbs the development ladder, major inflows of foreign development assistance tend to decrease. The long-term priorities of donors interested in poverty reduction were shifting away from South Asia toward sub-Saharan Africa. In 2015, Bangladesh graduated from the World Bank's "low-income economy" category, becoming a "lower-middle-income" country. BRAC, or at least the donor-funded part of it, was becoming a victim of Bangladesh's success—a success that BRAC had helped create.

BRAC Bangladesh responded to this new reality with two strategic shifts. First, microfinance began subsidizing other programs for the first time. Prior to 2016, the entire microfinance surplus had been reinvested in the program. Not a taka had been transferred to health, education, or other donor-supported programs. In 2016, it began using a big chunk of the surplus—more than $20 million annually—to cross-subsidize health, education, graduation, and other programs.

Second, major donor-financed programs like health and education were told to begin experimenting with ways to recover a greater portion of their costs. In this "free-to-fee" transition, participants would need to pay small fees for services. Parents were now asked to pay a small fee for putting their children in BRAC schools, for instance, though allowances were made for ultra-poor households. Turning participants into paying clients upended the dynamic between the organization and the people it served, and some programs had difficulty adapting. The results of these ongoing experiments will determine the direction of many of BRAC's traditionally donor-subsidized programs.

⋆ ⋆ ⋆

In response to the downtick in donor funding, BRAC might have shifted more attention to regions with greater need, particularly sub-Saharan Africa. But international operations were facing their own set of challenges. For about the first seven years, BRAC Afghanistan had achieved extraordinary success, and the government welcomed BRAC with open arms. This created a sense that international expansion would be easier than it proved to be. Even in Afghanistan, a host of problems forced it to close its microfinance program in 2012. The issues included instability caused by the ongoing war, which led to several employees being kidnapped and at least one killed, and mismanagement—sometimes outright fraud—by members of BRAC's own staff. Several people were fired when the misconduct emerged, but the damage was done.

Other countries faced their own problems. Microfinance in South Sudan also had to shut down shortly after a civil war broke out in 2013. BRAC Haiti, which opened in the wake of the 2010 earthquake, proved too difficult to manage from Dhaka, eleven time zones away, and wound down after several years. A number of projects in African countries—in education, agriculture, and health—also ended due to lack of funding after their initial start-up grants, and social enterprises, including a seed farm in Uganda, had yet to achieve profitability.

"I don't know whether I've done the right thing by extending our programs abroad," Abed said in 2015. It was a rare moment of self-doubt. "If we don't really make a difference in people's lives, then why are we wasting people's time?" He linked some of the challenges, especially in Afghanistan, with the sudden death of his loyal disciple, Amin, which left fast-growing operations with inadequate supervision. But the real problem, as he saw it, was that operations were underfunded. In Africa, in particular, donors had not supported BRAC's expansion to the extent he had initially hoped. Raising money had been easy for Abed in Bangladesh. He failed to recognize that this was partly due to his extraordinary persona: the native son, an accountant no less, who sacrificed a corporate career to raise his country from the ashes. This did not readily translate into raising large sums for global operations.

To be sure, there were promising exceptions. One was microfinance. Following the closures in Afghanistan and South Sudan, and a surprisingly fast recovery from the devastation of Ebola in Liberia and Sierra Leone in 2014, microfinance was going strong in all seven countries in which it operated. BRAC achieved notable success in Africa with some other programs, including a network of girls' empowerment clubs called Empowerment and Livelihood for Adolescents. Adolescent girls would receive vocational training paired with "life skills" training from older girls and young women, covering issues like menstruation, peer pressure, sexual health, and emotions. Though it originated at BRAC in Bangladesh, the program achieved far greater success abroad than it did at home. In a randomized controlled trial (RCT), researchers in Uganda found that, after four years, it caused a 48 percent rise in employment, a one-third drop in reported cases of rape, and a similar drop in early pregnancy. This happened across the villages where the clubs operated compared to similar villages with no clubs. RCTs also recorded positive results from the same program when it ran in Sierra Leone and South Sudan. At one point the clubs had sixty thousand members in Uganda. The program had trouble maintaining girls' interest over longer periods of time, however, and it proved hard to raise the money to keep it going at such a large scale.

Then there were the graduation programs. The studies on the BRAC ultra-poor graduation program in Bangladesh had traveled far, landing on desks at foreign aid agencies, private foundations, the World Bank in Washington, and universities. One of the institutions most interested was Consultative Group to Assist the Poor (CGAP), a partnership of donors and development banks housed at the World Bank. CGAP's reach was wide, and its name carried weight. Among those working there was Syed

Hashemi, the former Grameen researcher who had become a promoter of the graduation approach. According to Hashemi, people lauded BRAC's results but questioned whether the approach had global application. "People said it works in Bangladesh and nowhere else," he said.

In 2006, pushed by Hashemi and other proponents, CGAP set up a partnership with the Ford Foundation to pilot and evaluate graduation programs with unprecedented rigor. They launched programs in Ethiopia, Ghana, Haiti, Honduras, India, Pakistan, Peru, and Yemen, teaming up with a group of independent researchers—including Abhijit Banerjee and Esther Duflo, by now two of the most widely known champions of generating evidence using RCTs—to evaluate the results. Notably, local organizations, not BRAC, ran the pilots in each of these places. They followed the same approach BRAC had used with Shahida and Amina, giving women assets like cash, goats, and cows, plus in-person coaching in microentrepreneurship, health care, and other social issues—all for a period of two years, after which the women "graduated" from the program.

The result was a massive RCT involving twenty-one thousand participants in six of these countries. The results did not merely suggest that graduation programs *could* work outside Bangladesh. They *did* work. Revenue, income, total consumption, and indicators of physical and mental health all rose significantly. Even three years after the intervention began—that is, a year after participants stopped receiving benefits—the economic gains were sustained. By the standards of most development interventions, this outcome was remarkable. Reporting their results in *Science* magazine in 2015, the researchers noted that where so many previous attempts to help the poorest have failed, this one, with only a two-year intervention period, succeeded on nearly every measure.[1]

This became new and promising territory for BRAC. It meant that it could parlay its direct experience into advising others on how to implement these kinds of anti-poverty programs. It did not have to do everything itself; scale could come through others. By 2020, there were already about a hundred programs worldwide that imitated this approach and called themselves "graduation" programs, and BRAC was advising several of them. BRAC then received $60 million from the Audacious Project, a collaborative of wealthy donors, to work with governments to adopt and scale up graduation programs with a goal of lifting twenty-one million people out of ultra-poverty by 2026.

These were bright spots in an otherwise cloudy picture for BRAC's international expansion, however. It says something that the domain where BRAC left its biggest mark outside Bangladesh, graduation, was the one area where it was not implementing the programs directly. Commenting on his father's move to expand internationally, Shameran Abed said, "I don't think he fully appreciated the challenge of taking BRAC into other countries."

★ ★ ★

When he made his pledge to Zafrullah to help fund the low-cost dialysis service, Abed failed to mention one thing: he did not actually have the power to write a check on behalf of BRAC. For that, he would need to convince Musa, who was now officially the head of the organization. And Musa was not immediately sold on the idea of granting such a large sum to Zafrullah, his old boss.

Musa's door faced Abed's office across an expanse of carpet on the executive floor of BRAC headquarters, and, from his desk, he kept an eye on who was coming and going, including journalists, politicians, and other notable visitors. One day, he spotted Zafrullah going in to see Abed. Musa greeted him but did not ask the purpose of his visit. Zafrullah was in Abed's office for two or three hours, according to Musa.

The next morning, Abed walked into Musa's office, sat down, and explained the concept. Abed had already worked out the financial mechanics. There would be one hundred machines, with three shifts serving five hundred people per day. The patients would be charged on a sliding scale according to their ability to pay, with VIP cabins offered for the wealthier ones. The poorest 10 percent would receive services free of charge. Laborers and rickshaw pullers would come at night, and when the day broke, they would go back to work. Abed told Musa of his intention to contribute 100 million taka. "If you agree," he added.

Musa found the cause worthy, given the financial ruin of kidney disease. "But who will manage it?" he asked Abed. He himself did not have the bandwidth to oversee it, and, having briefly worked for Gonoshasthaya Kendra at the start of his career, he had doubts about whether Zafrullah would run it according to BRAC standards. Musa and Abed spent several days going back and forth on it.

This was a new position for Abed. He was not used to anyone questioning him except his family. A few days later, he asked Musa whether he had made his decision. The executive director again wavered.

Abed grew impatient and reminded Musa that people's lives were at stake. "If you, as executive director, have any problem giving this from the BRAC account, just tell me," he said. "I'll go to my relatives and friends. I'll raise this money myself and give it to Zafrullah Chowdhury."

Feeling like a child having his ears boxed, Musa relented.

The only thing left to do was coax the money out of Yunus. Abed, Yunus, and Zafrullah were by now recognized around the world as the three elder icons of Bangladesh civil society, with more awards and citations between them than could fit on a page, including a knighthood, a Nobel Prize, and three Ramon Magsaysay Awards. Yet when Abed and Zafrullah came to Yunus's offices at the Grameen Bank headquarters, it was one of the first and only private meetings between the three men. Abed and Yunus were not old friends the way Abed and Zafrullah were, and, despite the overlap in their work—and the fact that they were two of the most famous Bangladeshis in the world—they had maintained a respectful distance from one another over the years. Nevertheless, if one person could convince Yunus to contribute something to Zafrullah's project, it was Abed.

At their meeting, Yunus agreed to have Grameen match BRAC's contribution, but, as per Yunus's rule of never giving away money, it would be an interest-free loan, not an outright donation.

Yunus laughed when recalling the story. Zafrullah brought Abed "just to put pressure on me to do something," he said. It worked. "He got the big gun to convince me."

The Gonoshasthaya Dialysis Center opened in May 2017, overseen by a trust jointly managed by the three organizations. Zafrullah Chowdhury was one of the first patients.

26

THE WORLD'S MOST PERSECUTED

Bangladesh had long been a synonym for calamity in the eyes of the world, and the 2010s did nothing to change that. In April 2013, an eight-story garment factory on the Dhaka outskirts collapsed while Abed was en route to Uganda for a series of internal meetings, killing 1,134 people. The garment business, along with remittances from foreign workers sending money home, had become Bangladesh's largest source of export revenue. The business was rife with corruption and exploitation of low-wage labor. Cracks had appeared in the building the day before, and the owner had willfully ignored an engineer's warnings that it was on the verge of collapse. Workers had been ordered to go back inside to their deaths.

With rescue workers still searching for survivors in the rubble—and before he even returned to Dhaka—Abed's byline appeared in the *New York Times* opinion pages. He was one of the few prominent Bangladeshis discussing the tragedy at length in the Western press. "The victims were among the most vulnerable in our society—hardworking people making an honest, but meager, living," he wrote. "Many died manufacturing clothing for Western brands." Dispite the unease Westerners might feel about wearing clothes made in such conditions, he stressed the importance of continuing to buy Bangladeshi-made garments, for these low-paying garment sector jobs had in fact given many women hope. "Partly because many women and their daughters now take garment industry jobs—even in factories where workers' rights are virtually nonexistent—families living in poverty have changed their vision of the future." He called for Western buyers to finance better safety standards and for workers to be allowed to unionize. "Their organized power is the only thing that can stand up to the otherwise unaccountable nexus of business owners and politicians, who are often one and the same."[1]

The collapse of the Rana Plaza building was a momentous event that shook the conscience of the country. According to Asif Saleh, who by now had been promoted to senior director, when Abed returned to Dhaka, he asked what BRAC had done to respond. He had been trying to take a step back from the day-to-day running of the organization but erupted in rage when he found that, without him there to issue orders, BRAC had sat by, doing almost nothing. "He was furious," Asif said, who quoted him as saying (or rather shouting), "BRAC is an organization for the people, and if we cannot mobilize to stand behind the people who need the support the most, there is no point for us to even exist."

★ ★ ★

Fast forward two years. Muhammad Musa came on board as executive director with big ideas, some of which were controversial within the organization. The new executive director wanted to turn BRAC into a leader in emergency response, which engendered plenty of internal skepticism—including from me.

I had joined BRAC's US affiliate organization, BRAC USA, in 2011, as the manager of communications for North America. I had no previous experience in nonprofit work or international development. My background was in journalism, which may explain why I ended up writing many of Abed's speeches. Despite my lack of expertise in international development, the area to which Musa had committed his decades-long career, after five years at BRAC I had spent enough time with the founder, other senior managers, and rank-and-file staff to have a sense of what was realistic to achieve. Or so I thought.

Musa wanted to beef up BRAC's capacity for disaster relief, so it would become known for its humanitarian response to crises like earthquakes, cyclones, and refugees. The latter, especially, was emerging as the defining international crisis of the 2010s. Disaster relief was nothing new for BRAC, of course. Abed had launched the organization to help returning war refugees, and other human-made and natural catastrophes had prompted several of its more recent moves into new territories, including Afghanistan, Sri Lanka, and Haiti. Even so, when disaster struck somewhere in the world, BRAC was not viewed as one of the world's go-to charities. Those would include the International Committee of the Red Cross, International Rescue Committee, and Musa's former employer, CARE International, which responded to dozens of disasters each year and reached millions through its emergency programs.

Musa wanted to change this, even if it went against the grain of how BRAC self-identified. We were a development organization, not a disaster-relief agency. Providing for people's immediate needs in the wake of catastrophe was all well and good, but, as Abed had learned in 1972, it had little to do with putting a permanent end to people's misery.

It did not help that Musa began preaching this creed during the "funding crisis" of 2016, when BRAC was in the midst of laying off thousands, including many long-serving employees. Donor funding for BRAC International, its arm overseeing non-Bangladesh operations, had dropped several years in a row. Not for the first time, many thought BRAC had finally spread itself too thin, and yet its new leader seemed to be suggesting more foreign ventures.

I had already heard about Musa's ambition, so during a visit to Bangladesh in 2016—the same visit on which I first met Shahida Begum and heard her story of the fox that killed her goat—I visited his office on the nineteenth floor to hear for myself. By responding quickly to global emergencies, Musa told me, BRAC could capture donor funding while gaining footholds in new territories where its services were badly needed. The aspiration was noble, but it seemed detached from the organization's current reality. "You and what army?" I asked.

Musa assured me that the money would come as long as BRAC responded quickly. We would hire the army, in other words. It could start with as few as three people—an analyst, a photographer, and a writer—who would land on the ground in the immediate aftermath of a crisis and make themselves and the organization visible. We would use the material they produced to solicit funding from donors, who tended to respond quickly to bad news. There was nothing cynical about recognizing that. It might also help us replace some of the donor funding that was dissipating as Bangladesh became a less poverty-stricken country.

Providing essential services like food, shelter, medicine, and latrines would also lay the groundwork for long-term anti-poverty programs. Musa had seen this all play out during his decades of service with CARE, including, most recently, during the aftermath of Typhoon Haiyan in the Philippines in 2013 and the Nepal earthquake of 2015. He was confident future disasters would follow the same pattern.

Musa had a chance to prove this to skeptical colleagues sooner and more emphatically than anyone might have anticipated. Given Bangladesh's history, it should have come as no surprise that the next global emergency took place in BRAC's own backyard.

* * *

Shah Alam, a slight man with a graying goatee and a lungi, emerged from the mosque in the village of Anjuman Para, where he was the imam. At the water pump, a younger congregant prepared for prayer, washing his hands and feet, rubbing his teeth and gums with a finger, and then swishing and spitting. Behind the mosque, a herd of water buffalo walked to the nearby Naf River along a path lined by purple morning glories.

It was 2018. Shah Alam described the scene in this exact spot about a year earlier. The Naf River is a muddy, swamp-flanked estuary that forms part of the 130-mile-long border with Myanmar in Bangladesh's far southern coastal strip, in the district of Cox's Bazar. One night in August 2017, a stream of people in rags began walking up the path where the water buffalo were now walking. They had crossed the border from Myanmar in the dark. "It was midnight, so everyone was sleeping when they began to arrive," he said. "We were woken up by the sound of the people." The people spoke Rohingya, a language that is closely related to Bengali and mutually intelligible with Chittagonian, the language of the region.

They came in the hundreds, then thousands, wading up from the river through swamps and rice paddies. Two thousand people settled in the village the first night. They brought their dead with them. Many told stories of families being shot, women raped, their babies taken from them and burned alive by the Burmese military.

As fellow Muslims, the people of Anjuman Para invited the guests to eat with them for the Eid al-Adha feast as they waited for entry to nearby refugee camps. They kept coming. They slept everywhere—in the school, people's homes, and the courtyard of the mosque. For the Bangladeshis old enough to remember, the refugees could have been the ghosts of 1971.

While sharing the story with me, Shah Alam pointed to a spot in the distance where the Myanmar border fence was visible. He described the plumes of smoke visible the next day—Rohingya villages razed to the ground. I recalled the story of Sarabala, one of the first BRAC participants, who held her daughter and watched her home burn while fleeing Sulla by boat.

The genocide against the Rohingya people of neighboring Myanmar was a human-made catastrophe that shocked the world. In August 2017, an unprecedented wave of people began crossing Bangladesh's eastern border, including children still bleeding from gunshot wounds. A stateless people denied citizenship in both Myanmar and Bangladesh, the Rohingya have been called "the world's most persecuted minority." The Myanmar government denies their very existence, insisting they are Bangladeshi immigrants, even though they have lived in Myanmar since long before Bangladesh existed. Periodic waves of persecution since the 1970s had already displaced about three hundred thousand Rohingya into camps along the border.

In the weeks to come, seven hundred thousand more crossed over, creating the world's largest refugee settlement, a sprawling camp of one million souls living in makeshift huts of sticks and plastic bags on hilly, swampy land. They had almost no food, no place to defecate, and no medicine for the dysentery that began running rampant. The situation required extraordinary relief measures, and BRAC had an opportunity to be one of the lead responders.

According to Musa, Abed had also been skeptical of his plans to pursue large-scale emergency-relief projects. The founder was prioritizing grander goals, including the global eradication of extreme poverty. In September, as he did every year, Abed visited New York for meetings coinciding with the annual UN General Assembly session, including one with Bill Clinton at his midtown Manhattan office. The ex-president considered Abed a friend and had recorded a warm video greeting for his eightieth birthday. The two men talked about becoming grandparents before turning to the business at hand. It was less than a year after the election of Donald Trump. Abed told Clinton he was concerned about preserving momentum on the UN's Sustainable Development Goals, particularly the first goal, eradicating extreme poverty. He asked for Clinton's help promoting BRAC-style graduation programs worldwide. Clinton was sold on it, at least enough to talk up BRAC's graduation approach with Paul Kagame, the president of Rwanda, the next day.

In this context, one can certainly see why short-term disaster relief might seem less important than global policy changes that might affect the lives of hundreds of millions. Nonetheless, as Abed hobnobbed with Clinton, senior managers in Dhaka had more immediate concerns. A team descended on Cox's Bazar, the nearest city to the Rohingya camps, and visited the makeshift settlements on a scouting mission. Named for a minor officer in the East India Company, Cox's Bazar was normally a beach resort town, boasting one of the longest expanses of unbroken sand in the world. It was now the epicenter of the world's most horrifying refugee crisis.

The scene at the camps was overwhelming. For Musa, it evoked memories of his childhood. He had been fourteen and living in Dhaka when the Liberation War broke out. He and his family, including his pregnant mother, fled on foot. It took them seventeen days to reach a camp on the Indian border. Allen Ginsberg had written of a million "starving black angels in human disguise" on the road to Calcutta; Musa had been one of those, walking past the dying and the dead, fearing for his and his loved ones' lives. In the crowded settlements outside Cox's Bazar, filled with malnourishment and trauma, he saw the same fear he had known then.

When the team returned to the hotel that evening, many cried. If there was any lingering resistance to intervening, it disappeared that night. They began to strategize. Musa insisted on mobilizing BRAC's full institutional might, and he wanted to do so without wasting another hour. The only man who might have slowed him down was thousands of miles away. "I was lucky," Musa later reflected, "that the week that I started the Rohingya project, Abed *Bhai* was in New York."

Musa recalled the initial plans from the sanitation team. In line with BRAC's mantra of piloting small before scaling up, they had proposed starting with no more than twenty formally constructed toilets. Musa rejected this idea immediately. "I was doing back-of-the-envelope calculations," he said. "I saw that one million people would need thirty-five thousand toilets." The camps already had some limited infrastructure, but with the population expected to triple, the government, the military, UN agencies, and private relief agencies would struggle to meet that need, even working at breakneck pace.

The basics of a decent pit latrine are simple. It consists of a set of concrete rings placed in a hole in the ground, covered by a slab with a hole in it. The point is to separate people from the feces they produce. Ideally, there is a housing over it for a modicum of privacy. The rings and the slab are crucial, for without them the hole will not last long, especially on the muddy hillsides outside Cox's Bazar.

At ten o'clock that night, Musa placed a call to Reaz Uddin of the microfinance program, who was accustomed to receiving late-night orders from his superiors. He was the one who, ten years earlier, had endured Amin's wrath for meeting but not exceeded his target, driving all night through dense fog for a dressing-down by his boss.

Musa instructed Reaz to call all sixty-four BRAC district offices across the country and tell them to spend the day buying every available ring and slab in the district.

The team stayed up until three o'clock in Cox's Bazar, planning and budgeting. Early the next day, Musa ordered the transport division to mobilize a fleet of flatbeds to visit every district office that evening and load them with concrete rings and slabs. They would set off for Cox's Bazar after a day of purchasing, arriving the morning of the second day. He soon learned there would be twenty-two trucks coming, with some making multiple stops at districts along the way.

Musa then called Asif, the senior director in charge of communications, and told him to print twenty-two banners with BRAC's name on them. Get a video cameraman, a still photographer, and a writer, he added, and alert the media that the trucks would be arriving. "The day after tomorrow," he said. "I want that picture in the newspapers, and at the bottom, I want it saying that BRAC has stepped up its operations for Rohingya refugees."

The photographers were ready when the fleet of trucks began arriving the next morning, stacked with concrete latrine slabs and rings from all over Bangladesh. Two days later, BRAC received its first call from a major donor, Australia's Department of Foreign Affairs and Trade, offering $3 million to support the operations. The money began pouring in.

Abed once told an internal audience—perhaps half joking—that he was probably not the best person to lead BRAC since he was so poor at communications. Musa had no compunction about publicizing the work. Field staff fanned out through the camps with vests, hats, and umbrellas in bright magenta, BRAC's signature color, with a prominent logo. In a YouTube video, Asif led viewers on the tour through smoke-filled tents, introducing a child who had been shot in the head. "I had no idea before I came here of the actual scale of the humanitarian crisis," he told the camera. "Wherever you are, however you can, help is really needed. This is a national emergency."

By mid-October, a month after operations began, BRAC had built ten thousand toilets serving about 415,000 people, installed more than a thousand tube wells for clean water, and immunized 167,000 people against cholera. To restore a sense of normalcy to the lives of children, it opened child-friendly spaces and learning centers for the Rohingya children. BRAC was one among many, as there were countless other aid and development groups working in the camps, providing food, water, medical care, and shelter, including far more recognizable names like UNICEF, Save the Children, and Doctors Without Borders. Yet when the *New York Times* published "Helping the Rohingya," a list of organizations responding to the crisis, BRAC was at the top of the list—and not because it was first alphabetically.[2]

Abed could be stingy with praise. If you did something well, you would be lucky if he told you once. After Abed's return from the United States, the executive director took his boss on a tour of the camps. To the extent that the word "success" is appropriate in such grim circumstances, the program was no doubt a success.

The two men had breakfast together at the hotel the next day, before Abed's flight back to Dhaka. Mindful of his cholesterol, Musa pushed one of his egg yolks to the side and left it on his plate. As they were getting up to leave, Abed peered down at Musa's plate and, pointing to the uneaten egg yolk, scolded him for wasting food, given the privation they had just witnessed. Chastened yet again, the executive director sat back down and finished his egg. He then walked Abed to his airport car and, as he was getting in, gently prodded him. "Abed *Bhai*," he said, "you haven't given me any feedback."

Abed looked up from his seat. "Excellent program," he said. "Thank you." Then the driver shut the door.

★ ★ ★

Abed would not have stood in Musa's way in responding to the Rohingya crisis, according to Asif Saleh, who by now was Abed's son-in-law and would eventually succeed Musa as executive director. "When [Abed] came back and he visited the camps, you could tell that he was so, so proud—like 'Yes, this is BRAC. This is exactly how I expect the organization to be.' He was happy that without his day-to-day instructions, we went ahead and did that—the exact counter to what happened with Rana Plaza, when nobody moved without his instruction."

Subsequent phases of the Rohingya program saw BRAC take halting steps beyond immediate relief needs. With help from Lego Foundation and Sesame Workshop, the makers of *Sesame Street*, BRAC launched a $100 million expansion of its "Play Labs"—centers for play-based learning already piloted in East Africa and elsewhere in Bangladesh—in the Rohingya camps. With a heavy dose of academic input from BRAC University and a consortium of global scholars on early-childhood development, these centers would help children six and younger heal from trauma.

The transition to long-term development has proven difficult, however, in part due to the tragic political status of the Rohingya. They remain a stateless people, unwanted by either government. The chance of peaceful and voluntary repatriation to Myanmar seems remote, and yet the Bangladesh government has resisted efforts that might make their stay seem permanent, like the construction of concrete dwellings in the Cox's Bazar encampments or allowing them to work. Creating safe spaces for children to play and learn was one thing; creating sustainable livelihood options for adults was more problematic. BRAC made some headway by getting permission from the government to launch production centers for Aarong textiles. But the vast majority remained reliant on external food aid.

The politics of the Rohingya question are thorny, both domestically and internationally. BRAC was able to grow as large as it did in part because Abed insisted on leaving Bangladesh's messy internal politics to the politicians, steering it away from any hint of partisanship, preferring the quiet politics of empowering the powerless. If he met with the prime minister, he would generally follow up with a meeting with the opposition leader. Non-Bangladeshi observers of BRAC often make the mistake of overestimating its stature inside the country, with some even calling it a "parallel government." This makes the management of BRAC cringe. As large and reputable as the organization is, it cannot do much without the blessing of the state.

When it comes to refugee relief, BRAC has had to navigate the political sensitivities that come with visibility. Public sentiment, initially welcoming of the Rohingya, began to sour, especially in the communities surrounding the camps. The residents of Anjuman Para, the settlement on the Naf River, told me they regretted welcoming the Rohingya. A portion of BRAC's aid was subsequently redirected to these "host communities," in part to assuage their resentment.

Officially, BRAC employees were (and still are, as of this writing) forbidden from calling the Rohingya "refugees." Following the government's nomenclature, they are Forcibly Displaced Myanmar Nationals (FDMNs); they do not live in "camps" but in "makeshift settlements." Both terms are politically loaded, as they imply a certain status under international law that the government is unwilling to grant. BRAC, meanwhile, remained active in Myanmar, where it needed to be mindful of the safety of its six hundred staff—more than 90 percent of them Myanmarese—serving ninety thousand low-income families with microloans as of 2019.

As of this writing, the Bangladesh government is moving ahead with a plan to transplant a huge portion of the Rohingya refugees, about one hundred thousand of them, to an offshore island called Bhasan Char, a low-lying, uninhabited land created by silt from the massive Meghna estuary emptying into the Bay of Bengal. Human rights groups expressed shock when the idea was first raised, likening it to an offshore prison, vulnerable to being swept away in a cyclone. But the government is serious about it, even constructing concrete homes and storm shelters.

The story comes full circle here, for this island is not far from Manpura, where Abed and his Dhaka friends led an efficient relief effort that drew international praise following the November 1970 cyclone. Located about midway between Chittagong and Manpura, it is likely Abed would have flown over this spot on the helicopter visit that caused him to reassess his life's priorities. He would not have seen the island, however, because it did not exist. Bhasan Char, about fifteen square miles in area, rose from the sea around 2006 amid the shifting soils of the Ganges Delta.

⋆ ⋆ ⋆

Prior to the Rohingya crisis, there may have been a lurking suspicion that BRAC, with its aging founder and chairperson, was becoming a dinosaur, no longer able to move quickly even when it wanted to. There were times when its bureaucracy seemed sclerotic, its institutional habits built for another century. The rapid response dispelled this notion.

Musa, it turned out, was cut from Abed's cloth in at least one sense: both were perfectly content to take a proposed solution and multiply its scale by a thousand or more. The problem with most social-impact organizations, Abed once said, is that they are not ambitious enough. They are content remaining small and beautiful. Tinkering around the edges was not his style; he sought systems change, which led him to constantly challenge those around him, asking whether what they were doing was big enough to confront the problems they were trying to solve.

Abed praised Musa for giving the organization the confidence that it could still take on large new projects. For at least his first two years on the job, Musa said he felt like Abed was watching him closely. That changed with the Rohingya program. "After the Rohingya program, he was not even looking at what I was doing," Musa said.

That said, there was much else to be concerned about besides the day-to-day running of BRAC, including the university, the bank, and BRAC International. "I don't have any retirement plan, but I am semiretired in the sense that I come to the office about ten o'clock," Abed told a video interviewer in 2017. "I used to come at eight in the old times. I used to go home at seven. I still go home at seven, but then I take a rest in the afternoon." He nodded toward the corner of his office, where a daybed near the window overlooked the Korail slum, nineteen floors below. It is questionable whether the average person would classify such a schedule as "semiretired."

After 2017, he began to feel a little more comfortable taking a modest step back. There was little doubt that Abed's eventual retirement was in sight.

27

IF I HAD A LITTLE MORE TIME

The funding crisis abated after about four thousand layoffs in 2016, and within a year the number of full-time staff in Bangladesh was back up to its previous level, about sixty thousand, partly due to the thousands of people added to the ground in Cox's Bazar. As had happened many times before with BRAC, what seemed like a crisis was merely a hiccup.

There remained, however, one change for which BRAC could never have fully prepared. In July 2019, I visited Bangladesh, as I did often, to fill in some of the remaining gaps in my research for this book. I went on a long road trip, from the northern reaches to the southern shores, meeting participants in one of the earliest BRAC programs in Rowmari, survivors of the 1974 famine, and paying a return visit to Shahida, whose story begins this book. I visited Abed's primary school in Pabna and saw the *haor* areas submerged in the summer.

When I returned, I visited Abed in his office and sat across from his desk, as I had many times before. I asked how he was doing.

"Honestly?" he began. He then shared with me the latest news about his health. He had recently begun feeling strange and alarming symptoms, perhaps suggestive of a neurological disorder. He would lose the sensation in his right arm and feel it momentarily paralyzed, for instance. A series of tests, including a brain scan, were inconclusive. He consulted Viquar Chamoun, a consultant neurologist in the United Kingdom and the son of two of his oldest friends, Runi Khan and Viquar Choudhury—the woman whose phone call to Chittagong prompted the post-cyclone relief effort in 1970 and the man with whom he had cofounded BRAC. Chamoun looked at the results and suggested he undergo further diagnosis during a visit to London, which he did. From London, he went to The Hague for the BRAC International board meeting, but, while there, he was called and told to return to London immediately for a biopsy, as the brain scan had yielded disturbing results.

The biopsy results confirmed that Abed had glioblastoma, the most aggressive form of brain cancer. Treatment meant invasive surgery followed by chemotherapy and radiation; with this aid, he would likely have about twelve to eighteen months to live. Without treatment, he would have about four months.

It was early July. Abed considered the quality he wanted for his remaining life and the disruption that treatment would cause to his family and the organization he had founded. His father had died at seventy-three and his grandfather at seventy-two, and he had long expected that he would die around that age. Officially, he was now eighty-three; biologically, he was eighty-four. He opted not to receive treatment and immediately came home.

He shared this news with the tone of someone relaying a shift in strategy. He seemed mildly frustrated with the inconvenient timeframe. "I was a little unhappy that the time is too short," he said. "If I had a little more time, maybe six months to a year, it would be better, rather than four months."

There was much work to be done to prepare BRAC for his departure. Although he had stepped back from day-to-day affairs, he was still, both formally and in spirit, the glue that held the BRAC family together. He alone chose the members of the governing boards of BRAC, BRAC International, and BRAC Bank. The same held for the trustees of BRAC University. He still chaired the boards of all four organizations. "I won't be there, so who is going to do the kinds of things I do?" he asked. "What one person used to do, can a well-intentioned committee do the same thing? That's what I am asking myself." Not wanting the news to distract from shifts in governance he was already preparing, nobody knew beyond close friends and family. He only told me in case I needed to ask him something more for this book.

He hardly seemed distraught that his own death was close enough to affect his calendar. He would not be able to accept invitations or make commitments beyond November. I told him he seemed dispassionate, almost analytical. He laughed. "No, I'm not too unhappy as to what I've done," he said.

Not too unhappy as to what I've done. I repeated the words back to him, and he laughed again. "I think I have used my life to improve the situation or the condition of a fairly large number of people on this planet," he said. "But I wish I could do more."

He said he only had one question for the doctors: Is it going to be painful? They explained that, in the coming weeks and months, the brain would be attacked by the cancer, and he would gradually lose the effectiveness of his hands and feet, followed by other impairments, and eventually would lose the ability to speak. But he would not be in great pain. Quoting Keats, he said he looked forward to a death in which he would "cease upon the midnight with no pain."

He did not believe in an afterlife. "I'm happy that this is not clouding my mind at all," he said. Beyond figuring out who would govern BRAC, he expressed concern about being able to spend quality time with his children and extended family before being debilitated—and not being a burden as the disease took its toll.

"BRAC remains my constant preoccupation," he said. "Will it be run well? Will it survive? How long will it survive? If it survives, will it continue to do good for the people it's supposed to serve? That's what I'm worrying about. I just hope that I've created an organization which will continue to be a force for good in the world. That's all."

He paused and looked around his office, cluttered with waist-high stacks of books. "And then I'm thinking that all this junk that I have—after I'm dead, people are going to go through this and throw it away. Maybe I should start doing some of that myself."

I began thinking of all the small details of his story, things I always assumed I could check with him later. I had a list of questions, and we began bouncing haphazardly around the decades, trying to pry out more of the mundane details that made up a life. I asked for details about his 1971 visit to the prime-minister-in-exile in Calcutta, seeking permission to fund the bombing of the Pakistan Navy. We talked about his travels with Marietta in the early 1960s, when "our life was less constrained by thinking about the future." We spoke of Khushi's notorious letter and his proposal to Sarwat.

I asked him what it was about T. S. Eliot that he loved so much. He didn't have a good answer, beyond pointing out that Eliot could write phrases like "mixing memory with desire," *The Waste Land*'s opening evocation of the nostalgia of spring. He quoted the section called "Death by Water" about Phlebas, a drowned Phoenician sailor who

> Forgot the cry of gulls, and the deep sea swell
> And the profit and loss.
> A current under sea
> Picked his bones in whispers.

This was about as close as Abed got to being wistful or sentimental.

We met once more in July before my flight back to New York. As I opened the door to his office, I almost took a step back from the smell of cigarette smoke. "Have you been smoking again?" I asked. "Those things will kill you." He was in good humor and laughed. Despite his terminal diagnosis, Sarwat still didn't allow him to smoke at home, so in the time he had left, he was enjoying all the cigarettes he could at the office.

My list of questions did not seem to get any smaller and would keep growing until he was no longer able to answer.

In Dhaka, the future management and governance of the BRAC family of organizations began falling into place. Muhammad Musa had already shifted to the executive directorship of BRAC International. Earlier in the year, he had decided, for family reasons, that he needed to relocate to the United States. Abed refused to let him leave BRAC, eventually charging him with turning around the struggling international operations.

In late July, Abed appointed Tamara, his daughter, to be managing director for enterprises, reporting directly to the board. She would also take over as chair of the board of trustees of BRAC University. Shameran, his son, would remain in charge of microfinance (the biggest revenue generator) and the ultra-poor graduation program. The executive director, overseeing all the social programs, would be Asif Saleh, who had joined BRAC in 2011 after twelve years with Goldman Sachs. Initially in charge of communications, Asif had been promoted over the years to oversee strategy and a widening range of programs. He was also now Tamara's husband and the father of one of Abed's three grandchildren.

In August, Abed announced "an important life decision" to staff around the world. He would be stepping down as chair of the governing bodies of both BRAC Bangladesh and BRAC International. To replace him as chair of the board of BRAC Bangladesh, he recruited Hossain Zillur Rahman, an eminent research economist and policymaker, and head of the Power and Participation Research Center (PPRC). A sort of research think tank, PPRC had been the source of the original research that Abed had credited with sparking the creation of the ultra-poor graduation program. To chair BRAC International and a newly created Global Board of BRAC, whose purview was yet to be fully established, he appointed Ameerah Haq, a senior UN official and the senior-most Bangladeshi within the UN system. Abed described it as a retirement. He did not divulge the real reason he was stepping down.

In his final letter to staff, Abed wrote that no one should ever be a "passive recipient of charity." He pointed out that BRAC's consistent ethos has been giving people hope, investing in confidence, and reminding them of their own self-worth. "I have spent my life watching optimism triumph over despair when the light of self-belief is sparked in people," he wrote. "As a team, I want us to keep lighting these sparks."

By September, two months after the diagnosis, Abed's functioning began to deteriorate, much as the doctors had predicted. His ability to carry on a conversation was largely undiminished, but he commented that his mind was not functioning the way it once had. His eyesight was fine, but the cancer had made it difficult to read words on a page. Though he was not in physical pain, this fact alone must have dismayed him greatly, as he had been a voracious reader his whole life.

He came to the office less and less, spending time with his children and grandchildren, including a helicopter trip to the Hasan estate in Baniachong, where he grew up. He insisted on moving about on his own for as long as he could and took great pleasure in his favorite foods, like beef *shatkora*, a dish made with the rind of a bitter citrus native to Sylhet. In one of the last pictures of him standing up, taken by Sarwat, Abed is at the stove making a pot of chicken *rezala*. His recipe was simple: chopped onion, ghee, ginger paste, coriander powder, red chili powder, yogurt, and whole chilis. It was the same dish he had made for an elderly E. M. Forster.

Lying in bed, he would review correspondence aurally and verbally, often giving input with his eyes closed. He requested several of his oldest friends, including the Chens, Cole Dodge, and Jon Rohde, come to Dhaka for one last visit. The only people told of his illness were professional acquaintances he notified in writing, including Bill Clinton and Bill and Melinda Gates, and close family and friends whom he was able to tell in person. On October 26, he made his last public appearance at the ceremonial laying of the foundation stone for the long-planned new campus of BRAC University.

I saw him again at his home in November. He had asked me to visit from my home in New York, as though there were some last thoughts he felt important to share. I left that night on the familiar twenty-four-hour journey via Dubai and visited Abed's apartment as soon as I arrived. He was lying on his bed, facing the ceiling, his face puffy from the steroids administered to reduce cerebral swelling. He skipped the customary greeting and said what was on his mind. "Do you know how long it took me to get to London?" he asked.

"What exactly are you referring to?" I asked, perplexed.

Without sitting up, Abed explained that, in 1954, when he first left East Pakistan for his education in the United Kingdom, it took him thirty-six hours to get there. He named every layover on a succession of short-haul flights in propeller planes: Calcutta, Karachi, Tehran—there was some hassle there, he recalled, due to the coup orchestrated by the CIA the previous year—Baghdad, Rome, Geneva, and London. "Most people went by ship," he said. "I was one of the first to go by plane." His own brother had gone to the United Kingdom six months earlier and had taken the train to Bombay to board the MS *Batory*, a Polish ship that had evacuated troops from Dunkirk before becoming a flagship carrier of the Polish Ocean Lines, for the voyage to Southampton.

"I also want to talk to you about Humayun Kabir's father," he added. He then shared the story about Golam Kabir—also the father of Kaniz Fatema, the original head of the BRAC education program—who had come to visit while he and Humayun were living together in Glasgow. The older Kabir slept in the same room as the two younger men and was a terrible snorer. "We couldn't sleep at all!" Abed said.

These were the two things on his mind, and I could not help but be amused that he had called me across the oceans to share these facts. But a life is a collection of memories, and Abed's was fading. He didn't have the energy to tell me more but invited me to come back the next day with additional questions. "We can go through some of these parts again and freshen up a little bit," he said.

He told me he had developed a huge appetite for sweets. "Now that I've got this cancer, I'm eating more sweets than I ever did," he said. "Apparently cancer likes sweets." He then thanked me profusely. In his final days, Sarwat said, he was effusive in his gratitude for even the smallest things.

That was our last real conversation, for his condition deteriorated quickly. I saw him a few days later when he put on a suit and paid one final impromptu visit to his office. One of his aides pushed him in his wheelchair to his regular spot behind his desk, where he smoked a cigarette with shaking hands.

In late November, he received a final bedside visit from Zafrullah Chowdhury. Though Abed was weak, they spoke at length. According to Zafrullah, Abed told him, "We must do something so that Marietta and her contributions are remembered." Zafrullah soon made plans to name a hospital ward after Marietta Procopé, Abed's first love.

On November 27, Abed was admitted to the hospital with difficulty breathing. Though there had been no official announcement of his terminal illness, word was out that his health was declining. A joint message from Asif and Musa, the executive directors of BRAC and BRAC International, informed the staff of his hospitalization, adding that he "does not want the matters related to his health to distract us from our vital work on the ground. Let's respect his wishes."

Abed died at a Dhaka hospital on the evening of Friday, December 20, 2019, with his family by his side. Islamic custom calls for a swift burial, so, on Sunday morning, following the dawn prayers, his body was bathed in the Azad Mosque in Gulshan. With its congested streets, Gulshan was no longer the leafy suburb it had been in the late 1960s, when Abed began socializing with the doctors from the nearby cholera lab.

The first threads of light were barely visible when the plain mahogany coffin arrived at the BRAC Center. Close family, friends, and colleagues paid their last respects next to an open casket in the small auditorium. The *namaz-e-janaza* funeral prayer took place in the plaza in front of the building. Then the coffin was loaded onto a light-duty truck covered with white flowers and the BRAC logo, and Abed left work for the last time.

Bangladesh was experiencing the first cold wave of the season, and a thick blanket of fog covered the country. By the time the body arrived at the Army Stadium for the public funeral, several thousand people were already waiting under a gray sky. At least ten thousand people attended the funeral, including senior leaders of both the Awami League and the opposition Bangladesh National Party, whose fighting has marred the country's politics for decades. It was a rare occasion when the two parties appeared at an event together.

At Dhaka's Banani Graveyard, Abed was buried next to Bahar, his first wife and the mother of his children. Though he had initially been reluctant to enter into an arranged marriage with her, she went on to become the love of his life, his partner and companion at the helm of BRAC, and a believer, like him, in the vast untapped potential of the powerless.

* * *

We yearn for heroes. Only sometimes do we get them. To be sure, Abed believed in the great men of the past; he read them, he recited them. A colleague once asked Abed which historical figures he would invite to his dinner party. He mentioned Shakespeare. "It would be nice to have a word with him," he said. Yet Abed also believed that "civilization is not the product of a few great men," as he said in 1980, upon receiving his first major award, but the product of all men and women, both known and unknown.

He was born into a life of plenty in a world full of want. In the world he lived and died in, he saw men and women finding their voices and speaking their truth, building meaning in their own lives, however they saw fit, through struggle and creative action. Poverty was a deprivation of this basic human capacity, and breaking free of it, as he said in his 2015 speech accepting the World Food Prize, "is part of the ongoing process of becoming fully human." The words echoed Paulo Freire, who wrote that freedom—not granted, but acquired by conquest—is "the indispensable condition for the quest for human completion." Heroes, for Abed, were almost beside the point. In any case, they often weren't who you thought they were.

Abed championed the routinization of tasks, similar to an assembly line or a large corporation. *The Economist* once called BRAC "one of the most businesslike" nonprofits in the world. His preoccupation with efficiency and self-reliance is indeed part of the organization's DNA, and yet these are pragmatic and transactional concerns. They never obscured his life's true purpose, which was enabling oppressed people to liberate themselves from the clutches of hunger, exploitation, and fatalism.

Humankind, in Abed's view, had made a fundamental shift in his lifetime. His generation likely saw more change than any before it in terms of empowering people to shape their own destinies. Yet the despair that pervaded centuries of human existence—the tenacious myth that widespread poverty and suffering is, as Abed said, "ordained by a higher power, as immutable as the sun and the moon"—is still with us. Becoming fully human means overcoming that myth. The journey continues.

EPILOGUE

Rabindranath Tagore's *Gitanjali* contains an untitled poem about a musician who spends his days stringing and unstringing his instrument, pained by "the agony of wishing" as his long-awaited audience fails to show its face. "The song that I came to sing remains unsung to this day," the poet mournfully declares.

Abed said, near the end, that he was glad his life had not been wasted. Thanks in part to his work, millions recognized not only that a better world was possible but also that they themselves had the power to bring it about. Yet the notion of work unfinished, of a song unsung, was part of his dying message. He was not a man to look back; he did not dwell much on the memories recorded in these pages. He mainly thought about what more needed to be done.

In 2010, Stephen Sackur, a BBC interviewer, asked Abed whether he was an optimist. Abed laughed and replied, "How can you be in development without being an optimist?" If he were inclined toward pessimism, he probably would have chosen a different field, he added. There were limits, however. His compatriot Muhammad Yunus often spoke of people one day having to go to a museum to see what poverty looked like. Abed would give this a wry chuckle, and when Sackur quoted it to him, he replied that he was "not as optimistic as Professor Yunus."

Abed was generally not a fan of grand, sweeping statements or unrealistic goals for humankind's future. The Alma Ata Declaration of 1978, signed by 134 governments at an international conference in the Soviet Union, was considered a major milestone in global health, as it put forward the goal of "an acceptable level of health for all the people of the world by the year 2000." Years later, asked what he had made of it, Abed replied with a joke that had been common among skeptics at the time: "Is it health for all by the year 2000, or health for all in two thousand years?"

His view on ending poverty began to shift as global objectives became more realistic and measurable. The Millennium Development Goals, adopted by the UN in 2000, targeted a halving of the global poverty rate by 2015. Incredibly, the world met that goal five years early, driven mainly by the rising fortunes of China and India. Bangladesh was also high on the list of fast climbers. Partly as a result of this progress, Abed began expressing even greater optimism in the last decade of his life. Where he used to speak of "poverty alleviation," he began using the words "poverty eradication."

Abed was likely swayed by an emerging consensus among global policymakers that poverty—or at least the most extreme forms of it—could indeed be removed from the face of the earth by 2030, much like smallpox had been eradicated in the 1970s. The World Bank qualified the expectation somewhat, defining "eradication" as less than 3 percent of people living on the 2005 equivalent of $1.25 a day, later updated to $1.90. In any case, poverty was clearly on the retreat. By 2013, in every region of the world, including Africa, the number of people living in extreme poverty was dropping for the first time in recent memory.

That year, Abed went to Budapest to give a speech at the convocation ceremony of Central European University, where he received the Open Society Prize from his friend George Soros. On his Kindle, Abed had recently been rereading Karl Popper's *The Open Society and Its Enemies*, the book after which the prize was named, which he had first read fifty years earlier. In the speech, he reflected on Popper's belief that claims to "prophetic wisdom"—the type of "sweeping historical prophecies" about the future of humankind that left little room for doubt—were among the enemies of any free and open society. In contrast to utopian goals, Popper embraced "piecemeal social engineering" or solutions that are effective, if lacking in elegance. For Abed, there was an element of that pragmatism in BRAC, in its avoidance of ideological prescriptions, readiness to adapt, and willingness to learn from its own mistakes. "The vision of BRAC is a world free from all forms of exploitation and discrimination," Abed said. "I am sometimes asked if such a world is really possible—whether I believe that poverty can be truly eradicated. The truth is, I believe it can be." But there was no prophetic wisdom in this, he added. Humans had made poverty; only their hard work and creativity, "an ongoing and arduous task rather than a historical certainty," would unmake it.

By 2018, the outlook for eradicating extreme poverty by 2030 had turned bleaker, with the World Bank warning that to meet the 3 percent goal, the economies of the world's poorest countries would have to grow at a rate "that far surpasses their historical experience."[1] Donald Trump was just one of many inward-looking nationalist leaders who seemed more concerned with protecting their own countries than creating better conditions for the poorest. The global refugee crisis did not help matters. While Abed was urging Bill Clinton to re-energize the world behind the UN's post-2015 Sustainable Development Goals, the latest and worst episode of this crisis was already taking place on Bangladesh's eastern border.

One cannot help but wonder what Abed would have made of the world in 2020 had he lived to see it. Shortly after he died, a global pandemic, which is ongoing as of this writing, ground the world's economies to a halt. The most vulnerable were the rising poor—the millions who remade their lives thanks to the types of changes Abed set in motion. These include people like Shahida, who built a new life for herself through sweat, grit, and goats. The threat to gains in women's equality is especially dire. In addition to the increased risk of maternal mortality, women have a greater chance of infection from the virus, as they are usually tasked with caregiving. Violence against women also tends to increase when people are locked at home. BRAC saw this result when the Ebola epidemic raged in Liberia and Sierra Leone, which saw a spike in teenage pregnancies during the outbreak.

There was fear, early in the pandemic, that COVID-19 might unravel decades of gains. The estimates as of June 2021 were more optimistic. According to the World Bank, the number of people in extreme poverty rose in 2020 for the first time in decades, but it was still below 2015 levels, and an uncertain forecast for 2021 suggested it may have already begun decreasing again at the pre-pandemic rate. The projected recovery will be uneven, with extreme poverty in sub-Saharan Africa likely to continue to increase.[2] All of this is extremely uncertain; in late 2021, COVID-19 was surging in Uganda, disrupting BRAC's activities there. If true, however, it would mean about five years of progress may have been lost overall, with some countries lagging further behind. In any case, extreme poverty eradication is unlikely to happen by 2030.

If there is a heartening aspect of the current situation, it is that those who have struggled with poverty seem to have a limitless store of resilience—often far more than richer people. When Ebola hit Liberia and Sierra Leone, BRAC had to shut down microfinance for seven months. When it reopened, clients repaid most of the loans they had taken out before the crisis. Women were eager to reestablish their credit, for they wanted to restart their lives quickly, and they needed capital to do so.

During a three-day global strategy session with BRAC senior leadership in May 2019, shortly before he was diagnosed with cancer, Abed lost his temper several times when people suggested it was time for BRAC, now at about one hundred thousand employees worldwide, to consolidate. "I don't want you guys to think we're too big," he said, according to his son, Shameran. "There's still a lot of stuff to do. One hundred thousand people is not enough. Continue to grow and become four hundred thousand people." The strategy BRAC's leadership agreed on sets a lofty goal of reaching 250 million people globally by 2030, a number Abed came up with. "His idea was to give them something big to aim for—and let them keep working at it," said Shameran. (In June 2021, Shameran Abed took on the executive directorship of BRAC International, the entity overseeing all operations outside Bangladesh.)

If Abed were here today, he would likely remind us that setbacks are rarely as insurmountable as they seem—and that optimism will eventually triumph over despair.

ACKNOWLEDGMENTS

During the years-long process of researching and writing this book, Nawrin Nujhat proved to be more than a translator, fixer, pep-talker, and traveling companion. On our journeys through the backroads, rivers, and traffic jams of Bangladesh—including an epic road trip from Rowmari in the north to Patuakhali in the south—I gained a better and more sensory understanding of the country. Only someone with Nawrin's sensibility would point out that a passing market town smells like a mix of fish and sawdust. I also learned from Nawrin of the sweet scent of night-blooming jasmine (an aroma reminiscent of sorrow, according to the poets) and the most famous desserts of each city and district.

I am indebted to Rachel Kabir, the head of the chairperson's office at BRAC headquarters in Bangladesh, for numerous edits and proofreads, and also for opening a window into Bangladeshi language and customs, often over lunches and late-evening suppers on the nineteenth floor of the BRAC Center. I am grateful to many others who have ridden those elevators, including Shajedur Rahman Rokon, for memories and connections formed during his many years at BRAC; Shararat Islam, for translation and other invaluable help during my first trip to Sulla in 2015; the staff of Shuruchi, the best restaurant in the world; Rakib Avi; and many other colleagues who have turned into friends.

Closer to home, I feel honored to have worked alongside amazing people at BRAC USA (both versions 1.0 and 2.0) over the past ten years. They are too numerous to name here, though I am especially grateful to my immediate supervisors, Donella Rapier and Dan Stoner, for their support in pushing this project through to the end and to Susan Davis for being a champion in its early stages. Thanks, also, to Doris Prodanovic and Ally Feldman for volunteer transcribing and note taking.

Emma Riley, a postdoctoral researcher in the Department of Economics at the University of Oxford, did me the enormous favor of visiting the Bodleian Library to dig through the Oxfam archives, unearthing old emails that tell the story of the scuttled BRAC-Oxfam merger from the Oxfam side. Collette Chabbott provided guidance for the chapter on the BRAC education program based on research for her book, *Institutionalizing Health and Education for All: Global Goals, Innovations, and Scaling Up* (2015). Stephen Smith, chair of the Department of Economics and professor of economics and international affairs at George Washington University, deserves thanks just for letting me bounce ideas off him while walking along the Potomac. Martha Alter Chen, who appears many times as a supporting character in the BRAC story (and serves as chair of the BRAC Global Board, as of 2022), opened up her archive of old photos. Her book *A Quiet Revolution: Women in Transition in Rural Bangladesh* (1983) is a valuable portrait of the early years of BRAC. I am also indebted to the scholarly work of the late Catherine Lovell, author of *Breaking the Cycle of Poverty: The BRAC Strategy* (1992). My friend Jen Sacks gave creative input at the proposal stage, while June Thomas and Keith Miller offered valuable copyediting suggestions.

I am grateful for the reflections of the many people I interviewed for this book. Cole Dodge was especially helpful on nearly all aspects of the BRAC story, answering question after question. Manzoor Hasan helped fill in gaps in the Hasan family story. David Nalin reviewed chapter 17 in detail, and Richard Cash offered comments on the manuscript in its entirety, not just the chapters that included him. Others added shape and color to the narrative, even though not all could be credited in the text. In addition to those whom I have quoted directly, these include Lady Syeda Sarwat Abed, Tapan Kumar Acharjee, Kaosar Afsana, Faruque Ahmed, Jalaluddin Ahmed, Kutubuddin Ahmed, the late Moudud Ahmed, Ghulam Fatema Ahsan ("Anu"), Shamma Alam, Lynn Bickley, Viquar Chamoun, Lincoln Chen, Najma Hafeez, Anadil ("Dilly") Hossain, Ariful Islam, Safiqul Islam, Sirajul Islam, Andrew Jenkins, S. N. Kairy, Sudhir Nath, Rashida Parveen, Kamal Quadir, Bidhubhusan Roy, Reeta Roy (president and CEO of the Mastercard Foundation), Simone Sultana, Sabina Yasmin, and Hossain Zillur Rahman.

George Greenfield of CreativeWell, my agent, deserves a massive amount of credit for agreeing to represent an unknown author writing a book about a subject whom (unfortunately) most people have never heard of. The same goes for Jon Sisk of Rowman & Littlefield, the publisher, for finally bringing Abed's story to the world.

Thank you to my parents, Doug and Janet MacMillan, for your incredible support over the years, including helping care for Isabella when I had to fly to Bangladesh at a moment's notice. My mother deserves extra credit for proofreading this entire manuscript and (of course) finding countless errors. Finally, I think I may have mentioned this project in its earliest stages on my first date with the woman I later married. Thank you for sharing this journey with me, Alex.

NOTES

INTRODUCTION

1. *Economist*, "The Path through the Fields," November 3, 2012.
2. Pamela Das and Richard Horton, "Bangladesh: Innovating for Health," *Lancet*, November 21, 2013. Accessed November 15, 2021, at http://dx.doi.org/10.1016/S0140-6736(13)62294-1.

CHAPTER 3

1. Leo Amery, *The Empire at Bay: The Leo Amery Diaries 1929–1945*, edited by John Barnes and David Nicholson (London: Hutchison, 1988), cited in Lawrence James, *Churchill and Empire* (New York, London: Pegasus, 2014), 184.
2. Archibald Percival Wavell, *Wavell: The Viceroy's Journal*, edited by Penderal Moon (London: Oxford University Press, 1973), 78.

CHAPTER 4

1. Piri Halasz, "Great Britain: You Can Walk Across It on the Grass," *Time*, April 15, 1966.

CHAPTER 5

1. Cornelia Rohde, *Catalyst: In the Wake of the Great Bhola Cyclone* (self-published, 2014), 51.
2. Ibid., 58.

3. Ibid., 59.
4. Ibid., 65.
5. Ibid., 67.
6. Ibid., 89–90.
7. Ibid., 99.
8. Sydney H. Schanberg, "A Western Group Aided Pakistanis," *New York Times*, January 3, 1971.

CHAPTER 6

1. Gary J. Bass, *The Blood Telegram* (New York: Vintage Books, 2013), 77–78.

CHAPTER 7

1. I am indebted to Julian Francis, then Oxfam's field director for northern India and Nepal, for providing a copy of Bennett's typewritten report.

CHAPTER 9

1. Paulo Freire, *Pedagogy of the Oppressed* (New York and London: Continuum, 1970; 1993), 60.
2. Ibid., 54.
3. Ibid., 87.

CHAPTER 10

1. Leon Clark, "A Consultant's Journal: Bangladesh," *World Education Reports*, no. 13 (1976).
2. Freire, *Pedagogy of the Oppressed*, 98.

CHAPTER 11

1. *The Net: Power Structure in Ten Villages* (Dhaka: BRAC Prokashana, 1980).
2. Ross Kidd and Krishna Kumar, "Co-opting Freire: A Critical Analysis of Pseudo-Freirean Adult Education," *Economic and Political Weekly* 16, nos. 1/2 (1981): 27–36. Accessed June 7, 2021. http://www.jstor.org/stable/4369408.
3. Aminul Alam, interview with Ian Smillie, audio, n.d.

4. Mohiuddin Alamgir, *Famine in South Asia: Political Economy of Mass Starvation* (Cambridge, MA: Oelgeschlager, Gunn & Hain, 1980), 142–43, cited in Amartya Sen, *Poverty and Famine: An Essay on Entitlement and Deprivation* (Oxford: Clarendon Press, 1981), 134.

5. Cole Patrick Dodge and Paul D. Wiebe, "Famine Relief and Development in Rural Bangladesh," *Economic and Political Weekly* 11, no. 22 (1976): 809–17.

6. Ibid., 814.

CHAPTER 12

1. Interview by Tarun Khanna, Cambridge, MA, April 24, 2014, Creating Emerging Markets Oral History Collection, Baker Library Historical Collections, Harvard Business School.

2. Ernst Friedrich Schumacher, *Small Is Beautiful* (New York: Harper & Row, 1973), 50.

3. Ibid., 55.

4. Ibid., 31.

CHAPTER 14

1. Aminul Alam, interview with Ian Smillie, audio, n.d.

2. Interview by Tarun Khanna, 2014.

3. "Melinda Gates Answers Questions, Part II," *New York Times*, January 11, 2012.

CHAPTER 15

1. Aminul Alam, interview with Ian Smillie, audio, n.d.

CHAPTER 17

1. Joshua Nalibow Ruxin, "Magic Bullet: The History of Oral Rehydration Therapy," *Medical History* 38, no. 4 (1994): 363–97.

2. David R. Nalin et al., "Oral Maintenance Therapy for Cholera in Adults," *Lancet* 292, no. 7564 (1968): 370–72; R. A. Cash et al., "A Clinical Trial of Oral Therapy in a Rural Cholera-Treatment Center," *American Journal of Tropical Medicine and Hygiene* 19, no. 4 (1970): 653–56; David R. Nalin and Richard A. Cash, "Oral or Nasogastric Maintenance Therapy for Diarrhoea of Unknown Aetiology

Resembling Cholera," *Transactions of the Royal Society of Tropical Medicine and Hygiene* 64, no. 5 (1970): 769; D. R. Nalin et al., "Oral (or Nasogastric) Maintenance Therapy for Cholera Patients in All Age-Groups," *Bulletin of the World Health Organization* 43, no. 3 (1970): 361–63. All cited in Ruxin, "Magic Bullet," 384–89.

3. "Water with Sugar and Salt," *Lancet* 312, no. 8084 (1978): 300–301.

4. A. Mushtaque R. Chowdhury and Richard A. Cash, *A Simple Solution: Teaching Millions to Treat Diarrhoea at Home* (Dhaka, Bangladesh: University Press, 1996). I am indebted to the authors of this book, as well as David Nalin, for much of the programmatic and scientific information in this chapter.

5. Sk. Masum Billah et al., "Bangladesh: A Success Case in Combating Childhood Diarrhea," *Journal of Global Health* 9, no. 2 (2019).

CHAPTER 18

1. Bill Drayton, "The Citizen Sector Transformed," in *Social Entrepreneurship: New Models of Sustainable Social Change*, edited by Alex Nicholls (Oxford: Oxford University Press, 2006), 45.

CHAPTER 19

1. Tessa Bold et al., "What Do Teachers Know and Do? Does It Matter? Evidence from Primary Schools in Africa" (Washington, DC: World Bank Group, 2017), 8.

2. Dharampal, *The Beautiful Tree: Indigenous Indian Education in the Eighteenth Century* (Coimbatore: Keerthi Publishing House, 1995), 355, cited in James Tooley, *The Beautiful Tree* (Washington, DC: Cato Institute), 213.

3. Chitra Naik, "India: Extending Primary Education through Non-Formal Approaches," *Prospects* 13, no. 1 (1983): 61.

4. Pankaj S. Jain, "Program Success and Management of Integrated Primary Education in Developing Countries," *World Development* 25, no. 3 (1997), 353.

5. Alan Rogers, *Non-Formal Education: Flexible Schooling or Participatory Education?* (New York: Springer US, 2007), 209. Rogers shared the date of his interview with Abed in a personal correspondence with the author.

CHAPTER 20

1. Manzurul Mannan, *BRAC, Global Policy Language, and Women in Bangladesh: Transformation and Manipulation* (Albany: State University of New York Press, 2015).

CHAPTER 21

1. Since neither had a chance to tell their side of the story, their names have been changed.

2. Syed Hashemi, "Those Left Behind," in *Who Needs Credit? Poverty and Finance in Bangladesh*, edited by Geoffrey Wood and Iffath Sharif (Dhaka, Bangladesh: University Press, 1997), 253.

3. Timothy Evans, Alayne M. Adams, and Rafi Mohammed, "Demystifying Nonparticipation in Microcredit: A Population-Based Analysis," *World Development* 27, no. 2 (1999), 426.

4. Imran Matin and Rabeya Yasmin, "Managing Scaling Up Challenges of a Program for the Poorest: Case Study of BRACs IGVGD Program," in *Scaling Up Poverty Reduction: Case Studies in Microfinance*, papers presented at the Global Learning Process for Scaling Up Poverty Reduction and Conference in Shanghai (Washington, DC: CGAP/The World Bank Group, 2004), 91.

5. Oriana Bandiera et al., "Can Basic Entrepreneurship Transform the Economic Lives of the Poor?" IZA Discussion Paper No. 7386 (2013), available at SSRN: https://ssrn.com/abstract=2266813.

6. Abhijit Banerjee and Esther Duflo, *Poor Economics: A Radical Rethinking of the Way to Fight Global Poverty* (Philadelphia: Public Affairs, 2011), 22–28.

7. Esther Duflo, "Human Values and the Design of the Fight against Poverty," *Tanner Lectures* (Cambridge, MA: MIT Press, 2012), 40–44. Accessed June 6, 2021. https://economics.mit.edu/files/7904.

8. Quoted in Matin and Yasmin, "Managing Scaling Up Challenges of a Program for the Poorest," 86.

9. Nicholas Kristof, "The Power of Hope Is Real," *New York Times*, May 21, 2015.

10. Fazle Hasan Abed, "Building Human Capital Means Investing in the Science of Hope" (New York: Thomson Reuters Foundation, 2018). Accessed June 18, 2021. https://news.trust.org/item/20181017120852-ak1io.

CHAPTER 23

1. Internal Oxfam report, "Draft OI [Oxfam International] Delegation Visit to BRAC, Bangladesh," April 17, 2001, Oxford, Bodleian Libraries, MS. Oxfam DIR/2/3/3/65.

2. Naomi Hossain and Anasuya Sengupta, "Thinking Big and Going Global: The Challenge of BRAC's Global Expansion," IDS Working Paper 339 (Brighton, UK: Institute of Development Studies, 2009), 13.

CHAPTER 24

1. *Economist*, "BRAC in Business," February 20, 2010.

CHAPTER 25

1. Abhijit Banerjee et al., "A Multifaceted Program Causes Lasting Progress for the Very Poor: Evidence from Six Countries," *Science* 348, no. 6236 (2015).

CHAPTER 26

1. Fazle Hasan Abed, "Bangladesh Needs Strong Unions, Not Outside Pressure," *New York Times*, April 28, 2013.
2. Tiffany May, "Helping the Rohingya," *New York Times*, September 29, 2017.

EPILOGUE

1. "Poverty and Shared Prosperity 2018: Piecing Together the Poverty Puzzle" (Washington, DC: World Bank), xi.
2. Daniel Gerszon Mahler et al., "Updated Estimates of the Impact of COVID-19 on Global Poverty: Turning the Corner on the Pandemic in 2021?" *World Bank Blogs*, June 24, 2021. Accessed June 30, 2021. https://blogs.worldbank.org/opendata/updated-estimates-impact-covid-19-global-poverty-turning-corner-pandemic-2021.

A NOTE ON SOURCES

This book relies mainly on original research in the form of interviews with primary source participants and access to BRAC's internal archive of reports, proposals, and program documentation. When providing information about BRAC programs, I used both types of sources, sometimes drawing from multiple sources even within a single sentence. I have not provided detailed citations for facts and figures about BRAC programs in the interest of not overburdening the reader with notations. When people's memories conflicted with the written record, I relied on the written record.

Unless another citation is provided, words that are attributed to people and in quotation marks are usually direct quotations from author interviews. Where these quotes capture historical conversations, the words generally reflect what a person said they recalled hearing or saying. There are a few exceptions, which I hope are obvious from the context: These are where I have dramatized the dialogue for narrative purposes, such as in chapter 10 (quoting the BRAC facilitator and respondents in the first Freirean lessons), chapter 11 (Abed's first encounter with Amin and Kadbanu's confrontation with the imam), and chapter 21 (the Union Council hearing on the case of the poisoned cow).

I am indebted to the authors of *Catalyst: In the Wake of the Great Bhola Cyclone*, by the late Cornelia ("Candy") Rohde (self-published, 2014), and *A Simple Solution: Teaching Millions to Treat Diarrhoea at Home*, by A. Mushtaque R. Chowdhury and Richard A. Cash (Dhaka: University Press, 1996). These provided much of the material for chapters 5 and 17, respectively. I am also indebted to Ian Smillie, the author of *Freedom from Want: The Remarkable Success Story of BRAC, the Global Grassroots Organization That's Winning the Fight Against Poverty* (West Hartford, CT: Kumarian Press, 2009), which charts the development of BRAC through 2009 from the perspective of a seasoned development professional. Not only was Smillie generous with his personal time in allowing me to interview him and answering subsequent emails, but he also provided me with audio copies of his own interviews for *Freedom from Want*, including two with the late Aminul Alam, who died before I began researching this book.

Several of my interviewees passed away during the writing of this book, and I feel grateful to have had the privilege of spending time with them in their final years. These include Faruq Choudhury, Nayeemul Hasan, Soraiya (Putul) Hossain, Tajul Islam, Viquar Choudhury, Zakaria Khan, and, of course, Sir Fazle Hasan Abed.

INDEX